CHRIST AND CAESAR IN MODERN KOREA

SUNY Series in Korean Studies

Sung Bae Park, Editor

CHRIST AND CAESAR IN MODERN KOREA

A HISTORY OF CHRISTIANITY AND POLITICS

WI JO KANG

STATE UNIVERSITY OF NEW YORK PRESS

This book is dedicated in loving memory of Dr. Jung Young Lee

Published by
State University of New York Press, Albany

For information, address State University of New York Press,
State University Plaza, Albany, NY 12246

Production by M. R. Mulholland
Marketing by Theresa A. Swierzowski

Library of Congress Cataloging-in-Publication Data

Kang, Wi Jo, 1930–
        Christ and Caesar in modern Korea : a history of Christianity and politics /
Wi Jo Kang.
        p.   cm. — (SUNY series in Korean studies)
        Includes bibliographical references and index.
        ISBN 0-7914-3247-5 (hardcover : alk. paper). — ISBN 0-7914-3248-3
(pbk. : alk. paper)
        1. Christianity and politics — History.   2. Korea — Church history.
I. Title.   II. Series.
        BR1325.K36   1997
        322'.1'09519 — dc20   96-12877
                                                                                      CIP

10 9 8 7 6 5 4 3 2 1

CONTENTS

PREFACE

Socrates called the human being a "political animal," while humankind has often been referred to as "homo religiosus," or "religious human," as well. These two descriptions indicate how important both politics and religion are to human life in history and society. Yet, attempts to understand the interrelationships between politics and religion are few, probably as a result of certain Western notions about the separation of church and state.

However, since the introduction of Christianity to Korea in the modern age, its impact has been greatly dependent upon Korea's political situation. Indeed, an important reason behind Christianity's success in Korea has been its frequent identification with the political movements of Korean nationalism, the independence movements, democracy, and Korean reunification.

In recent years, Korean Christians have made significant contributions toward human rights, justice, and democracy and against dictatorial governments of Park Chung Hee, Chun Doo Hwan, and President Roh Tae Woo. Christianity is a spearhead of the democratic movement in Korea and must be reckoned with as a significant political and spiritual force. This author strongly believes that studying the development of Korean Christianity in relation to Korean political history will give a better understanding of the contemporary Korean situation. The present work was initiated with a grant received from the National Council of Churches in the United States to write a book on the history of Christianity in Korea. It was initially intended that this work would be co-authored by Dr. R. Pierce Beaver, then of the University of Chicago, and myself. Since that time Dr. Beaver has passed away. Thus, the responsibility for writing the history fell entirely to me.

Meanwhile, I felt that a chronological history would be of little interest to the English reading public at this time, since two outstanding books on Korean church history, one by Allen Clerk, and the other by Professor Min Kyung Bae, have been published by the Christian Literature Society of Korea in Seoul. Therefore, on the basis of my research and personal knowledge of Korean church history, I have decided to write this work as an interpretive history of the development of Christianity in relation to the political development of modern Korea.

I am deeply grateful to the National Council of Churches in the United States for its financial support in the initial stages of my research. I also thank my relatives and friends in Japan and Korea, who facilitated my travels to those countries as I gathered research and original documents. The inspiration to complete this book comes from the courageous Christians in Korea and abroad who continue their unceasing witness to God's justice, peace, and love both for individuals and nations.

In the last stages of completing this book, my student assistants have helped me in revising and editing. I am deeply grateful for their labor of love. However, I am responsible for any mistakes in the book.

In this work all East Asian family names are written first, followed by given names. Exceptions are made for well known names such as Syngman Rhee, John M. Chang, and others.

1

KOREAN POLITICS OF ISOLATIONISM AND ROMAN CATHOLIC ENCOUNTER

The political tragedy of modern Korea resulted from the longevity of the Yi dynasty. The Yi dynasty initiated its rule in 1392, a century before the first voyage of Columbus to America, and it continued into the twentieth century until 1910, when Japan formally annexed Korea. During these long years of rule, the Yi family adopted Neo-Confucianism as a political ideology and system of rule that kept Korea in total isolation. The only country that had access to Korea was China. Confucian family ethics were thus reflected in the political realm in the interaction between big brother China and smaller brother Korea.

It was the introduction of Roman Catholicism that initially challenged Korea's political attachment to China and broke Korean isolationism. The first Korean contact with Roman Catholicism is reported to have come through the Japanese soldiers who invaded Korea in 1592. When Toyotomi Hideyoshi dispatched his troops to conquer Korea, a Roman Catholic general, Konishi Yukinaga, was among them. About eighteen thousand Catholic soldiers were in General Konishi's division. The soldiers were Japanese converts, the result of missionary work by St. Francis Xavier, who came to Japan in 1549, and his Jesuit successors. At Konishi's request, Fr. Gregorio de Cespedes, who was working in Japan as a Jesuit missionary, came to Korea with a Japanese assistant to minister to the Japanese troops. But Father de Cespedes' ministry was limited exclusively to the Japanese soldiers, and there is no evidence that it had any direct influence on the native Koreans.

The real foundation of Catholicism in modern Korea was laid in the eighteenth century by Koreans who visited and studied in China. Matteo Ricci, an Italian Jesuit missionary, began his work in Beijing in 1601. His knowledge of Western mathematics and sciences, plus his appreciation of Confucianism, attracted the attention of the Chinese royal court and the literati. His successors also served the imperial court, firmly establishing the Roman Catholic church in the Chinese capital. To Korean visitors to Beijing, the Roman Catholic church seemed influential, so they became interested in learning more about the teaching of this new faith. When they returned home, they brought with them not only knowledge of Western science and astronomy, but also books that told about "the Lord of Heaven,"[1] and the Catholic church's teachings.

These books on the teachings of the Roman Catholic church appealed to Korean scholars who were searching for new ideas. Many accepted Catholicism as a new branch of philosophical learning and called Christianity "Western learning." Among these scholars was Yi Pyŏk, whose friend, Yi Sŏng Hun, was about to accompany his father to Beijing as the Korean envoy in 1783. Hwang Sa Yŏng, a Korean Catholic, writes in his memoirs:

> When Yi Sŏng Hun was about to go to Beijing with his father, Yi Pyŏk visited him and told him secretly "In Beijing there is a temple of the Lord of Heaven (Catholic church) and there are some Western priests. Go to see them and get a copy of the Sacred writings. Ask them to baptize you and that will certainly please them. Then they will give you many precious things."[2]

Yi Sŏng Hun was impressed by the enthusiasm of Yi Pyŏk and promised to visit the churches in Beijing to seek more information about their teaching. While in the Chinese capital, Song Hun was converted and baptized. He received the baptismal name Peter, which proved to be a prophetic symbol, since he became a foundation stone for the Korean Catholic church. When "Peter" Yi returned to Korea, he baptized his friend Yi Pyŏk, who took the baptismal name John the Baptist. These men baptized others, and the followers of "the Lord of Heaven" increased.

As the numbers of Roman Catholic adherents grew in Korea, the archbishop of Beijing took note. In 1790 he instructed Korean Catholics to abolish the practice of ancestor worship. Accordingly, Korean Catholics burned their ancestral tablets and shunned the ancient practices. As a result, the government became alarmed and began prohibiting envoys from bringing Catholic Christian books out of Beijing.

The Korean government operating under Confucian ideals considered Catholicism to be *sa-kyo,* an "evil religion," because of its proscription of ancestor worship. This made Catholics appear to be unfilial and thus disloyal members of Korean society. The natural outcome of this conflict, considering the rapid spread of this "evil religion," was persecution. Yet, despite fierce repression, Korean Catholics withstood the persecution bravely.

They stood firm because they had a strong sense of pride in having laid the foundation of this new religion themselves. Christianity had been introduced by native leaders returning from China rather than by strangers from faraway lands. It spread rapidly among Koreans with very little need for foreign missionary assistance, creating strong bonds among the Catholics and inspiring loyalty to their faith. Many converts, especially the former Confucian literati, became unemployed and were displaced in society as a result of internal political conflicts. They were considered "foreign Koreans" and gravely mistreated. But their faith remained their source of inspiration and hope for future change in their social status. Even when some Catholics renounced their faith, persecution continued; the only other alternative for Korean Catholics was to withstand persecution.

The first organized persecution took place in 1791; John Baptist Yi was one of the first martyrs. In spite of the storm, the church's work in Korea not only continued but increased. However, the members of the Korean church had no ordained priesthood to minister to them, nor was there an organized hierarchy to unite and direct the faithful. To remedy this, Korean Catholics tried to develop their own hierarchy and elect priests, but in 1789, Bishop de Govea of Beijing objected, informing them that it was not permissible for them to choose priests in that manner. Since it was also not permissible for them to administer the sacraments—baptism was the only exception—the bishop acknowledged the problem and promised to send an ordained priest.

In February 1791, Jean dos Remedios, a priest from Portuguese Macao, was appointed to go to Korea. After a long and hard midwinter journey, he reached the Manchurian border but was unable to cross. He returned to Beijing and died soon after. In September 1794, a Chinese priest, James Chu, was sent by the bishop. He succeeded in secretly crossing the border and became the first official Roman Catholic missionary to enter Korea and work among Koreans. Father Chu was able to minister openly to the people for six months; then he had to take refuge in a Christian home to avoid arrest. His two guides and an interpreter were apprehended and were ordered to reveal his hiding place. Though tortured and finally beheaded in June 1795, they never disclosed Father Chu's hiding place. After Father Chu had been in hiding for three years, a public proclamation by the government legally outlawed him. When he read the proclamation, he left his hiding place and voluntarily surrendered himself, not wishing to further endanger the lives of his Korean friends. On May 31, 1801, he was martyred at the age of thirty-two.

Father Chu's death left Korea without a Catholic priest for thirty-three years. Meanwhile, persecution continued, and Korean Catholics, abandoned, stood alone, surviving especially harsh persecutions in 1815, 1819, and 1827. Korea was not forgotten by European missionaries, however. In 1829, the great French missionary society La Société des Missions Etrangères de Paris resolved to found a mission in Korea directly attached to the Holy See. In 1832 Barthelemy Bruguière, then a missionary in Siam (Thailand), volunteered to go to Korea. Unfortunately, he died before crossing the Korean border, but in 1836 Fr. Pierre Philibert Maubant, a French priest, successfully crossed into Korea. The following year another French priest, Jacques Chastan, joined Maubant in Seoul. On December 19, 1839, Laurent Marie Joseph

Imbert came to Korea as vicar apostolic. There was undoubtedly much rejoicing among Korean Catholics at the arrival of these missionary priests, especially the bishop. The joy over their arrival was short-lived. Confucian politicians further enforced Korea's politics of isolationism, forbidding any contacts with foreigners. In 1839 a new storm of persecution swept through the country. Bishop Imbert and Fathers Maubant and Chastan were arrested with 130 Korean Catholics and executed. Again the young church suffered a blow to its leadership.

At this time there was a young pious Korean student in Macao, Andrew Kim, sent there by Father Maubant to study at the seminary. He knew of the need for priests in Korea, and he labored to bring in more European missionaries. Early in 1843, Kim returned to Korea at Uiju with a group of Korean merchants, but he fell under suspicion and was forced to return to China. From there he tried to help Jean Joseph Ferreol enter Korea when the latter was appointed bishop in December 1843. It proved too dangerous for the bishop to enter at that time, so he returned to Macao. Then in 1844, Kim and eleven other Korean Catholics, none of whom had any navigating experience, sailed in a small fishing boat to Shanghai, where Bishop Ferreol met Kim and ordained him into the priesthood. Later, in that same small boat, Father Kim smuggled Bishop Ferreol and Fr. Nicholas Daveluy into Korea. Father Kim continued such efforts to bring more missionaries in by sea, but he was soon arrested as a traitor to his country. Andrew Kim, the first native Korean to be ordained a priest, was beheaded on July 25, 1846, at the age of twenty-six.

Two decades later, in 1866, the politics of isolationism was at its peak and marked the bloodiest period in the history of Roman Catholicism in Korea. Taewonkun was an ardent isolationist and a strong ruler who despised foreign intervention. Still, he was rather indifferent to the spread of Catholicism in the early period of his rule. As a matter of fact, his wife, Min, was sympathetic toward Catholic teachings, and Pak, the nurse of the young king, was a devout Catholic. Some high officials in Taewonkun's government were also Catholic converts.

Trouble began in January 1866, when a Russian war vessel appeared at Wonsan Harbor and threatened to open Korea by force for Russian trade. Taewonkun was greatly upset by the Russian demands and sent a special envoy to China to consult with Chinese officials concerning the matter. Meanwhile, John Nam, a government official and a Catholic, saw this as an opportunity to gain religious tolerance in Korea. He suggested that Taewonkun seek an alliance with France and England which would aid in thwarting the Russian advances.

Another leading Korean Catholic, Thomas Kim, asked Berneau, the French bishop in Seoul, to assist the government in solving the "Russian problem." The bishop assured him that he would try to approach the regent. Kim also wrote a letter to Taewonkun suggesting that the most effective way of resisting Russian aggression would be to sign a treaty with France and England. In the letter he suggested that an anti-Russian alliance with France and England could easily be made through the French bishop in Seoul. The regent responded favorably to the suggestions and expressed a desire to see the bishop, but as it turned out Bishop Berneau was away from the capital by that time. When he returned, the Russian warship had voluntarily left Korea, and the regent no longer felt any need to see him.

Shortly after, the envoys who had returned from Beijing started a rumor that the Chinese government was executing all Europeans who were in China. Taewonkun, encouraged by the rumor and determined to pursue a more strict isolationist policy, began a bloody persecution. Between February 26 and 28, 1866, Bishop Berneau, Fathers Bretenières, Beaulieu, and Borie, and several leading Korean Christians were arrested. On March 8 the four foreign missionaries were beheaded. Father Pourthie and Father Petitnichols were executed three days later. Fortunately, three priests—Ridel, Calais, and Feron—were visiting remote country districts during the early stages of the persecution, and they managed to escape. With the courageous assistance of Korean Catholics, Fathers Ridel and Feron were reunited in May 1866. About a month later, they were informed that Father Calais was also alive, and soon the missionaries exchanged letters from their hiding places.

According to the rules of La Société des Missions Estrangères, Feron—who had been in Korea longer than the other two priests—became the leader. Feron directed Ridel to leave Korea and report to concerned Catholics in China. After a difficult time in obtaining a boat and completing the voyage, Ridel and eleven Koreans reached Chefu, China, in July. Ridel soon met with Admiral Pierre Gustavus Rose, commander of the French Indo-China fleet at Tienjin, and reported on the persecution of Catholics in Korea.

Admiral Rose relayed the report to H. de Bellonet, the French chargé d'affaires in Beijing. Bellonet became furious at hearing the news and wrote to Prince Kung, the Chinese premier, on July 13, 1866:

Sir:

I grieve to bring officially to the knowledge of your Imperial Highness a horrible outrage committed in the small kingdom of Corea, which formerly assumed the bonds of vassalage to the Chinese empire, but which this act of savage barbarity has forever separated from it.

In the course of the month of March last, the two French bishops who were evangelizing Corea, and with them nine missionaries and seven Corean priests and a great multitude of Christians of both sexes and of every age, were massacred by order of the sovereign of that country.

The government of His Majesty cannot permit so bloody an outrage to be unpunished. The same day on which the king of Corea laid his hands upon my unhappy countrymen was the last of his reign; he himself proclaimed its end, which I, in turn, solemnly declare today. In a few days our military forces are to march to the conquest of Corea, and the Emperor, my august Sovereign, alone, has not the right and the power to dispose, according to his good pleasure, of the country and the vacant throne.

The Chinese government has declared to me many times that it has no authority over Corea, and it refused on this pretext to apply the treaties of Tientsin to that country, and give to our missionaries the passports which we have asked from it. We have taken note of these declarations, and we declare now that we do not recognize any authority whatever of the Chinese government over the kingdom of Corea.

I have, etc.,
H. de Bellonet[3]

In September 1866, with a flagship, *Primaguet,* and two gunboats, *Deroulede* and *Tardif,* Admiral Rose began an invasion of Korea. Father Ridel accompanied him as an interpreter, and three Koreans went as guides. The small fleet left Chefu on September 18; it docked two days later near Inchon Bay. On the September 19, Admiral Rose dispatched the *Deroulede* to test the possibility of sailing upriver to Seoul. The next day the *Deroulede* reported that passage up the Han River was possible and the admiral ordered his ships to proceed. However, the *Primaguet* soon struck a rock, and only the two gunboats continued the voyage.

On Sunday, September 23, Father Ridel led the sailors in a celebration of mass on the deck of the *Deroulede.* On the following day the ships approached Seoul to find that the Korean government had sent ships to block the river against them. The French ships fired upon, and sank, two Korean boats, but Korean land troops returned fire, and the French ships were unable to proceed any farther.

The fleet had to return to China, but the idea of a conquest was not abandoned. The admiral increased the number of his ships and returned to Korea with six hundred marines in October of that year. On October 14, the marines landed at Kanghwa and fired on several Korean forts. Again the Koreans fought back, and the expedition failed. Even threats of a French invasion did not stop the persecution. On the contrary, it became more intense, and the country's door to any foreign influence closed more tightly than ever. By 1870, over eight thousand Christians suffered martyrdom.[4]

However, Korea's isolationism and the persecution of Christians were not to go on forever. In October 1873, Taewonkun retired from the regency and

Queen Min became the new ruler. Soon the numbers of foreign ships on Korean shores increased, and in 1876, Korea opened her long-closed door by signing the Treaty of Amity with Japan. In 1882, Korea signed a treaty with the United States, and shortly thereafter Great Britain, Germany, and Russia all established diplomatic relations in Korea.

France, however, had more difficulties establishing official ties because of the tension that still existed due to the presence of French Catholic missionaries and the invasions by French gunboats in previous years. In addition, the purpose of other Western nations in making treaties with Korea was commercial, while that of the French was to gain freedom for the propagation of the Roman Catholic church and protection for French missionaries. The Korean government was unwilling to grant France such concessions, but eventually those countries that already had diplomatic ties with Korea pressured the court into making a treaty.

In 1886, the Korean-French Treaty was signed, and as a result, the work of the Catholic mission progressed much more favorably. Major Korean ports, such as Inchon, Pusan, and Wonsan, were opened to the French, and French missionaries were able to continue work among the unemployed literati and the common people. The antagonistic attitude of government officials toward the missionaries did continue, but at least it was no longer necessary for priests to disguise themselves or to celebrate mass in secret.

Then in August 1890, Fr. Gustave C. Mutel, who had been in Korea before and who was at that time the dean of a seminary of the Foreign Mission Society of Paris, was appointed the new bishop of Korea. Before his departure, a special mass was held for him at the seminary he served on September 21, 1890; it was held in conjunction with a mass commemorating the deaths of early missionaries to Korea. In the service, the head of the seminary spoke these words to the new bishop of Korea: *"Florete flores marturii"* (Bloom, flowers of martyrdom). Father Mutel left Paris on November 26, 1890, and arrived at Inchon on February 22, 1891. He was welcomed by cheering Korean Catholics and missionaries, and the Catholics' work progressed.

The use of military force by the French to invade Korea, and thereby to introduce Roman Catholicism to the country, constituted illegal acts of imperialism. Also, the actions of Korean Catholic converts were at times treasonous. Hwang Sa Yŏng wrote a secret letter to the French bishop in Beijing, asking him to encourage the French naval forces to attack Korea. It was Hwang Sa Yŏng's hope that such an attack would end the Yi government's isolation and would also promote the toleration of Roman Catholic missionary activities, for the continuous isolationist policies of the Korean government kept Korea blind in a time of rapid change. The end of isolation was necessary! The persistence of Roman Catholic missionary work in Korea made contributions to end the politics of isolation and to open Korea to the outside world, although that opening eventually resulted in the demise of the Yi dynasty.

2

INTRODUCTION OF PROTESTANTISM AND THE OPENING OF KOREA

Dutch seamen made the first Protestant Christian contact with Korea in the seventeenth century. In 1628, three sailors, all members of the Dutch Reformed church, were stranded in Korea by a storm, and they made the country their home. Two of the three later died while fighting on the side of the Koreans against invading Manchu soldiers. The survivor, Jan Janse Weltevree, "Pak Yŏn," as he was called in Korea, married a Korean woman. He served as a military trainer in Korea and was well accepted by the people.

In 1653, there was another shipwreck involving the Dutch ship *Sparrow Hawk*, which landed on Cheju Island in southern Korea. Of the sixty-four crewmen, twenty-eight drowned, and the thirty-six survivors were captured by island authorities and sent to Seoul and other places in southwestern Korea. In 1666, eight of the captives were able to escape after a fourteen-year imprisonment. Since a small number of Dutch sailors lived in Korea for many years, it is reasonable to suppose that some first exposure to Protestant Christianity was made via these men. There is no documentary evidence of any conversions from these contacts, however. Yet, if other sailors had as strong a faith as that revealed in the account of the shipwreck, imprisonment, and life in Korea of Hendrik Hamel, bookkeeper of the Dutch vessel *Sparrow Hawk*, then it is likely that Koreans took note of Christianity.[1]

Aside from these unexpected visitors from shipwrecked vessels, there was little contact with Protestant churches until the nineteenth century, though of course Roman Catholic influence was becoming more and more prevalent. One significant contact early in the nineteenth century by Protestants was made by the Reverend Karl Gutzlaff. Gutzlaff came to Korea in 1832 as an interpreter for the British ship *Lord Amherst*, which had been sent to open trade relations with Korea. Gutzlaff was trained at the famous center of pietism in Halle, Germany, and sent to Thailand in 1828 as a missionary for the Netherlands Missionary Society. Gutzlaff's main contributions were in the distribution of Christian literature.

In later years he went to Macao and explored the Chinese coast, "Loo-Choo" Islands, and other places, with an interest in starting new missions. On July 17, 1832, Gutzlaff wrote in his journal, "A stiff breeze brought us in sight of Corea. A merciful providence has protected us through many dangers, along the coast of China, and O that we were truly grateful!"[2] The *Lord Amherst* arrived at an island near Hwanghae Province in central Korea, and the British sent a letter via local officials to the royal court in Seoul. The effort failed to elicit any response, so the ship sailed south and anchored in Basil's Bay in Chung Chong Province. Again a petition was sent, along with gifts for the king, in the hope of establishing a commercial trade agreement.

While waiting for an answer, Gutzlaff had the chance to make contact with the local people. Before sailing to Korea, he had obtained the Chinese Scriptures from Robert Morrison, the first Protestant missionary to China. Gutzlaff distributed these and other tracts to the people and undoubtedly tried to witness personally to them, but his stay in Korea was too short to leave much impression. The mission of the *Lord Amherst* to open Korea for trade failed, and as a result Gutzlaff had to leave after only one month. He left Korea, saying:

> In the great plan of the eternal God, there will be a time of merciful visitation for them. While we look for this, we ought to be very anxious to hasten its approach by diffusing the glorious doctrine of the cross by all means in our power. . . . The Scripture teaches us to believe that God can bless even these feeble beginnings. Let us hope that better days will soon dawn for Corea.[3]

Thirty-three years after Gutzlaff's visit, a Scottish missionary, Robert J. Thomas, went to Korea. Thomas was sent as a missionary to China by the London Missionary Society. He and his wife left Scotland in July 1865, arriving at Shanghai soon after this time. Shanghai's climate proved to be too warm for Mrs. Thomas, so Thomas journeyed to Hankow seeking cooler conditions, but while he was gone, his wife died. After her funeral, Thomas went to Chefu, China, and there met two Roman Catholic Koreans at the home of the Rev. Alexander Williamson of the National Bible Society of Scotland. Thomas then decided to go to Korea with these men. Williamson provided copies of the Scriptures, tracts, and expenses for the journey, and Thomas was on his way, arriving in Hwanghae Province in September 1865.

In December 1865, Thomas returned briefly to China for a visit. Early in 1866, he sought transportation for the return to Korea. When he heard about the upcoming departure of the American schooner *General Sherman* to open trade relations between Korea and the United States, he applied for passage and subsequently was offered a free trip if he would serve as interpreter. Thomas accepted, and the ship arrived in Korea in August 1866. The *General Sherman* entered the Taedong River and proceeded toward Pyongyang, today's North Korean capital. While they were en route, the governor of Pyongyang Province sent to inquire about the nature of the ship's visit. When he was informed of its mission, the governor notified them that it was impossible to open trade relations at that time. He asked the Americans to leave, but they did not. To the eyes of the Koreans this was an invasion and intrusion of foreigners, yet the ship continued, taking advantage of heavy rains and high tides, until it became stuck in mud. Soon after, the ship was attacked and burned by the Koreans. The entire crew was killed. Since no crew member survived, the historical account of the *General Sherman's* fate is incomplete, but missionary Harry Rhodes gave this version:

> At Sook-Syum, Preston, the owner of the ship and his Chinese interpreter went ashore and met the governor of Pyongyang and the commander of the garrison. The commander and three of his men went out to visit the ship. The ship's crew asked to see his insignia of office, which had been given to him by the King, and refused to give it back. Then the four men were forced into the ship's long boat and taken up the river. The Koreans on shore offered a large reward to any one who would rescue their comrades. A man by the name of Pak Choon Kwun rowed out in a scull to the "long boat" which was having difficulty getting up the rapids. . . . The Koreans attempted to jump into the scull. The general and one of his men were saved but the other two were drowned. . . . Firing from the ship continued off and on for two weeks, during which time twenty Koreans were killed and a large number wounded. Meanwhile the ship was hopelessly grounded in the mire and the crew began to sue for peace. They sent a man and an interpreter to make apologies to the governor. The men were bound and ordered to send for the rest of the crew if apologies were really meant. But this order was suspected to be a ruse and as soon as a note on paper was sent back, firing from the ship was resumed. The Koreans now determined to burn the *General Sherman* and sent down against the ship a large scow loaded with pine branches of fire, on September 3, 1866. The crew in attempting to escape, jumped into the water and were killed as they came ashore.[4]

Missionary Thomas, too, was killed when he reached the shore.

Still, Protestant Christian witness to Koreans began to increase. In the year following Thomas's death, Alexander Williamson, who had given Thomas Bibles when he first visited Korea, journeyed to the northeastern part of China near the Korea-China boarder. On this trip he visited the "Korea Gate" and sold Christian books to Korean merchants who were doing business in the border area. From 1873 on, John Ross and his brother-in-law, John McIntyre, both Scottish Presbyterian missionaries, preached the gospel to Korean residents in the China-Korea border region. In 1876 McIntyre baptized his first Korean converts; in 1881 Ross baptized eighty-five Koreans in the northern valleys of Manchuria, and in 1884 he baptized several more. With the help of Korean language teachers, Ross and McIntyre translated the Gospel of Luke in 1882, and five years later they translated the entire New Testament into Korean.

Among the Korean language teachers was Sŏ Sang Yun, an itinerant medicine merchant who frequently visited the northeastern region of China. On one of these trips he became ill and was cared for by McIntyre. His concern moved Sang Yun to assist the missionaries in their translation of the New Testament. During the course of their work, Sŏ Sang Yun and his brother, Sŏ Kyŏng Yun, were converted. After completion of the New Testament, the two brothers returned to their home in Uiju but found themselves no longer welcome. They then moved to Sorae on the west coast of Hwanghae Province. There the two men established a Presbyterian church, and Sŏ Kyŏng Yun became one of the first Protestant, Korean-ordained ministers.

Thus the work of Ross and McIntyre in northeast China laid the foundation for Protestantism in Korea. Koreans who were converted in China took back to their homeland Protestantism, a movement which was to have quite an impact on Korean politics. This significant impact of Christianity was to be felt after the opening of Korea, which ended Korea's politics of isolationism.

Meanwhile, in the neighboring country of Japan, the Tokugawa military government had ended in 1868 and established Meiji imperial rule. This opened the way for Japan's modernization, and its government now struggled to build a rich, modern nation with an up-to-date military force. William E. Griffis, who taught and lived in Japan in the last part of the nineteenth century, wrote about the modernization of the Japanese navy as an example: "Since 1868 the Japanese navy, modelled after the British and consisting of America and European ironclads and war vessels, has been manned by crews uniformed in foreign style."[5] The battleship *Unyo-Kwan,* part of the new Japanese navy, cruised the mouth of the Han River in September 1875 and landed some troops near Kanghwa Island. Korean soldiers were able to repel them, but in retaliation the Japanese ship attacked the fort of Yongjon-Chin before returning to Japan.

When the *Unyo-Kwan* brought back news of this "Kanghwa incident," it aroused Japanese anger and stirred imperial ambitions. The next year, Japan sent its envoy, Kuroda Kyodake, to the Han River with several demands and the Japanese fleet to back them. Kuroda demanded that the Korean government render an official apology for the Kanghwa incident, open ports to Japanese vessels, and sign a trade agreement with Japan. Because of the threat of the fleet, the government had no choice but to concede to the demands. A Treaty of Amity was signed on February 26, 1876. This treaty, which was Korea's first major involvement in international relations, signaled the beginning of a gradual loss of independence. The treaty was established not by Korean willingness, but by the military threat of Japan.

Although Korea's independence and sovereign rights were formally recognized in the treaty of 1876, Japan's goal was to colonize Korea by rooting out the strong political influence China exerted there. China was consequently alarmed by this development and wanted to stop Japan's growing power and influence in Korea. As one means of diffusing growing Japanese influence, China encouraged Korea to make more treaties with other nations, including the United States.

On April 8, 1878, two years after the Korean-Japanese treaty, the U.S. Senate passed a resolution which stated:

> That the President of the United States be, and hereby is authorized to appoint a commissioner to represent this country in an effort to arrange by peaceful means, and with the aid of the friendly means, and with the aid of the friendly offices of Japan, a treaty of peace and commerce between the United States and the Kingdom of Korea, and the sum of $50,000 or so much thereof as may be necessary, is hereby appropriated out of any money in the Treasury not otherwise appropriated to defray the expenses of said commission.[6]

In the following year, the U.S. Navy Department sent the *U.S.S. Ticonderoga,* commanded by Commodore R. W. Shufeldt, on a world cruise in the general interest of American commerce, and in particular to sign a trade agreement with Korea. Through the efforts and diplomatic skills of Shufeldt and with the aid of Li Hung Chang, who directed Chinese foreign policy, Korea and the United States signed a treaty in 1882. Griffis wrote:

> Schufeldt arrived in the *Swatara* off Chemulpo May 7th. Accompanied by three officers, Commodore Shufeldt went six miles into the interior to the office of the Korean magistrate to formulate the treaty. Though surrounded every moment by curious crowds, no disrespect was shown in any way. Two days afterward, the treaty document was signed on a point of land in a temporary pavilion opposite the ship. Thus, in the most modest manner the negotiations were concluded, and a treaty with the United States was, after repeated failures, secured by the gallant officer who, by this act of successful diplomacy, closed a long and brilliant professional career.[7]

The Korean-American Treaty was important to the Korean people, not only because it was the first treaty made by Korea with a Western nation, but also because the treaty honored Korean independence and sovereignty and provided for "perpetual peace and friendship" between the two nations. Article 1 of the treaty stated:

> There shall be a perpetual peace and friendship between the President of the United States and the King of Chosen (sic) and the citizens and subjects of their respective Governments. If other powers deal unjustly or oppressively with either Government, the other will exert their good offices, on being informed of the case, to bring about an amicable arrangement, thus showing their friendly feelings.[8]

The United States, however did not honor the treaty agreement when Japan threatened Korea for annexation.

Meanwhile, the Japanese influence in Korea grew rapidly, and a pro-Japanese faction developed among Korea's political leadership. This progressive faction came to be called the "Dongnip" (independent) or "Kaehwa" (progressive) party. The leaders of this group, Kim Ok Kiun, Pak Yŏng Ho, Sŏ Kwang Bŏm, and Hong Yong Shik, visited Japan and saw the progress being made through the selective importing of Western culture. These leaders keenly felt the need for similar reforms in Korea. Being young and vigorous, they campaigned aggressively for political and cultural reforms.

Wherever there are progressives promoting change, however, there are also conservatives interested in maintaining the status quo. Korean conservatives opposed Japanese influence in their country and sought to preserve the traditional isolationist policy. In the 1880s, this faction, the Sadae party, held control of the government under Queen Min.

The progressive party plotted to overthrow this conservative government in a coup d'état with the help of Japanese troops in Seoul. In 1884, after China had been defeated by the French in Indochina, Korean progressive and anti-isolationist factions estimated that China's weakness would prevent it from coming to the aid of the established government. The progressives conferred with the Japanese minister, Takezoye Shinichiro, and plotted to wipe out both conservatives and pro-Chinese officers in the government. On December 4, 1884, a dinner party was held to celebrate the completion of the new post office building in Seoul. Many foreign dignitaries were present, but the Japanese minister was not. About an hour after the party began, a fire broke out in the new post office building. The fire spread, and soon the city was in chaos. The leaders of the coup d'état ran to the palace and asked the royal family to move to a safer place. When the royal family and the conservatives were prepared to leave, they were met by Takezoye and two hundred Japanese soldiers. The leading conservatives were quickly executed. A new government was formed.

On December 5, the day after the coup, outraged Koreans asked Chinese General Yuan Shikai to intervene. Yuan sent a messenger to Takezoye asking why the palace was surrounded by Japanese soldiers and why government officials had been killed. He demanded that the Japanese soldiers leave immediately. When Takezoye refused to answer, Yuan ordered Chinese and Korean soldiers to attack the palace. Japanese and progressive party troops battled Yuan's army most of the day, but by early evening they were forced to retreat. The royal family had moved to the northeastern part of the palace grounds. From there they managed to escape. Forty-eight hours after the coup began, the new progressive government ceased to be. Many leaders of the coup, including Kim Ok Kiun, escaped to Japan, but some, such as Sŏ Jai Pil, fled as far as the United States.

Although the coup of 1884 failed, and its alliance with a foreign power to overthrow the government was a shameful episode in Korea's political history, some positive aspects can be discerned. Despite ties to Japan, the coup's leaders hoped to maintain national sovereignty and independence by their actions, ending the dominating influence of China in Korea. They also hoped to establish diplomatic links with other nations on an equal basis, thus ending the long years of isolationism. Further, they wanted to end the long and despotic rule of factions and family clans, develop the country's industry, and provide equal job opportunities for all. However, the fatal flaw was that these reforms did not reflect general public sentiment at that time, and any hope of popular support was lost because of the progressives' alliance with Japan. Japan was Korea's traditional enemy, and the progressive leaders maintained a naive ignorance of its imperialistic ambitions. It is questionable whether the success of the 1884 coup attempt would have ended Korea's isolation or whether it would have hastened Japan's usurpation of Korean power.

From a Christian perspective, the political upheaval of 1884 led to another epoch-making event, becoming the stepping stone for furthering Protestant mission work in Korea. Part of the progressive plot involved the assassination of Prince Min Yŏng Ik, the most powerful conservative leader. Though he was not killed, he was badly wounded. In the emergency, Dr. Horace Allen, the first Presbyterian medical missionary in Korea, who had only been in the country a short while, was called on to help the critically wounded prince. When Dr. Allen first saw him, the prince's condition was critical:

> After being rushed across the city under an escort of native troops I found the foreign representatives and the high native dignitaries spattered with blood and terribly agitated, while the host of the evening, Prince Min, was lying at the point of death with arteries severed and seven sword cuts on his head and body.[9]

The missionary doctor immediately began treating the wounded man, thereby assuming an awesome responsibility for the prince's life. The doctor stayed on and took care of Prince Min, but his job was certainly not an easy one. Dr. Allen exercised patience, care, and skill, and after three months of treatment, the prince fully recovered.

Dr. Allen's success in bringing the prince back to health won the confidence of the Korean government and the royal court. He received a government position as physician to the royal court. In this position of prominence Dr. Allen laid a solid foundation for the eventual success of Protestant Christianity in Korea, as well as his own involvement in Korean politics.

3

The First Protestant Missionary and Political Involvement

It was usually not considered wise for missionaries to be involved in the politics of the country where they served, nor in the diplomatic service of the country whence they came, nor even in the politics of the mission agencies that dispatched them! This was especially true in Korea where political factionalism and power struggles were many. The missionaries in Korea were particularly warned in an article in *Foreign Missionary* that "nothing could be more uncalled for, or more injurious to our real missionary work, than for us to seem to take any part in the political factions of Korea."[1]

At first, Dr. Horace Allen was cautious not to become involved in politics. In 1885 he wrote to the Presbyterian Mission House in New York, "I have been honored by a committee waiting upon me to ask me to present an address of welcome to the returning British Consul, General Aston, but have thought it best to stay out of politics, and have, therefore, respectfully declined.[2]

How was it, then, that Allen eventually became such an active diplomat in an alien country? Two important factors which contributed were Allen's personality conflicts with General Foote, the American minister in Seoul, and his ideological conflicts with fellow missionaries, especially Horace Underwood, the first ordained missionary in Korea.

Allen's difficulties with Foote peaked after the coup attempt of 1884. Foote was jealous of Allen because of his growing popularity at the Korean court, and Allen's diary relates an incident that illustrates the level to which their professional relationship had dropped:

> I told General Foote the same regarding Allen's decision to stay in Seoul and not take refuge in Chemulpo after the coup and then he urged me to come and live in their place, but I soon learned from his remarks that what I expected was true, namely, that he cared not a bit for our safety but simply desired someone to look after his own effects. I asked him to ask for a guard for my place and then I would come and do as he requested. He finally promised to send my message but afterwards told me he had

forgotten it. Mr. Foote, however, in his endeavors to assure me he had really forgotten it, assured me that my opinion was true, namely that he lied.[3]

After that, Allen and Foote made no secret of their dislike for each other.

Allen's involvement at the court also proved a trial for his missionary colleagues. Most of the Korean royal family, especially Prince Min Yŏng Ik, whose life Dr. Allen had saved, were conservative and pro-Chinese. In contrast, most missionaries, especially Horace G. Underwood, favored the progressive, pro-Japanese Koreans. The pro-Japanese view of these missionaries was clearly expressed in the *Foreign Missionary* in 1885:

> Dr. Hepburn expressed the fear that the national temperament of the Koreans is more Chinese than Japanese; that a strong anti-foreign and conservative feeling will characterize them for many years. He makes special mention, however, of the very liberal spirit and progressive notions for the Koreans now in Japan, and expresses the hope that if they do return and are restored to the confidence of the Government they will be good friends of the missionary and of national progress.[4]

The relationship between Allen and Underwood was strained from the beginning. Allen wrote in his diary after their first meeting, "Yesterday evening Mr. Underwood came to us. . . . Mr. Underwood seems smart and businesslike but he is rather conceited and rash. I am afraid he will get us into trouble."[5]

Allen had other difficulties with Underwood and the other missionaries besides those involving his close association with the royal family. Allen had his doubts concerning evangelistic practices, and he was always cautious about beginning open, active mission work. However, Underwood was zealous to promote his mission "cautiously but without apology" and to "preach and take the consequences."[6] Similar criticisms of Allen also came from the Methodist missionaries and even from a medical colleague, Dr. John Heron. Allen became disillusioned and disgusted, writing in one angry mood:

> Mission work is a farce. I am kept busy by various duties, yet have an easy time. Heron has every other week wholly to himself and all but 2–3 hours of other weeks. Yet he does not study. Underwood has as much leisure. So have the Methodists. I think it is a pretty soft thing.[7]

Out of Allen's unhappiness came a growing desire to get away from Seoul and from his countrymen there. An ideal opportunity eventually arose. In 1887 the Korean king decided to open a legation in the United States. He asked Allen to be its foreign secretary as well as a guide to the Korean members of the envoy.

Allen's first step toward becoming a diplomat was escorting these representatives to Washington.

While he was glad to leave Seoul, this new job was no easy one. Guiding uninitiated diplomats through a strange land was long and tiresome work, from the very first experience on board ship:

> They persist in standing upon the closet seats which they keep dirtied all the time and have severely marked with their hob-nailed shoes. They smell of dung continually, persist in smoking in their rooms which smell horribly of unwashed bodies, dung, stale wine, Korean food, smoke, etc. I go regularly every morning to see the minister and get him up on deck. I can't stop long in their rooms as I have had to point out lice to them on their clothes.[8]

The difficulties Allen was to face had just begun. When the diplomatic party landed in San Francisco, they went to the Palace Hotel, and Allen recounts another incident there:

> Arriving from our ship we entered the elevator at the Palace Hotel in San Francisco. It was quite a little room with divans along the sides. Some of the Koreans had comfortably seated themselves, while others were standing about seeming to wonder why we were all put into so small a room, when the operator pulled his rope and we began to shoot skyward. With horrified exclamations, as one man they seized me, exclaiming about earthquakes in the greatest alarm. After that, when stopping at hotels, they insisted on having rooms low enough so they might dispense with the use of elevators. It was amusing to see them go clattering up the stairs in their sandals, a sort of foot gear not meant for stair climbing and used in a country where the houses are of one story, without stairs, and where the shoes are left outside the door on entering a house.[9]

But eventually Allen escorted the delegation safely to Washington, D.C., and presented them to President Grover Cleveland, as he wrote:

> In 1888 I escorted a Korean minister, and his suite of twelve, to Washington, and established them there, the first Korean legation to be established out of Asia. It was in January that this unique party burst upon our capital, clad in delicately tinted silkgowns, and wearing their hats in the house. And such hats! They were made of glossy black horsehair, silk and bamboo, with the crowns, shaped like truncated cones, rising from rims six inches across.[10]

Though his task was sometimes difficult, sometimes humorous, Horace Allen performed it patiently and faithfully for the benefit of Korea. He could write his friend Prince Min Yŏng Ik and report to him truthfully that everyone in Washington received the Korean legation very favorably.

After the Korean diplomats were settled and the legation firmly established, Allen began trying to raise American business interest in Korea. He extolled the Korean people and their culture in newspaper and magazine articles, hoping to attract American financiers and businesses by explaining Korea's economic potential and promise of prosperity. Allen wrote of his efforts:

> I tried to raise a loan through James H. Wilson of Grant Co. . . . He is the financial authority in New York apparently, on Eastern matters. The result was unsuccessful. Later on several gentlemen visited me in Washington asking a franchise for gas lighting in Seoul.[11]

More American business leaders began to respond. In the summer of 1888, Allen succeeded in forming a syndicate which included some of America's leading capitalists of the day. One of them was W. T. Pierce, who wanted to establish a gold mill. Allen rejoiced and wrote in a letter to Prince Min, "I now have some encouraging news for you. The mining expert Mr. Pierce has found gold enough in Korea to warrant the erection of a mill and machinery."[12] Pierce later sent a telegram to Allen, about which Allen wrote, "Pierce telegraphed us for the mining land, his telegram which he wrote: 'one machinist foreman was sent, one machinist, four assistants.'"[13] From that small start, W. T. Pierce went on to develop the most modern mechanized gold mine in Korea.

To be sure, Allen's success in bringing American business into Korea had roots in selfish economic motives quite apart from any perceived benefits to the Korean people. Nevertheless, his efforts stimulated some crucial economic development in Korea as a result of American enterprise, and Koreans began to enjoy more of the advantages of modern science and technology. Before the end of the nineteenth century, Americans developed Korea's first modern gold, silver, and coal mines; an electric railroad; a modern water system; and a steam railroad. Allen boasted:

> America built Korea's first steam railway . . . and is now in successful operation with American equipment over a standard gauge track and a ten span steel bridge of two thousand feet in length. Although this road is but twenty-five miles long, connecting the capital with the port of Chemulpo, it was the forerunner of the extensive system of railways now built.[14]

With the involvement of American enterprise, the progress toward modernization in Korea was amazing. In the last decade of the nineteenth century, Korea had "one of the most extensive and successful gold mining properties in Asia" employing "over half a hundred white men and some thousands of Asiatics in the operations of its mines and mills, and all the many accessories necessary to the successful conduct of so large a property."[15] In Seoul, the first Korean electric railroad was built by Americans in conjunction with an electric plant, which was itself one of the largest single plants in Asia. The firm that built this electric plant also constructed the Seoul waterworks system of which Allen again boasted:

> This plant is so extensive as to provide for all probable future wants, and although the supply could not well be better, a complete filtration system is being installed for greater perfection: so that as in the matter of light the Koreans passed from the tallow dip to electricity, in the matter of a water supply they will jump from wayside wells to mountain water carefully filtered and delivered at the door or in the houses.[16]

Thus Korea was well on its way to complete modernization. American enterprises had developed many more of Korea's natural resources and could have easily industrialized the nation had not Korea been bothered by the colonial aspirations of surrounding powers. Indeed, at that time Korea could have become one of the most modern, industrialized nations in Asia. Unfortunately, its development was constantly hindered by its neighbors, especially Japan, and by its own internal weakness and political corruption. The country lost a prime chance to develop its resources for its own people. Still, Dr. Allen continued to believe that Korea could blossom into a modern nation. When neighboring powers interfered with Korea's freedom and sovereignty, Allen went to great lengths to oppose their encroachments. These efforts were among Allen's greatest contributions in Korea's modern history.

One significant triumph of his work to maintain Korean independence came at the time when Allen was asked to guide the Korean legation to Washington. This mission was a diplomatic insult to the Chinese, who wanted to keep Korea as a vassal state of China. Yuan Shih Kai, the Chinese representative in Seoul, tried to stop the envoy's departure with the help of the former regent, Taewonkun, as noted by Allen: "[Yuan Shih Kai] is trying to prevent the departure of the mission."[17] In his diary entry on September 23, 1887, Allen also wrote:

> Minister Pak Chung Yang [the leader of the legation] was to meet me outside city gate and at once to proceed together. He did not appear. Next day I learned that he had been recalled by the King who had been

intimidated by the Chinese representative who produced a telegram to Li
Hung-Chang to declare war if the mission was sent [to the] U.S.[18]

The Korean king was very worried by the Chinese reaction and called upon
Allen for advice, but Allen strongly urged him to carry out the mission for the
sake of Korea's sovereignty and integrity. With this encouragement, the king
became determined to send the diplomats to the United States in spite of the
threat. He asked Allen to seek further support for the venture from the Russians
and Americans in Seoul. Allen wrote, "[The king] asked me to linger . . . [and
requested that I present these] matters to Americans and Russians and see whether
they would back him up in sending off the mission."[19]

    In addition, Allen helped Pak Chung Yang stay with the American lega-
tion in Seoul and with the help of Hugh N. Dinsmore, the American minister in
Seoul, arranged passage on the *USS Omaha* for the Korean diplomats. China
was prepared to prevent their departure from Chemulpo and sent a fleet to stop
them, but the attempt failed because the Chinese did not dare to tangle with an
American warship. Allen recounted the incident:

> Yuan Shih Kai attempted to prevent the departure of the mission
> but was embarrassed by the fact that a foreigner was connected with it.
> Then the American Government dispatched the Naval Vessel *Omaha* to
> transport the mission to Nagasaki, which further complicated matters for
> the Chinese. As they were steaming down the bay the *Omaha* passed be-
> tween the lines of a Chinese fleet sent to intercept them and for a time
> they were greatly alarmed by the salutes until they were assured that, in-
> stead of being fired upon, Chinese powder was actually being burned in
> honor of their departure.[20]

The presence of Dr. Allen in the legation and his position as its secretary thus
helped make possible the Korean diplomat's safe departure for the United
States.

    However, Chinese efforts to prevent their success continued in Wash-
ington. When the mission arrived, the Chinese minister wanted to introduce the
Koreans as vassal envoys of China, but Dr. Allen would not allow this and again
lobbied for Korea's sovereign rights, "It became my duty to defeat the demands
as well as the persuasions of the Chinese minister that we consent to be introduced by him."[21] By his efforts Allen successfully thwarted the Chinese attempts, and the Korean legation was established on its own terms.

    After the Korean diplomats were firmly situated in their legation, Allen
resigned his duties with them. Dr. Allen returned to Chemulpo and practiced
medicine for a short time there. Then he took up his former job at the government hospital which he had established. The U.S. government appointed Dr.

Allen Secretary of the United States legation in Seoul, in 1890. Seven years later, he became the United States minister and consul general to Seoul. Resuming his diplomatic career, Horace Allen continued to support the Korean king and other Korean leaders in order to preserve the independence and freedom of Korea.

In 1896, when the Korean Independence Association was formed to cope with a growing infiltration by foreign powers, Allen supported them wholeheartedly.

As Allen rightly perceived, the growth of Japanese power in the Far East was the main threat to Korea's independence. He constantly warned his government that expanding Japanese power was the greatest threat to world peace:

> The Island Empire of the Rising Sun is frequently torn and rent by terrible convulsions of nature. Advices from that country are to the effect that vast forces are feverishly engaged day and night in constructing all manner of warlike material; may this not portend an outbreak greater and more far-reaching than those natural phenomena to which the Japanese are more or less accustomed?[22]

Allen wanted to save Korea from Japanese imperial ambitions, and he believed there was hope. He wished to instill this hope in his superiors, but the attitudes in Washington always seemed to be pro-Japanese, especially those of President Theodore Roosevelt. Roosevelt liked Japan and often praised the country, once writing, "Japan is indeed a wonderful land. Nothing in history has quite paralleled her rise during the last fifty years. Her progress has been remarkable alike in war, in industry, in statesmanship, in science."[23] As far as Korea was concerned, Roosevelt felt that it belonged to Japan! The president said:

> With businesslike coolness the soldierly statesmen of Nippon have taken the chance which offered itself of at little cost retaliating for the injury inflicted upon them in the past and removing an obstacle to their future dominance in eastern Asia. Korea is absolutely Japan's.[24]

In 1903 Allen decided to travel to Washington to speak with the president in person. Allen started out from Korea in early summer, taking the newly opened trans-Siberian railroad: "In the summer of 1903 it chanced to be my good fortune to make a trip through Manchuria, Siberia and Russia on my way to America."[25] In going through the northeastern part of China and Russia, Allen had a chance to note the friendliness of the Russian people toward Americans and the good prospects there for expanded American trade. He wrote:

> As I saw the great consumption of American products in Manchuria, it seemed to me that we were the ones most likely to profit by the expenditure of those hundreds of millions of Russian roubles in the pacification of that vast territory. It seemed also that we, of all people, were regarded by the Russians with the greatest favor and that we had the best opportunity of all for cultivating intimate trade relations with that vast empire, as yet almost undeveloped.[26]

Allen's pro-Russian and anti-Japanese views were to encounter their exact opposites in the views of President Roosevelt.

Arriving in Washington, D.C., on September 29, 1903, Allen remarked in his diary, "Went to Washington by PA. R.R. got there in evening. Went Willard's Hotel."[27] He met with the president on September 30 and later wrote in his diary:

> I went to Dep't [sic] and stated things. Went to W. W. Rockhill and talked over matters. Called on President and told him he was making a mistake to Russia. He asked me if I had talked with Secretaries. I said I had. He then made an appointment (with) Rockhill and myself to meet him at 9:30 P.M. . . . Called on the Koreans in afternoon.[28]

Keeping his appointment, Allen met with the president and W. W. Rockhill that evening. Concerning Rockhill, Allen wrote, "Rockhill is a splendid person and a convincing talker. And he is the creator and sponsor for our Asiatic policy."[29] In his discussion with the president, however, Allen's pro-Korean and pro-Russian views clashed sharply with Roosevelt's pro-Japanese attitude. Allen wrote: "I said I did not believe that the Russian gov't were oppressive to their subjects, and the President spoke up very sharply and said 'We have awful assurance on their head' . . . I told the President I was sorry."[30] Likewise, Allen attacked Japan's aggressive behaviors, but it was beyond Allen's ability to sway the president's opinion. Roosevelt maintained his pro-Japanese views in Far Eastern affairs and in 1905 wrote to John Hay, the secretary of state, "We can not possibly interfere for the Koreans against Japan. They couldn't strike one blow in their own defense."[31]

Allen gained little in his conference with the president, but he resumed his work as American minister in Seoul and continued as much as he was able to oppose Japanese expansion in Korea. When he returned to Korea, he traveled through Japan and later remarked, "By encouraging Japan it seemed that we were egging them on to war, a war that would harm us."[32] As growing Japanese power further menaced Korean independence, Allen wrote to Secretary of State Hay, sharing with him the serious concern of the Korean king about the threat of Japan:

He falls back in his extremity upon his old friendship with America. . . . The Emperor confidently expects that America will do something for him at the close of this war (the Russo-Japanese War) or when opportunity offers, to retain for him as much of his independence as is possible. He is inclined to give a very free and favorable translation to Article I of our treaty of Jenchun [sic] of 1882.[33]

However, Allen's influence in Washington was minimal, and his letter persuaded no one.

At the Portsmouth conference which ended the Russo-Japanese War, Japan's paramount interest in Korea was recognized by the American government and forced upon Russia. With that, there was almost no hope of maintaining Korea's independence. Yet Allen did not cease his efforts in the Korean cause. He continually transmitted letters of protest from American residents in Korea and from Koreans themselves over Japanese conduct in the country. Allen constantly reported to Washington about the activities of the Japanese, but he went so far in supporting Korean independence that he finally aroused the ire of the State Department. In 1905 he was recalled to the United States and replaced by Edwin V. Morgan. There was little question that Allen was dismissed because he strove for Korean sovereignty in opposition to Japanese imperialism. Allen wrote about his recall in a letter to Pak Chung Yang:

I can see now that the Japanese, who are very strong in public favor in America as the result of their great war, arranged all this (withdrawal of the American Legation from Seoul) in Washington sometime ago and my recall was probably due to the fact that this course had been decided upon. I was regarded as too strongly in favor of Korea and therefore presumably opposed to the Japanese.[34]

When Allen returned home to the United States in the latter part of 1905, Korea was in Japanese hands under the name of a "protectorate." The first protestant missionary to Korea, Horace N. Allen, had been a friend of the Korean people and was closely involved in the political life of Koreans with a strong sympathy for Korea's independence. When Korea fell into Japanese hands, he fell with her. In his letter to Pak Chung Yang, Allen wrote:

This blotting out of the independent rights of such an ancient and kind people is most sad and regrettable, and Mrs. Allen has shed many tears over the fate of Korea, while tears have been in my own heart. . . . Sometime I must surely come to see my old Korean home which seems so dear to me.[35]

4

THE PROGRESS OF CHRISTIANITY AND THE AWAKENING OF KOREAN NATIONALISM

After Dr. Horace Allen's favorable acceptance by the royal family of the Yi government, the cause of Christianity, especially Protestant Christianity, advanced. The establishment of a medical mission by Dr. Allen led to the appointment of Reverend Horace G. Underwood in 1885 to begin evangelistic work in Korea. On July 4, 1886, the first woman missionary, Annie J. Ellers, joined the mission as a nurse. She was succeeded by Lillian S. Horton, a medical doctor, who arrived in Korea in 1888 and later married missionary Horace Underwood.

Methodist missionary activities in Korea were similar to those of the Presbyterians. Preparation for Methodist work there had begun in 1883 when the General Committee of the Missionary Society of the Methodist Episcopal Church appropriated five thousand dollars of its budget to be used in Korea. Dr. Robert Maclay, superintendent of the Japanese mission, visited Korea in 1884 to study the prospects, and the annual report of the missionary society for that year remarked as follows:

> The visit of Dr. Maclay fulfilled the highest expectations of those interested, and made the way clear for the early establishment of a mission in that country. A paper setting forth the desires and object of Christian missionaries was sent to the King, who returned a cordial acknowledgement with permission to open work, especially medical and school work.[1]

The Mission Society was now determined to open a mission in Korea. In the latter part of 1884, Dr. William B. Scranton was appointed to the task and was joined later by Rev. Henry G. Appenzeller. The Women's Foreign Missionary Society also sponsored Dr. Scranton's mother, Mary F. Scranton, as a missionary. Dr. Scranton, his wife, his mother, and Rev. and Mrs. Appenzeller set sail on the USS *Arabic* and arrived in Japan in February 1885. The Scrantons remained in Japan in order to learn the Korean language while the Appenzellers joined Presbyterian missionary Horace Underwood and traveled on to Korea.

On May 5, 1885, Dr. Scranton left his family in Japan, traveled to Chemulpo, Korea, and opened his Methodist mission in Seoul. In 1895, the Methodists in Korea were strengthened by the arrival of Dr. C. F. Reid, a Southern Methodist missionary from China. Bishop E. R. Hendrix of the Methodist Episcopal Church, South, also visited Korea that year to evaluate the situation.[2] Interest in Korean mission work by the Methodist Episcopal Church, South, had been aroused by a noted Korean convert, Yun Chi Ho, who had become a Christian in Shanghai through the influence of Methodist missionaries. Yun had later traveled to the United States and studied at Vanderbilt and Emory universities.

A few other Protestant churches followed the Presbyterians and Methodists in their attempts to nurture Christianity in Korea, among them the Anglican Society for the Propagation of the Gospel. C. F. Pascoe, keeper of records for the society, related some background on the opening of Anglican work in Korea:

> The idea of an Anglican Mission to Korea was originated in 1880 by the Rev. A. C. Shaw, one of the pioneers and founders of the Society's Mission in Japan. In view of the opening of Korea for foreign intercourse, Mr. (now Archdeacon) Shaw felt that the Society should be ready to take the lead in Missionary work there . . . when in 1884 a treaty was being negotiated between England and Korea the three English Bishops in China seized the opportunity to make an identical proposal. . . . In 1887 Bishops Scott (of North China) and Bickersteth (of Japan) visited Korea, and appealed to the Archbishop of Canterbury to take steps to insure the sending of a Mission from the church at home without delay . . . under Royal Mandate of Rev. C. J. Corfe whose services as a Naval Chaplain had received recognition in the highest quarters, was on All Saints' Day 1889 consecrated in Westminster Abbey first Missionary Bishop of Korea.[3]

Bishop Corfe arrived in Chemulpo on September 20, 1890, and went immediately to Seoul. In 1892 sisters of the Community of St. Peter (Kilburn) joined the Anglican work in Korea. The Anglican Church worked among the Japanese residents in Korea as well as among Koreans.

The Toronto University Young Men's Christian Association also had interest in Korean work and in 1889 sent J. S. Gale, who joined the Presbyterian (northern) mission. In 1904, the Seventh Day Adventist church was introduced by two Koreans returning from Honolulu, Hawaii. In 1907, the Oriental Missionary Society began its work in Korea, and in 1908, the Salvation Army initiated a slow but steady growth. Yet, comparatively, it was the Presbyterians who showed the greatest growth and had the greatest impact. This became especially true when Presbyterians from the United States and the Presbyterian churches of Canada and Australia eventually united their missions, shaping the character of Korean Protestantism.

Although Protestant work was started in Korea much later than in other portions of Asia, Korea proved a greater success than other Asian missions. An important factor in the Protestant success there surely had to do with successful medical work, since practically every denomination that began work in Korea started with medical care. Allen, Ellers, Underwood, and Scranton were doctors or had medical training, and each showed great compassion for a people lacking in modern medical knowledge and good hygiene. The work of the doctors was hampered both by disease and by superstition, but they combatted them with the integrated work of medicine and evangelism.

In 1885, Dr. Horace Allen opened the Royal Hospital in Seoul, but with the growing needs of and increasing demands for medical work, the Royal Hospital was expanded in 1904 into the Severance Medical Hospital and College. The man responsible for this expansion was Dr. O. R. Avison, who said the following concerning the contributions of medicine to Protestant mission success:

> We frequently learn that those who return to their homes teach their neighbors and establish regular services for worship and study. We are often surprised to hear from the itinerant missionaries of the number of places where they find groups ready for them to minister to and build up into regular churches.[4]

Besides medical work, missionaries also contributed to the education of the Korean people, which was another factor of the church's success. The Methodists were especially active in education, founding some of the most outstanding educational institutions in Korea. It was Dr. Scranton's mother who first realized particularly the lack of educational opportunities for women, so she invited women to classes in her home. The number of pupils increased so rapidly that it was necessary to open a more extensive women's school, and this was the beginning of Ewha Hakdang, which has become the largest as well as the oldest institution offering higher learning to women in Korea, now known as the Ewha Women's University. Other denominations also established a variety of educational institutions, including theological schools, all of which have produced not only church leaders, but also leaders for all segments of Korean society.

In addition to evangelism, medicine, and education, the Protestant churches helped to modernize the country by introducing updated technology via American business. American enterprise provided Korea with its first modern railway before the end of the nineteenth century. Also, in the last decade of that century, Korea possessed one of the most extensive gold mining operations in Asia. In 1884 Thomas Edison secured the rights for the first electric plant in

Korea and established in Seoul a waterworks system plus one of the largest electric plants in Asia.

The contributions of technology, education, and medicine, brought through Christian mission contacts, helped raise both the standard of living and patriotic nationalism. One of the most important factors in nurturing Korean nationalism was a style of mission used by most Christian missionaries known as the "Nevius Method." This method took its name from Rev. John L. Nevius, a Presbyterian missionary in China, who first promoted it in a series of articles published in the *Chinese Recorder*. The goal of the Nevius Method was to establish self-supporting, self-propagating, and self-governing national churches that did not depend on foreign missionaries or agencies to support their finances or their administration.

The method appealed tremendously to the Korean mind. The emphasis on *self*-support and *self*-government aroused the Korean spirit of independence long repressed under the influence of Confucian thought. Confucianism had made some positive contributions in Korea by promoting high ethical standards in family and personal relationships and by emphasizing the value and dignity of human beings. However, it had also created fragmented political castes based on differing interpretations of Confucian teachings and their application in society. Worst of all, it encouraged an attitude of political subjection to China, the country in which Confucianism originated. Korean officials, most of whom were Confucianists, believed that China was the world's only truly civilized country and that it was the center of the world. They saw China as a "big brother" to Korea, and Korea had to respect its big brother in order to be true to Confucianism. Although Korea was technically a sovereign and independent kingdom, it subjected itself to China in accord with this, even sending an annual envoy with tribute to the Chinese emperor.

Toward the end of the nineteenth century, however, progressive Koreans began to attack the conservatism of Confucianism. Some patriotic Koreans saw in Christianity hope for Korean unity. One such individual was So Jae Pil, who came in contact with Christianity while studying medicine in the United States. Upon returning to Korea in 1886, he dedicated his entire life to the cause of the nationalistic movement, and to enhance this work, he began publication of the first modern Korean newspaper, *Tongnip Shinmun* (the independent). The paper served not only to enlighten the Korean public on world affairs, but also to arouse popular desire for the preservation of national independence.

Publication of the newspaper was not an easy task. Sŏ Jae Pil had primary responsibility for collecting the news items, writing them up, editing them, and printing them, even though he was lacking in printing skills. Through his paper, So advocated for reform of the Yi government and for liberation from foreign domination. He promoted the cause by use of nationalistic phrases such as

"Korea for Koreans," "for the interest of the Korean people," and "by the Korean people." Bold efforts like those of So Jae Pil inspired the rise of nationalism in Korea. They were a key to its future success.

In addition to his newspaper, So organized a political group called Tongnip Hoephoe (the independent society) in 1896. It began as a group of thirty people committed to national independence and opposed to foreign encroachment in their country. The society organized public political rallies and speeches for the cause of Korean freedom and independence. In 1897, the members of the Independent Society designed and erected the Independent Arch in Seoul as a permanent sign of Korean independence. The arch still stands as a memorial to those first Korean nationalist leaders.

Christian leaders, who engaged in independence movements and showed appreciation for Korean culture and history, contributed to the awaking of Korean nationalism. In their quest for a national identity, Korean Christians began to reevaluate their cultural heritage. The adoption of a Korean alphabet, Hangŭl, in Christian literature instead of traditional Chinese characters became one important factor. Hangŭl, a phonetic rather than the pictographic alphabet commissioned by the fourth king of the Yi dynasty, Sejong, was the product of scientific linguistic research made by literary masters. It was completed in 1443 and nationalized by royal edict in 1446. Yet this new alphabet, designed for the common people, remained neglected for many years. It was especially rejected by the Confucian literati because it was too easily learned "even by women" who were not supposed to achieve such abilities. Even so, some fine literature developed during the Yi dynasty using this alphabet, and it survived because it was used by women and oppressed commoners, as well as for the translation of a few Buddhist sutras.

When Christian missionaries arrived in Korea, they began to use Hangŭl for all their printed matter. The entire Bible was translated into Hangŭl. In October 1889, several Protestant missionaries met at the home of Horace Underwood and organized the Korean Religious Tract Society, today known as the Christian Literature Society of Korea. Practically all Korean Christian literature, hymnals, and Bible translations continue to be published in Hangŭl. A prominent missionary explained how its extensive use of Hangŭl helped the missionary enterprise to succeed:

> This common, easy-to-learn, written language became the vehicle for popularizing the Christian message among all classes. It had not been widely used during the four centuries since its invention and years hence it may again fall into disuse. Before schools giving a modern education were extensively established in Korea, the women, children, and ignorant men in the church who never had the advantages of even an elementary education were soon learning the Korean alphabet and reading the Word

of God and other Christian literature. New missionaries were also able to read and write the alphabet after a few lessons and thus pursue their language study. The Korean written script therefore has been of incalculable benefit in the Christian propaganda and particularly in the production of Christian literature.[5]

Such progress in Christian evangelism helped in turn to awaken Korean national sentiment, cultural pride, and independent spirit, during the time of threat of colonization by foreign forces. Korean Christians were few in number, however, and foreign powers were great. Among the foreign nations that were most actively seeking to dominate the political affairs of Korea were China, Russia, and Japan. Among them, Russia longed for warm-water naval harbors in Korea, China wanted to maintain her traditional influence, and Japan was the newly rising imperial power of Asia. A noted Koreanologist, Cornelius Osgood, stated:

> China, Russia, and Japan were juxtaposed to Korea with armies close at hand. Each considered that the subjection of the Peninsula by either of the others would be not only an economic loss but a vital threat to its national security. And since none trusted another, Korea became from that time on, a pawn in an international conflict for power.[6]

The interest of these three powers in Korea brought about international conflict. It led to the Sino-Japanese War of 1894 which was a turning point for the eventual colonization of Korea by Japan.

The immediate cause of the Sino-Japanese War was related to the Tonghak rebellion of 1894. "Tonghak" or "Eastern Learning" was originally a religious movement with a strong nationalistic political sentiment, founded by Choe Che Wu in 1860. Choe was born in Kyongju, the ancient capital of the Silla kingdom, in 1828. In his youth Choe was acquainted with the classical writings of Confucianism and Taoism. He was also acquainted with Buddhism and the teachings of Roman Catholicism. During the time of his sickness, he believed that he had received a revelation from the "Lord of Heaven" and was called to find a religion for the people of Korea. On the basis of this belief, he completed a writing of the "Great Holy Scripture," which was based on the teachings of Confucianism, Buddhism, Taoism, and even doctrines of Roman Catholicism. Choe believed that Christianity was the religion of the "Lord of Heaven" for the Western people, and he called Christianity "Sohak" or Western learning. He called his religion "Tonghak" or Eastern learning, because it was to be the national religion for Koreans. The Tonghak teaching began to spread. It was popular among the Minjung, the people of marginality who were oppressed by government officials and landlords. Gradually the Tonghak movement developed into a political and social reform movement, which provided a certain basis of hope and liberation from oppression.

In the Tonghak movement Roman Catholic influence was apparent in the dogmatic and devotional manifestations of its leaders. When Choe Che Wu and his disciples were arrested, they were labeled as followers of the "Lord of Heaven" or Roman Catholics. Choe was beheaded in Taegu on March 15, 1864. His Tonghak movement was outlawed. However, the Tonghak sect continued its attack against the corruption of government officers. This appealed to the nationalistic sentiment of the Korean public, and the Tonghak movement continued to grow.

In February 1894, rebellion broke out in the Kobu County of Cholla Province led by Tonghak followers against corrupt local officials.

The rebellion spread quickly into most of Cholla and Chungchong provinces. Rebels conquered the major cities and county seats of these southern provinces and marched toward Seoul. Government soldiers were sent to stop them. The royal army was unable to crush the rebel forces. The Yi government of Korea, worried by these developments, asked China to send military aid. At the same time, without invitation from the Korean government, seven Japanese warships and seven thousand Japanese soldiers landed at Inchon.

The Tonghak rebellion was stopped before the Chinese actually participated in its suppression. The Korean king therefore asked the Chinese soldiers to leave Korea. However, the Chinese did not wish to leave, since the Japanese soldiers were also in Korea. Meanwhile, the number of Japanese soldiers in Korea was increasing, enhancing military tensions.

At that point, the Korean government requested that the Western representatives in Seoul help secure the withdrawal of the Chinese and Japanese troops. Representatives of the United States, Russia, France, and England, in a joint note, suggested the simultaneous withdrawal of Chinese and Japanese forces from Korea. The Chinese responded with a favorable answer, but the Japanese did not. Instead, Japan increased its hostile attitude toward China and demanded that the Korean government order the Chinese troops to leave the country.

In the early morning of July 23, 1894, Japanese troops invaded the royal palace and almost kidnapped the king. Taewonkun was again made regent, but the government was controlled by Japanese force. This Japanese-controlled government signed an agreement which authorized Japan to expel the Chinese forces. On July 25, the Japanese attacked and sank the British steamer *Kowshing,* which was transporting Chinese troops. China and Japan declared war.

The Sino-Japanese War ended with a Japanese victory. The Tonghak rebellion, which sought to liberate the Minjung, the common mass of people who were oppressed by the government, also failed. The uprising of the people left a folk song that is loved yet today by Korean people from all walks of life. The song tells of the grief over the death of Chon Bong Jun, the leader of the rebellion, who was also called "Nokdu," which means green peas. At the same time it is an expression of Korea's sorrow over its declining sovereignty and loss of independence.

> Bird, bird, blue bird
> Do not sit on Green-pea
> when the green-pea blossoms fall
> Chòngpo[7] saleslady goes away with tears.

Although the Tonghak rebellion failed, it was an epoch- making event, demonstrating the power of the common people to bring about political change. In the year of the Tonghak rebellion, which rightly can be called the "Peasant Revolution of 1894," the Korean government made some important political reforms, which were known in Korean history as "Kabo reforms."

Still, the Yi government was not strong enough to resist foreign challenges to Korea's sovereignty. Korean nationalism, aroused by the progress of Christianity and political-social movements such as the Tonghak, failed when faced with aggressors like Japan.

5

THE JAPANESE COLONIZATION OF KOREA AND CHRISTIAN PARTICIPATION IN RESISTANCE MOVEMENTS

After the Sino-Japanese War, the influence of the Japanese government in Korea grew stronger than ever. However, Japan was not yet to take full political hegemony in Korea. There was still Russia to contend with. Russian influence in Korea grew steadily after Russia acquired the Siberian frontier from China through the Treaty of Beijing in 1860, gaining a common border with Korea. In 1884, Russia sent Karl Waeber to the Korean court as an envoy, and he became the Russian minister in Seoul. During this time, anti-Japanese feelings grew in the royal family, due to the Japanese conspiracy to depose Queen Min. The plot was discovered before it could be carried out, and Queen Min ousted pro-Japanese politicians from the government.

The balance of power which Japan had earned after the Sino-Japanese War was now shifting to Russia. Japan reacted to this situation with savage and brutal madness. In the early morning of August 20, 1895, Japanese troops invaded the palace and murdered the Korean queen. Japanese soldiers burned her body on the palace lawn and buried it on a hill near the palace. Professor Conroy of the University of Pennsylvania wrote this about the Japanese assassination of the queen:

> This was a murder of the most heinous kind, planned in advance, perpetrated against a defenseless woman in her own apartments, and climaxed by the hideous body's burning on the lawn. Such an act must be adjudged utterly indefensible by even the minimum standards of civilized society. Even the most loosely constructed laws of war, the direct necessities of diplomatic intrigue, the most insistent demands of national security cannot excuse such murder most foul.[1]

After the murder of the Queen, the Japanese military force and the pro-Japanese cabinet politicians took over power again and dissolved the pro-Russian cabinet. However, the Korean public did not support the new cabinet. Anti-Japanese feeling mounted, and political unrest continued.

Russia used the political instability and unrest for its own imperialist ambitions. The Russian minister Waeber arranged for the Korean king, who was frightened by the Japanese, to take refuge in the Russian legation where he stayed for a full year. Foreign representatives could approach the king only through the Russian legation. As long as the king was in Russian hands, the hegemony of foreign powers in Seoul was also in Russian hands. Anti-Japanese Korean leaders took this opportunity to form a pro-Russian cabinet. Russia exploited this situation by acquiring economic advantages, such as lumbering rights in the southern area around the Yalu River, and the right to mine in the northeastern part of the Korean peninsula.

Such encroachments by foreign powers and their economic exploitation definitely threatened Korea's independence. In February 1897, King Kojong returned to his palace. Earnestly desiring to bring stability to the government and to maintain the sovereignty of the nation, the king proclaimed the new name of Korea, Dae Han, and he was crowned as emperor. He also proclaimed a new education law, established new school systems, and invited foreign advisors to assist in educational development. However, the king lacked creativity in his leadership and depended heavily upon foreigners.

Meanwhile, the rival powers, Russia and Japan, continued to exert their influence in Korea. In 1903, Russian troops began to occupy the mouth of the Yalu River. Japan protested and asked Russia to concede to Japan's interest in Korea. Then Russia, countering, suggested a demarcation line at the Thirty-ninth Parallel to divide Korea between itself and Japan. Japan wanted the whole of Korea, so they refused the Russian proposal.

In February 1904, Japan broke off diplomatic relations with Russia, and, without a formal declaration of war, the Japanese navy attacked Port Arthur, a Russian naval base in east Asia. The Russo-Japanese War of 1904 and 1905 had begun. To the surprise of the world, Japan was again the victor, successfully wiping out all its rivals in Korea. Japan used the advantage gained by the victory over Russia to put Korea under its fist, becoming even more arrogant in dealing with the Korean government. Korea sought help in the "good offices" of the United States, to maintain its independence in accordance with the Korean-American treaty of 1882. However, President Theodore Roosevelt and the United States were on the side of Japan, not Korea.

A peace treaty recognizing the Japanese interest in Korea was signed in September at Portsmouth, New Hampshire. The treaty negotiations were mediated by President Theodore Roosevelt, who received the Nobel Peace Prize because of his involvement in ending this war. In November 1905 Japan concluded with Korea the Protectorate Treaty, using a military threat to the Korean government. Japan justified colonizing Korea on the basis of this treaty. It was never signed by the king of Korea, so it was invalid. Still, Japan used this illegal treaty to usurp complete control over Korea.

As the Japanese absorption of Korea was taking place, more Koreans participated in resistance movements against Japan. But, after 1905, the anti-Japanese movement within Korea faced increased difficulties. More and more Koreans fled to Siberia, China, Japan, and even the United States. Most of these Koreans who went abroad participated in patriotic activities to restore Korea's independence.

Among those Koreans who immigrated to the northeastern part of China, then called "Buk Kando," there were Christian converts who wanted to escape Japanese rule and engage in political activities for the independence of Korea. Christian mission work extended itself to these Korean immigrants in China. In 1898, the Canadian Presbyterians had begun mission work among the Koreans there. Canadian missionaries, such as Reverend Robert G. Grierson, who was sympathetic to Korean Christian efforts toward independence, supported the work of Yee Dong Hui, who was both a Christian and a nationalist political leader. Grierson extended his work among the Koreans not only in China, but also among the Korean immigrants in the Russian port city of Vladivostok.

Many Christian leaders strongly believed that the success of Christian mission work among the Koreans was the best way to liberate Korea from Japanese rule. Among such leaders was Yee Sang Sŭl, who engaged in the Christian education of Korean youth in China as a way to gain independence from Japan. To achieve that purpose, he established a Christian church in Yongjŏng, which became a center of the Korean nationalist movement and Christian education. In church meetings, Yee Sang Sul preached both the gospel of Christ and the liberation of Korea.

Many Christians migrated from the northeastern Hamkyung Province of Korea to northeastern China and established a new Christian town, naming it "Kusechon" (salvation village). In 1911 a Presbyterian church leader, Ryang Hyung Sik, led his entire family to an isolated village in northeast China and established a church there, calling the village "Unhoe Chon" (village of grace). Such towns and villages with church-related names such as Town of Eternal Life and Village of Salvation were common among the Korean settlements in China. Although there were conflicts between the Korean immigrants and the Chinese residents, the Chinese generally sympathized with the Koreans' anti-Japanese political movements, for China, too, was threatened by the encroaching Japanese power.

When Korean Christians migrated to China, many missionaries and mission agencies from Europe and North America welcomed the Koreans because of their zeal for evangelistic outreach and their strong commitment to church life. Often, when the Japanese police sought to arrest the Korean nationalist Christians, missionaries rendered assistance to protect Koreans with the missionaries' extra-territorial rights, granted them by the Chinese government.

To Korean Christians in China, the nationalist movement for Korean independence was the same as the movement for the Christian gospel. Christian leaders led revival meetings asking Koreans "to believe in Jesus to save the nation" and to educate the children for the independence of Korea. Such nationalistic sentiment was shared by Korean Christians both inside and outside Korea. The identification of Christian mission work with the political independence movement was one important reason for this "miracle in mission history," the success of Christian mission work among the Koreans. It was also the reason why a pro-Japanese American scholar, who visited Korea in the early part of this century, complained about Korean Christians, saying that they were not motivated by moral and spiritual reasons, but by economic, social, and political factors.[2]

With such political zeal for independence, Korean Christians increased in numbers. The imperialist policy of Japan's military government extended its influence into China, and brutally suppressed Korean nationalists and Christians there. It was not unusual for the Japanese police to demolish entire Korean villages and arrest Korean nationalist leaders. In recent visits of this author to Korean towns in Northeast China, he noticed many monuments that were erected to commemorate Korean patriotic martyrs who had suffered death by the Japanese.

Among all of the political resistance movements of Korean Christians, the most shocking incidents were the assassinations of two prominent political leaders by Korean Christians. One incident took place in San Francisco in 1908 and another in Harbin, China, in the following year. The San Francisco incident was the assassination of a U.S. diplomat, Durham White Stevens, who was a chief advisor to Marquis Ito Hirobumi, the architect of Japanese colonization of Korea. Previously, from 1883 to 1904, Mr. Stevens had been a legal advisor to the Japanese legation in Washington and chief advisor to Marquis Ito. He was loved by the Japanese and paid by the Japanese government when he left Tokyo on March 3, 1908, to visit Washington, D.C.: "He was given an enthusiastic farewell at the station by nearly two hundred officials of the embassy."[3] When he arrived in San Francisco, on Sunday, March 21, he was welcomed by the Japanese dignitaries, including the Japanese consul general in San Fancisco, Mr. Koike Chozo. Then he made statements supporting Japanese polices in Korea, blaming the corruption of the Korean government, praising the goodness of the Japanese government, and stating that all Koreans wanted to be ruled by Japan.[4]

Mr. Stevens made the following statement in the *San Francisco Call:* "Japan is doing in Korea and for the Koreans what the United States is doing in the Philippines for the Filipinos, modifying its methods only to suit the somewhat different conditions with which it has to deal."[5]

The prominent San Francisco newspaper further reported: "Stevens denies that the Japanese are exploiting Korea for Japanese profit or that the revenues of the land are being used in maintaining an arm of Japanese office holders."[6]

There were then about one hundred Koreans living in San Francisco, and practically all of them belonged to the San Francisco Korean Methodist Church. Meeting at the church, they discussed what they should do about the false propaganda they read in the newspapers. One young student, whose name was Chun Myung Woon, expressed his desire to kill Mr. Stevens. Most Koreans at the meeting opposed such an act of violence, however, and wanted to see Mr. Stevens personally, in order to ask him to recant his statements. Five Korean representatives went to meet with Stevens at the Fairmont Hotel, where he was staying. They succeeded in meeting with him, but Stevens refused to recant any of his statements. The five Koreans then physically attacked him. The *San Francisco Call* gave a detailed report of the incident. It reported among other things:

> A discussion between D. W. Stevens . . . and five Koreans who called to see him at the Fairmont hotel last evening ended in a free for all battle, in which the lobby chairs of the big hotel were turned into weapons of attack after the dinner hour, at a time when the lobby was filled with guests, the struggle created great excitement. The Koreans, who are opposed to the Japanese administration of the country, objected to the pro-Japanese sentiments expressed by Stevens.

> Five Koreans called upon Stevens. He was not in at the time, so they seated themselves to await his return. Three of them were young men, presumably students; the other two were middle aged men. None of them was definitely known by Stevens.

> One of the young men, who spoke good English, addressed Stevens and said that they had come to express their appreciation of his services to Korea. He suggested that they withdraw to a spot where they might engage in a general conversation. Stevens withdrew with them to an alcove close to the ballroom off the lobby.

> The conversation continuing, one young Korean showed an excerpt from Saturdays Call, in which Stevens had said: "Japan is doing in Korea for the Koreans what the United States is doing in the Philippines for the Filipinos, modifying its methods only to suit the somewhat different conditions with which it has to deal."[7]

Mr. Stevens could have been killed in his hotel by the five Koreans who attacked him. After the attack, he feared for his safety and hastened

to leave San Francisco earlier than planned. The following morning he arrived at the San Francisco pier to ride a ferry to Oakland where he would
catch a train to Washington, D.C. Mr. Stevens stepped down from the Fairmont Hotel bus with the Japanese consul general of San Francisco, Koike
Chozo, who was accompanying Mr. Stevens to bid him farewell. As Stevens
bent over for his luggage, Chang In Hwan aimed his revolver at Stevens
and pulled the trigger. Chang's handkerchief became jammed in the chamber of the revolver, preventing it from discharging. Then Chang attacked
Stevens, striking him in the face with his revolver. Stevens fell to the ground;
recovering himself, he started after Chang. Then Chang Myung Woon, who
was also involved in the plot to assassinate Stevens, fired his revolver at
Stevens. The *San Francisco Chronicle* reported the shocking incident as
follows:

> Three shots that will be heard around the world rang out yesterday
> morning from the crowded pavement in front of the arcade of the Ferry
> building.
>
> Fired from the revolver of In Whan Chang, confessed assassin and
> avowed patriot of Corea, two of them [bullets] pierced the body of Durham
> White Stevens, an American and advisor of the Corean Council of State
> since the Japanese occupation of Corea in 1904, as he was alighting from
> an automobile in company with the Japanese Consul, Chozo Koike, in-
> tending to take the morning train for Washington; the third felled the friend
> and accomplice of the would be slayer M. W. Chun. In Corea the story
> of the shooting will be heard by a captive people with fanatic praise for
> Chang and Chun, who will be pictured as riding to the heavens on the
> backs of winged dragons.
>
> In Japan the report of the three shots will be regarded with contrary
> emotions, but local Coreans hardly expect that it will call a halt in the pol-
> icy which, they would have it understood, has added the name of Corea
> to that of Poland, Armenia and the Congo Free State.
>
> All the diplomatic world will be stirred by the attempted assassi-
> nation of the American who had served Japan well, if not wisely, and the
> narrow escape from harm of the Japanese Consul, who sat by his side,
> and the trials of the Coreans that will follow in the San Francisco courts
> will be watched by the nations.[8]

Mr. Stevens died in the hospital the next day from the gunshot wounds
he received during the attack. After the death of Mr. Stevens, Mr. Chun handed
out a written statement in Korean explaining the reason why he had assassi-

nated Mr. Stevens. The translation of his statement was printed on the first page of the *San Francisco Call* on March 24, 1908:

> This day I shot Stevens. I shot him because he was the main factor in the Japanese reign of bloodshed and oppression in Korea, and because he, as the head and advisor of the regime, was responsible for the deaths of our fathers, mothers and brothers, in Korea.

> Stevens is the advisor of the Korean government, paid by the Korean government, but who is working for the interests of Japan and against those of the nation who looked to him as an American for justice and good rule. He has endeavored to make the people of the United States of America believe that Japanese protection of Korea was the best thing for that nation in the present and would be so in the future. He lied when he said that the Korean people were happy under Japanese rule. So, for his falsehoods, I shot Stevens.

> I shot the man as an expression of the sentiment of the Korean race and its hatred of Japanese government. I knew I would die when I shot him, but so angered was I at his falsehoods and the misuse of his power that, with the knowledge of my own death, I shot him. What is life without liberty?

> How can I be calm, knowing our fathers, mothers and brothers in Korea are being murdered by agents of the Japanese government? A man in whose breast there is not a love for his country greater than all else and who can remain passive, knowing that the fathers, mothers and brothers of his country are being murdered, has no right to live.

> Stevens was the man who forced the Korean emperor to sign a treaty giving away the independence of his country into the keeping of Japan. Stevens is an enemy of the world and a disturber of its peace. Therefore, I shot Stevens.

> If I kill him and I die it will be a warning to others who take his place to rule justly and to deal with people in his care with kindness and humanity. I will make no complaint to the punishment that will be meted out to me and, should my act aid my country in struggles for freedom, I will die nobly and well.[9]

In October 1909, Ito Hirobumi, the most colorful political figure of Japan, was assassinated by a Catholic Christian. Ito had shaped modern Japanese politics after the Meiji restoration, and was responsible for the Japanese colonization of Korea. After 1905 Ito had become the resident general of Korea. He had attempted to annex Korea into the fold of the Japanese empire. Before this annexation, Japan had wanted to eliminate any opposition from Russia and Ito had arranged a meeting with Russian representatives in Harbin, China.

As the news of Ito's travel plans spread, Ahn Choong Gŏn prepared to murder Ito. On the morning of October 26, Ahn entered the Harbin railroad station dressed as a Japanese dignitary as if to welcome Ito. After Ito stepped off his special train, he was welcomed by the Russian delegates and army representatives, and he greeted the members of the diplomatic community. In that moment, Ahn took out his pistol from the right pocket of his overcoat and fired. Three bullets hit Ito, killing him and injuring three other Japanese officials, including the Japanese consul-general from Harbin, Kawakami.[10] Mr. Ahn had been born into a strict Confucian family, but he had converted to Roman Catholicism. Ahn Choong Gŏn was baptized when he was eighteen years old. While he was in prison, he was visited by Catholic priests and had left a will asking that his son, then six years old, become a Roman Catholic priest. Ahn was executed in a Japanese-operated prison in Lushun, China, on March 26, 1910.[11]

Ahn Choong Gŏn, Chang In Hwan, and many other Korean Christians who participated in political activities undertook them believing that they were fulfilling God's will to oppose the Japanese control of Korea. While not condoning the violent action of political assassination, we must note that they were opposing the Japanese force which was waging unjust war in Korea and East Asia. If Japan had adhered to the warnings of these Korean Christians to abandon their militaristic policy of expansion, Japan and the world could have been saved from the tragedy of subsequent wars. Instead, Japanese imperial activities of expansion continued, and in spite of the many heroic activities of the Korean patriotic resistance movement, Korea was annexed by the Japanese empire in 1910.

6

CHRISTIANITY AND THE JAPANESE
POLITICS OF OPPRESSION

From the beginning of Japanese rule in Korea, government officials were well aware of the important political role played by Korean Christians. The Japanese government strongly felt it would need Christian support if its administration was to succeed. With the intention of establishing friendly relations with Christians, Governor-General Terauchi Masatake invited nineteen leading Korean church leaders to visit Japan in fall 1910. These Christian leaders were treated royally and, in order to demonstrate the benefits of a friendly relationship with Japan, they were given the opportunity to observe the progress and the strength of modern Japan. Also, the Korean YMCA (Young Men's Christian Association), which had formerly received an annual subsidy of ten thousand yen from the Korean government for its educational work, continued to receive this money under the Japanese regime.[1]

Japanese policy seemed benevolent, despite the role Christianity was coming to play in promoting Korean nationalism. In fact, many Christian missionaries welcomed Japanese rule. One missionary wrote in praise of the Japanese:

> Prior to the annexation the administrative system was chaotic. By stern enforcement the Japanese have introduced quiet and order, have commenced to exploit the natural resources of the country, set up a judiciary, developed the beginning of an educational system, improved communication, and cultivated hygiene.[2]

Such wholehearted acceptance of Japanese rule by the missionaries was further reflected in a letter from Rev. Arthur J. Brown, secretary of the Board of Foreign Missions of the U.S. Presbyterian church, to a Japanese official, Hanihara Masanao: "Japanese administration is far better than Korea would otherwise have had and far better than Korea had under its own rule."[3]

Acceptance of the Japanese administration was not merely a friendly gesture on the part of the missionaries; it also became the official policy of the Presbyterian mission, the largest mission in Korea. Arthur Brown wrote:

What is the attitude of the missionaries toward the Japanese? There are four possible attitudes: First, opposition; second, aloofness; third, cooperation; fourth, loyal recognition . . . the fourth, loyal recognition, is I believe, the sound position. It is in accord with the example of Christ, who loyally submitted himself and advised His apostles to submit themselves to a far worse government than the Japanese, and it is in line with the teaching of Paul in Romans xiii.[4]

The missionaries advised Korean Christians to avoid political involvement in opposition to the Japanese, and Korean Christians also officially adopted the position of "loyal recognition." Consequently, any Korean Christians who were involved in political movement against the Japanese were "kept from responsible positions in the Church."[5]

Despite this official policy adopted by the leaders of the Christian churches in Korea, the Japanese government began to distrust them. It suspected that covert political activities were being carried on within the churches. As is the practice today, at that time Korean Christians gathered every morning for prayer meetings, conducted worship services on Wednesday evenings, and thronged to the church on Sundays from early morning until late at night. The Japanese police, wondering why they met so often, sent spies out among the people to discover the reason. Sermons preached by missionaries or Korean pastors that were deemed suspicious were thus reported to the authorities.

Suspicion of Korean Christians was especially strong in the winter of 1910 and 1911, during the revival movement called "Campaign for a Million Souls." This great evangelistic effort by Protestant churches in Korea aimed to bring 1 million new Koreans into the Christian faith. Many revival meetings were held, and fiery sermons were preached. These meetings, too, were carefully watched by Japanese government officials, who concluded that the meetings were political in nature because they did not understand the spiritual nature of the Christian activities.

Their suspicion developed into an open policy of oppression and hostility toward the churches. The culmination of this was the fabrication of the so-called conspiracy case. The conspiracy case was a typical example of a Japanese political maneuver against the Korean Christian churches; this incident bears careful examination.

In mid-October 1911, without any explanation, the Japanese colonial government began to arrest Korea Christian leaders from the cities where Christian populations were significant in number, such as Seoul, Pyongyang, and Sonchon. A missionary stationed in Sonchon reported: "Time after time arrests have been made, sometimes one or two and sometimes several at a time, until now there are fifty or more from our neighborhood. The parents and relatives of these men do not know why they were taken. The men themselves do not know why."[6]

Finally, the administration issued a statement accusing these Korean Christians of plotting to assassinate Governor-General Terauchi as he passed through Sonchon in late December 1910. The government explained the conspiracy case in the following words:

> In the course of the prosecution of a robber arrested in Sensen (Sonchon in Korean pronunciation), North Heian Province, in August, 1911, the fact that a gang of conspirators under the guidance of a certain ringleader had been trying to assassinate Count Terauchi, Governor-General of Chosen, was discovered.[7]

This "gang of conspirators" happened to be Christians! Since the attempted assassination was to have taken place in Sonchon, arrests of Christians in this town were so numerous that the Hugh O'Neill Jr. Industrial Academy, the largest Presbyterian mission school in the area, had to close.

Among the arrested was Yun Chi Ho, a man converted to the Christian faith in Shanghai, China, and educated in the United States. Previously, the Japanese had tried to get him to accept a government office, but he had declined in favor of serving the church. If he had accepted the Japanese offers, he would surely have escaped the accusation. Those accused were imprisoned without a public hearing until June 28, 1912, when finally 123 of them were indicted and brought to trial before the district court of Seoul. The details of the trial were fully reported in English by special correspondents of the *Japan Chronicle* from Kobe, Japan. The newspaper account of the first day of the trial included the following report:

The first man to be examined was Sin Hyopyom, aged 32.

By the Court: . . . revolvers were distributed among the students of the mission school in the presence of the principal, Mr. McCune. The men and the boys then proceeded to Syen Chuen [sic] station, but the Governor-General's train passed through without stopping. Is that so?

Accused: I do not know.

By the Court: All the questions asked were based upon your statements before the police and the procurator at the preliminary examination. Why do you now deny your own statements?

Accused: At the police office I said so on account of the hard treatment, and the reason I said "yes" at the procurator's office was that they told me if I should say "no" I would be carried again down to the police office and be teased (tortured) again.[8]

The tortures were carried out by the Japanese police to obtain certain statements which the authorities wanted to obtain. All of the accused complained
about being tortured at the police station. One prisoner said he was tortured
for four consecutive days. Another stated, "I was bound up for about a month
and subjected to torture. I still have marks of it upon my body." He then asked
permission to show evidence of the torture, but the court refused. Thus were
the "confessions" of involvement in the conspiracy obtained. One of the accused declared, "I was told by one of the officials that one man had been killed
as a result of torture, and I was threatened that if I did not stick to the statements I had made, I should meet the same fate."[9] A veteran missionary who
was in Korea during the trial later wrote in demonstration of the falsity of such
confessions:

> I was able to secure a copy of the so-called confession before the
> police of the elder in whom I was especially interested. To my surprise
> and consternation I found that he had apparently not only confessed to
> the police that he had conspired with others to kill the governor-general
> when he came to Pyongyang, but that several missionaries including my-
> self had attended one of their meetings and had urged the Koreans to be
> brave and kill the governor-general without fail. However, the record
> showed that the elder in his subsequent examination before the procura-
> tor had indignantly denied having had any part in or even knowledge of
> the alleged conspiracy.[10]

The accused were permitted to have lawyers, but they were only allowed
to meet together for a few moments just before the trial, and only in the presence of police. The case presented by the prosecution was lengthy, taking up
many volumes, yet the defense lawyers were not given sufficient time to study
those pretrial records. All of the examinations in court were conducted by the
judges themselves. There were no witnesses, and the only evidence presented
was the false "confessions."

On September 28, after three months, the trial came to an end, and 105
men were found guilty. Despite the seriousness of the accusations, the sentences
were light, since the court could not truly establish the guilt of those accused. Indeed, the case was full of holes from the start. On the dates on which the prosecution charged that Yun Chi Ho had met the other conspirators in Seoul, he had
been in Kaesong City. Also, the confessions stated that toward the end of December 1910, the conspirators had traveled to Sonchon to kill General Terauchi.
The investigation showed, however, that during the last six days of December,
the number of passengers arriving in Sonchon by two different railways did not
exceed seventy. Finally, in a curious twist, the court did not try any missionaries. If they had been involved in the meetings, handing out revolvers and urging

"the Koreans to be brave and kill the governor-general without fail," then they should have been charged as well. However, as missionaries were not called to account, neither were they allowed "to be called as witnesses for the defense."[11] it seems obvious that the entire trial was a total fabrication.

The Korean Christians now convicted of attempting to assassinate the governor-general appealed to the Seoul Appeals Court, and the court met fifty-one times between November 26, 1912, and February 25, 1913. The court reduced the ten-year sentences to six years of penal servitude, and some were even acquitted. However, the accused refused to accept the decision of the appeals court and went to the higher court of the governor-general. That court chose to reconsider only the cases of those sentenced to penal servitude, and the rehearing began on July 1, 1913, in the Taegu appeals court. It ended three days later, and the decision was announced on July 15. The court upheld the previous court's decision with minor changes in terms of sentences. Again the defendants brought the case before the higher court, but on October 9, 1913, the court ruled against any further hearing and upheld the judgment of the Taegu court.

There was no question that those prosecuting the conspiracy case had no case whatsoever. The government was unable to produce even the slightest evidence of a conspiracy on the part of Christians in Korea or abroad. This "conspiracy case" only further alienated Christians from the Japanese by its mockery of justice.

The handling of the case was criticized from the very beginning of the trial by noted lawyers and scholars. One such criticism was made by Dr. Charles Eliot of Harvard University, who visited Korea and Japan during the early investigations. He wrote to Dr. Arthur Brown:

> After I got to Tokyo, and while the preliminary investigation was still going on, I had several conversations with eminent Japanese about the treatment of the accused Christian Koreans. The two points I endeavored to make were, first, that no American would believe on any Korean evidence that a single American missionary was in the slightest degree concerned with the alleged conspiracy; and secondly, that the Japanese preliminary police investigation ought to be modified, and particularly, that counsel for the defense ought always to be present during all states of the preliminary investigation. Counsel for the defense might or might not take part in the proceedings, but should invariably be present. I represented that the standing of Japan among Western nations would be improved by judicious modifications of her preliminary proceedings against alleged criminals.[12]

The Japanese criminal code and the court procedure under which the Korean Christians were tried were severely criticized as being "archaic, barbaric, and uncivilized." The conspiracy case was well publicized outside of Korea, especially in the United States. Church officials in the United States who had missionaries in Korea had a special interest in the case. In July 1912, a delegation consisting of Dr. Arthur J. Brown; Bishop Luther B. Wilson; Rev. Frank Mason North, secretary of the Methodist Episcopal Board of Foreign Missions; and Dr. Ed F. Cook, secretary of the Board of Foreign Missions of the Methodist Church South visited Washington, D.C., to confer with the Japanese ambassador and the American government regarding the situation in Korea. The delegation reported:

> Before going to the State Department, we went first of all to the Japanese Embassy.
>
> We told the Ambassador of our contemplated visit to our government regarding the Korean situation, in order that he might know directly from us, not only that we were going but what we were going for.
>
> From the Embassy we went to White House, where we were received with equal cordiality by President Taft. After a short conference with him, we went to the State Department, where Mr. Knox, the Secretary of State, spent a long time with us, going over the whole situation with painstaking care. Mr. R. S. Miller, Chief of the Bureau of Foreign Affairs, who has been cognizant of the whole affair from the beginning, was also present.
>
> The interviews indicated that the responsible officials of our government had given a good deal of attention to the subject, that they had carefully read the documents that we had sent to them in advance, and that they had received voluminous information from other sources which they had studied with care.[13]

The church leaders in the United States concerned for the Christian cause in Korea interpreted the conspiracy case as evidence of Japan's political aim to suppress Christianity. Dr. Brown, the secretary of the Presbyterian Board of Foreign Mission, made a strong protest against the case and against Japanese political oppression of Christians:

> We cannot be indifferent to the effect of the present policy of the Japanese police upon a mission work which now represents approximately 330 foreign missionaries, 962 schools, a medical college, a nurses' training school, thirteen hospitals, eighteen dispensaries, an orphanage, a school for the blind, a leper asylum, a printing press, 500 churches, a Christian community of 250,000, property worth approximately a million dollars,

and an annual expenditure of over $250,000. This extensive work is being injuriously affected by the reign of terror which now prevails among the Koreans.[14]

The Japanese government was probably surprised and disturbed to hear the reactions from the United States. On February 13, 1915, the administration released all of the accused before the completion of their prison sentences. One missionary wrote, "The authorities were sick of the case and suppressed all reference to it in the papers."[15] However, the colonial government continued oppressive policies against the Christian churches in various ways. Japanese authorities never admitted to the existence of oppressive policies and were quick to point out that freedom of worship was guaranteed by the Japanese constitution, but subtle repressions prevailed.

In the area of medical works of the missionaries, the government was fully aware of the shortage of doctors and the great assistance rendered by medical missionaries. The need for doctors was so great that the government permitted some Japanese to practice medicine without official licenses and proper qualifications. Despite the obvious need, the government persisted in restricting the medical practice of Christian missionaries by making it unusually difficult for them to obtain licenses. On November 15, 1913, ordinance 100 was issued by the government requiring all who desired to practice medicine to apply for permission from the governor-general. The ordinance listed as qualifications:

1. Those qualified according to the law in force in Japan
2. Those graduated from medical schools recognized by the Governor-General
3. Those who have passed a medical examination prescribed by the Governor-General
4. Those Japanese subjects graduated from medical schools of good standing in foreign countries
5. Those foreigners who have obtained a license in their respective countries, in which qualified Japanese subjects are permitted to practice medicine.[16]

Without considering the difficulties of obtaining licenses under the requirements laid down in items 1 through 4, item 5 alone limited foreign medical practice in Korea to those of British nationality. Only Great Britain permitted Japanese subjects who had received medical training and certification in Japan to practice medicine in Britain. The ordinance was finally modified in July 1914 to allow more foreign doctors to obtain general licenses, but restrictions against the Christian missionaries were not altogether eliminated.

In the area of Christian education, there was also significant government pressure. General Ordinance 24, as contained in the "Revision of Regulations for Private Schools" issued in March 1915, excluded the Bible from all school curricula and required all teachers to learn the Japanese language within the following five years and teach only in that "national language."

On August 16, 1914, in order to supervise the propagation of Christianity, government Ordinance 83 stated that official permission had to be secured before opening a new church or employing any paid workers in a church. Such permission was very difficult to obtain. Some churches were never able to secure permission to build and eventually had to disperse as a result. Regulations such as these tightened control on all Christian activities.

The first governor-general of Chosen, Terauchi Masatake, left Korea in October 1916 to become premier of Japan and to organize a new cabinet in the Tokyo government after the resignation of Premier Kuma. He was replaced in Chosen by another army general, Hasegawa Yoshimichi, who had been in Korea as commander-in-chief of the Japanese garrison forces before the annexation. General Hasegawa arrived on December 10, 1916. As the new governor-general, Hasegawa did not effect the slightest change in the policies set by General Terauchi, but sought to continue them, as evidenced by the praise he gave to his predecessor's administration:

> My predecessor, by special command from the Throne, spent over six years of great industry in this country, and a glance at the result of his service shows that the administrative and judicial machinery, educational, industrial, and communication systems, and all other enterprises and provisions are in good working order. Indeed, signs are markedly in evidence that the new regime is bearing beneficent fruit throughout the country.[17]

Among its other policies, the new administration continued the politics of oppression on Christians in Korea. As before, church services were infiltrated by police, pastors were questioned about statements made in sermons, and Christian school teachers and evangelists were intimidated. For Korean Christians, it was unquestionably clear that the Japanese policies concerning the Christian churches were oppressive and that the "religious liberty" guaranteed by the Constitution of Japan was not being honored in Korea. Eventually, Korean Christians responded to such policies with open protest and by aligning themselves with other religious groups opposed to Japanese rule. The first public exhibition of this solidarity was the nationwide March First Independence movement of 1919.

7

CHRISTIANITY AND THE JAPANESE
POLITICS OF CULTURAL RULE

The March First Independence movement of 1919 was first and foremost a direct action by the Korean public against Japanese rule. Several domestic and international developments in the period contributed to the uprising. On the international scene, postWorld War I problems were straining relations among many countries. In January 1918, President Woodrow Wilson had announced his Fourteen Points for the settlement of the war, including the famed Doctrine of Self-Determination. Many Korean political leaders immediately applied this doctrine to Korea. Influential Korean nationalists abroad, especially those in China and the United States, sought ways to send Korean delegates to the peace conference held in Paris during April 1919. Petitions were also sent to world leaders urging them to support the movement for Korean independence.

On the domestic scene, a comprehensive land survey that had taken more than eight years to complete and cost the government 20 million yen had just been completed. The purpose of the survey had been to investigate land ownership, land values, and topography in Korea, but caused severe hardship for many Korean farmers. At the beginning of the survey, the government had announced that all land owners had to register their land in order to keep possession of it. However, because many Koreans were unaware of the requirement, they did not comply. Even when those who were aware tried to comply, the registration procedure itself was too complicated for many illiterate farmers. Besides this, there was a deliberate effort by a great number of Koreans not to cooperate with the government. Thus, as many failed to register, many lost their land. The government also took over large portions of land that belonged to former members of the Korean court, as well as religious temples, shrines, and other property, the ownership of which could not be clearly determined. The confiscated lands were sold to Japanese settlers at a very low price. With the completion of the survey and the resulting confiscations and sales of land, hostility toward the Japanese administration mounted.

King Kojong, the last king of the Yi dynasty, died unexpectedly on January 22, 1919. According to government sources, he fell ill of apoplexy on

January 21 and died the following day, but many Koreans believed, or at least wanted to believe, that the king was poisoned by Japanese authorities. News of the king's death spread, and people gathered in Seoul to mourn.

As all these elements came into place, leaders of the independence movement in Korea met secretly to organize a nationwide demonstration against Japanese rule. They were encouraged by the desire for independence demonstrated by Korean nationals living abroad, especially when Korean students in Japan held a rally at the Korean YMCA in Tokyo on February 8, 1919, and read a Declaration of Independence. This event prompted a decision by the leaders at home to declare the independence of Korea on March 1, two days before the funeral of King Kojong.

At two o'clock a crowd gathered in Pagoda Park in the heart of Seoul and heard the Declaration of Independence read by a student leader. Then the crowd began a march through Seoul, waving Korean national flags and shouting "Long live Korean independence!" Demonstrations also took place that day in Pyongyang, Haeju, Wonju, and Chinju, and the independence movement spread rapidly throughout Korea.

Korean Christians were active participants in this independence movement, although some Christians first opposed the drafting of the Declaration of Independence. Christian leaders proposed instead to present petitions to the government seeking independence, but when this was rejected by other religious leaders, some Christians withdrew from the movement. Still, sixteen of the thirty-three signers of the declaration were Christian leaders, among them Rev. Kil Son Ju, the first ordained Korean Presbyterian minister. Many Christian churches became gathering places for demonstrators to hear the declaration read. One American missionary who disliked such active participation by Korean Christians in the political movement wrote a year later:

> At Pyongyang, the so-called Christian capital, where the writer happened to be on March 1 last year, permission was secured from the police to hold memorial services for the ex-emperor in the chief churches. At the close of these services the declaration of independence was read in the churches and the first "mansei" were shouted. At Chinnampo, where I went on March 2, the mobs each time collected at the churches and started from there . . . to the streets for the demonstrations.[1]

The government placed primary blame on the Christians for instigating the protests and retaliated against them. Christian worship services were even more closely supervised by police, and many churches were ordered to close. Practically every Christian pastor in Seoul was arrested and jailed. Soldiers stopped people in the street in order to discover and punish more Christians.

The number of Christians arrested became so great that many Christian schools had to be closed. In some localities the police arrested all church officers. By the end of June 1919, the following numbers had been arrested:

Presbyterian	1,461
Methodist	465
Roman Catholic	57
Other	207[2]

Less than four months later, the number of Presbyterians in jail had increased to 3,804, among them 134 pastors and elders. In the course of this persecution, forty-one Presbyterian leaders were shot and six others were beaten to death. Twelve Presbyterian churches were destroyed, and the homes of many missionaries were searched by the police, resulting in more property damage. Some of the missionaries were physically attacked by soldiers and severely beaten. Under these conditions, the work of the church was disastrously affected. One missionary reported:

> With the launching of the Independence Movement in March, 1919, the work suddenly stopped. Everything was changed. Schools had to be closed, Bible classes could not be held, Bible Institutes could not finish, trips to the country had to be cancelled, visiting in homes by missionaries was found to be inadvisable, many of our churches found their pastors, elders, helpers, and other church officers carried off to prison; missionaries lost their secretaries, language teachers, or literary assistants; every way we tried to turn regular work seemed impossible.[3]

Of all the repressive measures taken against Christians, surely the most tragic was the massacre in the village of Cheamni, near Suwon. Horace H. Underwood, the noted Presbyterian missionary, reported the incident in detail. On April 16, 1919, he and some friends left Seoul to visit Suwon. Nearing the town, they saw a large cloud of smoke. While visiting in nearby homes, Underwood had the following exchange with a local farmer:

Underwood: "What is that smoke?"

Farmer: "That is a village that has burned."

Underwood: "When was it burned?"

Farmer: "Yesterday."

Underwood:	"How was it burned?"
Farmer:	(glancing around fearfully) "By the soldiers."
Underwood:	"Why? Did the people riot or shout for independence?"
Farmer:	"No, but that is a Christian village."[4]

Proceeding then to Cheamni the group learned that on the previous day, Japanese soldiers had arrived in the village and ordered all male Christians into the church. When they had gathered, about thirty in all, the soldiers fired on them with rifles and killed the survivors with swords and bayonets. Afterwards the soldiers set fire to the church and left.

Such violently oppressive measures were quickly criticized and deplored by church leaders in Korea and abroad. The Rev. Herbert Welch, bishop of the Methodist Episcopal church in Korea, visited Tokyo on his way to the United States, meeting with Prime Minister Hara Takashi on May 15, 1919. The prime minister in his diary, now an important document, described the meeting:

> I asked him to express his frank opinion on the Korean incidents. Then he said he is going to the United States to raise funds of two million dollars for the work of the church in Korea. But he feels quite uncertain about the future of the church in Korea in consideration of the severeness of the military rule, lawless actions of the gendarmeries and police, the oppression of Christians in various places, and discriminating treatment of Koreans by the Japanese and discrimination in education.[5]

The prime minister's diary also recounts that on the next day, May 16, an entire committee of Christian missionaries from Korea visited Tokyo to report the oppressive situation there to Japanese officials.

The atrocities perpetrated on Korean Christians by Japanese soldiers and police were reported as well in the United States and in Europe despite efforts by the Japanese authorities to conceal the facts through their control of the post offices, railroads, and press agencies. Upon learning of this persecution in Korea, the Commission of Relations with the Orient of the Federal Council of Churches of Christ in America sent a cable on June 26, 1919, to Premier Hara deploring Japanese actions and demanding administrative reform. The cable read: "Agitation regarding Chosen abuses increasingly serious, endangering good will. Cannot withhold facts. Urgently important you publish . . . that abuses have ceased and reasonable administrative reforms proceeding."[6]

On July 10 the commission received a cablegram from the prime minister stating:

I desire to assure you that the report of abuses committed by agents of the Japanese Government in Korea has been engaging my most serious attention. I am fully prepared to look squarely at actual facts. As I have declared on various occasions, the regime of administration inaugurated in Korea at the time of the annexation, nearly ten years ago, calls on us for substantial modification to meet the altered conditions of things.[7]

The desire for "substantial modification" seemed to have been sincere on the part of Prime Minister Hara. Already in early April he had seriously discussed with his cabinet the possibilities of recalling Governor-General Hasegawa, providing equal opportunity both for Japanese and for Koreans in education, abolishing the gendarmerie system, and generally treating Koreans without prejudice. To Hara's mind, it was clear that reform was needed if the Japanese administration was to continue, and he frequently brought up the Korean question in Tokyo cabinet meetings. On June 27, 1919, the cabinet discussed replacing Hasegawa Yoshimichi with Navy Admiral Saito Makoto as governor-general of Chosen. In his diary the prime minister wrote:

I visited Admiral Saito Makoto and consulted about his willingness to assume the position of Governor-General and he consented. In the evening I invited Mizuno Rentaro and asked him to become the Administrative Superintendent (the next highest post) in Chosen, and I received his consent.[8]

On August 4, 1919, the cabinet finally agreed to replace the governor-general and introduce political reforms. The Japanese emperor officially appointed Admiral Saito as the new governor-general on August 12. Saito Makoto was born in 1858. He had spent some time in the United States as a student and also as naval attaché to the Japanese embassy in Washington.

A week after Saito's appointment to the Korean position, on August 19, 1919, the Imperial Rescript Concerning the Reorganization of the Government-General of Chosen was made public. Among other things it stated:

We are persuaded that the state of development at which the general situation has now arrived calls for certain reforms in the administrative organization of the Government-General of Korea, and we issue our imperial command that such reforms be put into operation.[9]

With a sense of mission and orders to promote reform, Governor-General Saito arrived in Seoul on September 2, 1919. In a press conference on the train, he promised that his administration would be dedicated to promoting popular happiness, guaranteeing freedom of speech and press, and many other reforms. His administration was nearly short-lived, however, for when he left the station, Kang U Kyu, a sixty-year-old Korean, threw a bomb at him. It exploded and wounded thirty-six people, but the governor-general himself was not harmed. The assailant was said by some to have been an elder of the Presbyterian church, but other sources claimed he was a Confucian scholar.

Despite this near disaster, Governor-General Saito issued the Governor-General's Instruction to High Officials Concerning Administrative Reforms the very next day. This document stated:

> The official organization has been altered in such a way that either a civil or military man may be appointed as the head of the administration in Chosen. The gendarmerie system has been abolished and replaced by the ordinary police system. Further, improvement has been introduced in the matter of the eligibility for appointment of Koreans as officials.[10]

The instruction advised officials to avoid unnecessary red tape, to respect people's rights, to pay special attention to improvements in education and law enforcement, and to treat Koreans and Japanese alike as members of the same family.

Unfortunately, the promises made in the governor-general's declaration were not all successfully kept. The appointment of a civilian governor-general never became a reality; of Korea's eight Japanese governors-general, not one was a civilian. The gendarmerie system was abolished, but many of its members simply changed uniforms and were recruited into the civilian police. At the same time, the size of the police force was substantially increased, so that by 1919 it was almost tripled, and in 1920 there was not a village without a police station. Likewise, the treatment of Koreans and Japanese on an equal basis was never practiced, especially in education. Korean students studied in inferior segregated schools, and it was very difficult for them to attend the government-supported colleges. For example, when Keijo Imperial University was opened in 1924, only forty-four Koreans were registered as opposed to 121 Japanese.

Nevertheless, it remained a sincere desire of the Japanese authorities to review Korean problems in a new spirit as the government "attempted to meet (the issues) with a new administration."[11] This new spirit was manifested in government by "rule of culture," rather than by rule of force, and attempts at assimilation soon became evident in the policies instituted.

In early October 1919, Saito met with representatives of Korea's thirteen provinces and heard their complaints. The Koreans demanded freedom of speech, freedom of assembly, and freedom to publish Korean papers. By the end of 1919 newspapers in vernacular Korean began to reappear. The new administration also decreed that school teachers and railway officials could no longer carry swords. The wearing of military uniforms by all except soldiers was also prohibited.

The reforms brought about a change in policy toward the Christian churches. Admiral Saito had conferred with missionary leaders in Tokyo, and soon after his arrival in Seoul he met with local missionaries. He asked them to frankly express their opinions on the Japanese administration and to make suggestions. In response, the Federal Council of Protestant Evangelical Mission in Korea prepared a statement and submitted it in September 1919. After expressing gratitude for the planned reforms, the document went on to say:

> It was a keen disappointment to us, who had lived in Korea under the former government to find that what we had expected from the Japanese administration after annexation, was not forthcoming, but that military rule to which the country was subjected, restricted the religious liberty and educational freedom which had been enjoyed, introduced unjust discrimination against the Koreans, and eventually imposed upon the people such subjection and such harsh measures of oppression, as to call forth from them to the protest of the independence agitation of this year. The unarmed demonstrations at that time were met with such brutality . . . and we were forced for the sake of humanity to give expression to our protests.[12]

The missionaries also said, "We urge that religious liberty, which is already guaranteed by the constitution of the Empire of Japan, . . . be made effective," and then made the following important requests:

1. That fewer restrictions be placed upon the church and upon missionaries
2. That discrimination against Christians and against Christianity by officials not be allowed
3. That missionaries be allowed to include the teaching of the Bible and religious exercises in the curricula of church schools
4. That restrictions on the use of the Korean language be removed
5. That we be accorded more liberty in the management of our schools and freedom from unnecessary official interference
6. That teachers and pupils be allowed liberty of conscience
7. That the details of the management of our hospitals be left to the staff without interference from officials
8. That the censorship of Christian books be abolished[13]

Subsequent meetings between government officials and missionaries were frequent. Likewise, in Tokyo, Dr. Mizuno Rentaro, the newly appointed administrative superintendent for Korea, held a reception at the Imperial Hotel for prominent missionaries in Japan "to meet and to learn to know each other better," and to report changes in the policy toward Christians in Korea.

These changes were numerous and effective. The new administration established a Section of Religious Affairs in the Department of Education to foster both the expression of public opinion and the convenience of religious propagators. Three Japanese Christians were appointed to its staff. The government also decided to recognize the property of financial foundations used for religious purposes as "juridical persons," a decision which provided a more convenient method for the management of mission properties. The Seoul diocese of the Roman Catholic church was the first to take advantage of this new law. Other church bodies soon followed.

Significant changes were also made in regard to Christian education. The former administration had fixed a definite curriculum for all grades of Christian private schools that precluded additional courses on the Bible or religion. However, in March 1920, new regulations for private schools were issued. The only required subjects were on "morals" and the Japanese language. Religion was again allowed to be taught in Christian schools. Further modifications of the law in 1922 and 1923 permitted the Korean language to be taught and spoken in the schools.

Policies governing Christian work in general were also changed. Before reform, specific permission from the governor-general was a prerequisite for the opening of a new church or other religious institution. If this was violated, a severe fine was levied. In April 1920, new regulations came out abolishing the fines and requiring only that new church openings be reported to the government. The government still reserved the right to close buildings if the institutions were found to have been used as "places for concocting plots injurious to the public peace and order."[14]

These policy changes took place in a remarkably short time, as the administration now fostered a positive attitude toward Christian work. Church workers and government officials began to maintain close, friendly contact, and officials often praised the Christian church's contribution to the betterment of Korean life. The following statement by Dr. Mizuno at the Tenth Annual Conference of the Federal Council of Protestant Evangelical Missions in Korea on September 21, 1921, expressed this new attitude:

> I have made several trips into the country, and the more familiar I become with the conditions in the peninsula, the more do I realize how painstakingly you labor for the uplift of the people. . . . It can be said without any appearance of flattery that Chosen owes much of her advancement in civilization to your labors. . . . So we hold Christianity in high regard to give it every possible facility for its propagation.[15]

Christians in Korea certainly welcomed the change in administration and appreciated the new relationship it enjoyed with the government.

The churches' membership had declined in 1919 (the year of the independence movement), but had begun to increase under the new administration as the following statistics show:

Year	Number of Christians
1918	319,129
1919	296,487
1920	323,575
1921	355,114
1922	372,920[16]

Taking advantage of new opportunities, Christians held many evangelistic campaigns and revival meetings. The most notable activity was the observance of the centennial anniversary of the American Methodist missions.

Despite all these good signs, it would be overstating the case to conclude that Christians under the Saito administration enjoyed full religious liberty with no restrictions placed on Christian work. The Japanese maintained a distrust of Korean Christians, and spying on Christian church activities continued. One missionary wrote:

> They (the policemen) often insist on attending the services of the churches and schools and in regulating what is said and done. They frequent the halls of the schools and arrest the students on all sorts of suspicion. They censor all publications and often object to articles in the weekly church's paper.[17]

However, the greatest problem that Christians faced during this period arose from the worldwide economic depression. Some 80 percent of the Korean population depended on the land for their livelihood, but because of Japanese expansion onto the Korean farms, many farmers who had tilled their lands for generations lost their property. A missionary recounted:

> There are now immense Japanese holdings that once belonged to Koreans and hundreds of Japanese small farmers are taking the land and the place of a like or greater number of Koreans; for the man from Japan can farm more than a Korean can and always manage to get hold of the land.[18]

Korean Christian farmers were especially vulnerable to this change of ownership. Japanese landowners who were antagonistic to Christians would often take away the land rights from their Christian tenants and give them to other Japanese or to non-Christian Korean farmers. The financial plight of Christians was so serious that it severely hampered the churches' work.

A 1927 study of church giving in Korea concluded that the church was paying only half enough toward an adequate income for its church workers. The principle of self-support, said critics of the Nevius plan, had arbitrarily frozen the church at too low a level of development, intellectually and culturally. It simply didn't have the resources to train and retain qualified leadership.[19]

In 1927, Governor-General Saito left Korea to attend the Geneva Disarmament Conference. General Ugaki Kazunari became the acting governor-general for the five months he was away. After Saito returned from Europe, with his health failing, he resigned from the post of governor-general. When the news of his resignation reached Korea, the Executive Committee of the Korean Mission of the U.S. Presbyterian church sent a letter of appreciation to Admiral Saito for his friendly and liberal policies of cultural rule toward the church. In reply Saito wrote:

It is with deep gratitude I write to thank you for the expression of your kindly feeling for me. . . . As I look back on the past eight years and more during which I held office as Governor-General of Chosen I recall with much pleasure the cordial relation that existed between all of you and myself.[20]

In December 1927, General Yamanashi Hanzo was appointed governor-general. The policies of his administration followed those of his predecessor, though certainly his twenty-month term of service was too brief to effect any significant changes. Then, in August 1929, Saito was reappointed to a second term as governor-general of Korea in which he naturally continued his moderate policies and friendly relations with Christians. Unfortunately, this second term lasted only twenty-two months, for in June 1931 he was recalled to Tokyo. Saito continued to play a significant political role in these turbulent years of modern Japanese history as the premier and keeper of the privy seal and advisor to the emperor. Tragically, on February 26, 1936, this moderately old soldier was brutally killed, in his wife's presence, as a result of a militarist plot by ultrarightist army officers.

8

CHRISTIANITY AND THE
JAPANESE POLITICS OF WAR

After Admiral Saito Makoto's second term ended in 1931, General Ugaki Kazunari was appointed Korea's new governor-general. Ugaki, who served as acting governor-general from April to October 1927 while Saito was away on a diplomatic mission in Europe (as noted in the previous chapter) was no stranger to Korea and knew something about the policies of the Saito administration. Since he was considered an open-minded individual, Christians in Korea hoped that the new governor-general would not become hostile toward the Christian churches. Such a desire was expressed at the Federal Council of Protestant Evangelical Missions which met three months after Ugaki's inauguration. In February 1932, the new administration combined the Section of Religious Affairs with the Section of Social Affairs in the Department of Education. However, this was done to promote cooperation between religious and social educators, not to bring about particular policy changes concerning religious affairs.

The Ugaki administration seemed to maintain the conciliatory policies of the previous administration, and so the rule of culture did not yet disappear. The prevailing attitudes even resulted in awards being presented in recognition of the positive contributions made by missionaries in Korea. Dr. O. R. Avison, a medical missionary and educator, received the fourth degree of the Order of the Sacred Treasure from the emperor of Japan, and early in 1937 the Imperial Educational Association presented Dr. Samuel Moffett with a gold medal.

In Tokyo, however, the political climate was changing. The militarists were expanding their influence and engaging in terrorist activities to suppress liberal democratic elements in Japanese politics. They attacked Western ideas of democracy and demanded chauvinistic devotion to the emperor from the people.

Then, on the night of September 18, 1931, hostilities between Japanese and Chinese soldiers broke out after an explosion on the South Manchurian Railway near Mukden. It occurred without the sanction or knowledge of the official government in Tokyo. However, this "Manchurian incident" was an epoch-making event in the history of modern Japan, eventually leading to another disastrous world war. As a result of the incident, Japanese troops soon occupied the whole of the northeastern region of China, and on March 1, 1932, the state of Manchukuo was born. On September 15, Japan officially recognized the new state and withdrew from the League of Nations because the league refused to recognize the new nation and critized Japanese actions.

With the establishment of Manchukuo, Korea gained new significance regarding the communication, economy, and defense of the Japanese empire. The devotion of the Korean people to the empire became, from the Japanese viewpoint, more important than ever before, and as a means of making Koreans more loyal subjects, the Japanese administration began urging all Koreans to participate in Shinto ceremonies, for which an increasing number of shrines were built throughout the country.[1]

Shinto was the traditional folk religion of Japan, drawing from animism, shamanism, phallic worship, and ancestor veneration and centered around the village shrines. It was made the state religion during the Meiji Restoration and was closely identified with Japanese national life until 1945. Wherever the Japanese governed, Shinto shrines were built and the spirits of ancestors and Japanese deities, especially Amaterasu ō mikami, the sun goddess, were worshipped. Thus, as early as August 1915, regulations were made regarding how Shinto shrines were to be established in Korea and what forms of worship services were to be observed. Two years later, in March 1917, another regulation regarding the establishment of *jinshi,* or "lesser *jinja,* " was announced with the aim of fostering reverence for the Imperial ancestors in small towns and villages. In 1919, the Imperial Diet in Tokyo passed a resolution to establish a state shrine in the capital city of Korea. After seven years of labor and an expenditure of 1.6 million yen, the Seoul shrine was completed. It was intended to be the official shrine for the government-general's state ceremonies, and the location for the demonstration of the people's reverence and loyalty to the Japanese emperor.

To Christians, the presence of Shinto religion became a serious issue after 1935, when the government ordered all educational institutions, including private Christian schools, to pay obeisance by attending the shrine ceremonies. In previous years when the government had asked Christian schools to participate, Christians had been able to excuse themselves by participating in some other forms of constructive activities. Now things had changed. The militarists had further gained strength in Japan through their policy of national expansionism, and Shinto was to be used without exception as the government's method of political and military control.

On November 14, 1935, the governor of South Pyongan Province called a gathering of educators, but before the meeting he wanted all of them to visit Shinto shrines. Dr. George McCune, president of Union Christian College in Pyongyang, and Velma L. Snook, principal of Sungui Girls' High School, refused to do so. The governor ordered them to leave the meeting and gave them sixty days to reconsider their action. If the missionaries' attitude did not change in that time, he warned, their educational qualifications would be revoked. The missionaries held their ground even after sixty days, and in retaliation the government did indeed revoke their educational permits. Police guarded Dr. McCune's house and followed him wherever he went. On January 20, 1936, McCune was relieved of his college presidency and Snook was relieved of her principalship. Yet all the while, in trying to bring Koreans to the Shinto ceremonies, the government tried to persuade them that the rites had nothing to do with religion, but were instead patriotic acts: "The veneration of her illustrious dead in places specially dedicated to their memory has been a national custom of Japan for ages past, and the state ceremonies for this purpose are treated by the Government as distinct from those of a purely religious nature."[2]

On January 29, 1936, seven Christian leaders, including Yun Chi Ho and Ryang Chu Sam, general superintendent of the Korea Methodist Church, visited the Department of Education of the Japanese colonial government to address this issue. Mr. Watanabe, the head of the department, emphasized that attendance at the ceremonies was a civil, rather than a religious act—and that participation was simply a payment of the highest respect to one's ancestors.

Watanabe's arguments did not prove convincing. Korean Christians who had abandoned their own ancient practice of ancestor worship as idolatry were not easily convinced that paying such respect to Japanese ancestral spirits was not worship. In spite of the efforts to persuade them, most Korean Christians rejected the government's definition and refused to participate in the ceremonies. Many believed that bowing to the shrines violated God's commandment against idolatry, and the overwhelming majority of foreign missionaries also understood the shrine ceremonies as religious acts.

Roman Catholics especially, though they came to accept the government definition after 1936, took Shinto rites to be highly religious in nature. A Japanese bishop told his people in 1931:

> The Shinto Shrines, so the high authorities of the government tell us, do not maintain a religion, but as a matter of fact the ceremonies that are performed therein have a full religious character. Thus the sacred right of religious freedom, given to the people in Article 28 of the Constitution, is forgotten and violated by the ministry of education.[3]

Roman Catholics in Korea generally enjoyed a steadier growth after the Japanese annexation and had fewer conflicts with the Japanese administration. The main reason for this was that the Catholic presence in Korea was not as strong as the Protestant, and so Catholics lacked the political strength to confront the government. Moreover, Roman Catholics did not meet as frequently as their

Protestant friends for revivals and Sunday School meetings, so they aroused far
less suspicion.

Nevertheless, Catholics in Korea before 1936 understood that participation in the shrine ceremonies was idolatrous. This was changed by specific instructions from Rome. The story is told by Rev. Edward Adams, a veteran Presbyterian missionary in Korea, that in a meeting of educators called by the
government, Dr. McCune was challenged for his opposition to participation in
Shinto ceremonies. A Roman Catholic missionary who happened to be seated
next to McCune whispered to him, "The blood of the martyrs is the seed of the
church."[4] On May 25, 1936, the Sacred Congregation of the Propagation of the
Faith instructed Catholics in the Japanese Empire, including Korea at that time,
to accept the government order. Item 1 of this instruction said:

> The Ordinaries in the territories of the Japanese Empire shall
> teach their faithful that the ceremonies, conducted by the government
> at Jinja are civil affairs. According to the repeated, explicit declaration
> of the authorities and the common consensus of the educated, shrine
> ceremonies are mere expressions of patriotic love, that is filial rever-
> ence toward the royal family and the benefactors of their own nation;
> and that, consequently, these ceremonies have only civil value and that
> Catholics are permitted to participate in them and behave like the rest
> of the citizens.[5]

The instructions resolved the shrine issue as far as the Roman Catholics
were concerned. However, for Protestants, especially Presbyterians, the problem remained serious to the point that one mission report stated, "At present,
possibly no problem of missionary policy is more difficult than that occasioned
by the requirement of the Japanese government of attendance at the national
Shinto shrines."[6] Protestants continued to reject the government's insistence on
the nonreligious nature of shrine ceremonies. A typical explanation for their opposition can be seen in a statement by the mission of the Presbyterian church
of Victoria (Australia):

> We wish to express the high respect and loyalty which we hold to-
> ward His Imperial Majesty, the Emperor of Japan; this we do in gratitude
> for the blessings of good government. . . . But since we worship one God,
> alone, Creator and Ruler of the universe, revealed as the Father of Mankind,
> and because to comply with an order to make obeisance at shrines which
> are dedicated to other spirits, and at which acts of worship are commonly
> performed, would constitute for us a disobedience to His expressed com-
> mands, we therefore are unable ourselves to make such obeisance or to
> instruct our schools to do so.[7]

The opposition of Presbyterian groups was so strong that the Executive Committee of the Presbyterian Board of Foreign Missions soon felt compelled to recommend closure of the Korean mission schools:

> Recognizing the increasing difficulties of maintaining our Mission schools and also of preserving in them the full purposes and ideals with which they were founded, we recommend that the Mission approve the policy of retiring from the field of secular education.[8]

Some schools in Taegu and Seoul had difficulty closing at first because of Korean and missionary efforts to keep them open, but Pyongyang schools did not enroll any new students in 1937, and finally in March 1938 all schools were closed, including the Union Christian College.

The cordial relationship that had existed between the Christians and the government weakened, and the conciliatory policies of the Saito administration became only memories. In August 1936, a tough-minded militarist, General Minami Jiro, commanding officer of the famous Kwanto Army, became the new governor-general of Korea. With militarists in control in Tokyo, General Minami was able to place Korea under a firm military dictatorship as well. Then on July 7, 1937, less than a year after his appointment, shots were fired between Japanese and Chinese soldiers at the Lukowchiao, or Marco Polo Bridge, near Beijing. Using this "China incident" as a pretext, Japan began an all-out war, and the superior Japanese military might began to occupy major Chinese cities and strategic positions.[9]

As the war progressed, more support for the war effort was demanded of the Korean people, along with their unswerving loyalty to the Japanese government. In October 1937, the government decreed that the "Oath of Imperial Subjects" be recited publicly at all school and other organizational meetings. There were two forms of the oath, varied slightly for different age groups; the following is a translation of the junior age oath:

First: We are subjects of the Great Japanese empire.

Second: We, in unity of our minds, fulfill the duty of the loyalty and service to the Emperor.

Third: We endure hardships and become strong and good citizens.[10]

Meanwhile, government pressure on the Christian churches to participate in the Shinto ceremonies increased. It became more and more difficult to resist. In 1937, the Methodists, the second largest Protestant church in Korea, decided to comply with the government's request, agreeing with the government's claim that shrine attendance was a patriotic rather than a religious rite. In February

1938, the government called a conference of Christians intended to shape their thinking on the world situation at the time and to demand Christian support in the war ventures of the empire. The Presbyterians, at their general assembly meeting of September 1938 in Pyongyang, finally agreed to obey the government order regarding shrine ceremonies.

However, it should be noted that the "surrender" of the Presbyterians was affected by an unusual use of government pressure. Before the meeting of the four hundred delegates, each delegate was taken to a police station and simply told by the police to approve shrine participation. Then, when the session began, high-ranking police officials sat right in front facing the delegates. No debates or negative votes were allowed, and anyone who tried to leave was brought back by police escort. With little other choice, the assembly resolved that participation in Shinto ceremonies was not a religious act and therefore did not conflict with the teachings of Christianity. After the meeting the delegates did their obligatory obeisance at the shrine in Pyongyang.

The "official approval" of shrine attendance by the largest and most powerful Christian denomination in Korea proved an effective means of suppressing any further Christian resistance. The Shrine issue was solved as far as the government was concerned, but war was to bring about tougher and more oppressive policies against Korean Christians.

In May 1939, the government called a meeting of Christian leaders in order to form an organic union of all Christian denominations under the Nihon Kirisuto Kyodan (the United Church of Christ in Japan), which would allow for more effective control of the Korean church bodies. The gathering of over seventeen hundred leaders, representing forty-seven Christian organizations, instituted an organization called the "Chosen Kirusuto-Kyo Rengokai" (the Federation of Korean Christian Churches).[11] Cordial relationships already existed among the different denominations, but a unified church that was not prompted by a true ecumenical spirit could only be a superficial union. Indeed, Korean Christians paid the new body little attention, and the forced union actually hindered the ecumenical movement among Korean churches in future years.

The Japanese authorities made efforts to eliminate the influence of foreign missionaries in Korean church affairs by attempting to bring the Korean churches into closer contact with the Japanese. In October 1939, a union between the Methodists in Japan and Korea was discussed, and special representatives of the two bodies met at Aoyama Gakuin in Tokyo on October 18, and in the Kamakura Methodist parsonage on October 19. One significant agreement made at the meetings was that in important matters with the government authorities, the bishops of the two churches would confer. However, the bishop of the Japan Methodist Church would take charge of the matter of dealing with the government.[12]

Japanese pressures on Korean Christians to conform to Japanese war policies continued relentlessly. In 1940, in celebration of the twenty-six-hundredth anniversary of the founding of Japan, all Koreans were ordered to abandon their traditional Korean names and adopt Japanese names. Most Koreans had no choice but to follow the government order, for without a Japanese name it proved difficult to enter schools or to get a job. By September 1940, 80 percent of the Korean populace had changed family names. Likewise, the names of the Christian churches were also ordered changed. In November 1940, the Salvation Army became the Salvation Society, and in June 1941 the Methodist church became the Methodist society.

In this way, government interference in church affairs increased more and more, and any activities of which the government disapproved became excuses to imprison church leaders or expel missionaries. The Day of Prayer Incident in September 1941 was a typical example. Christian women throughout the world observed the World Day of Prayer during the last week of February. Korean women had joined in this observance with their sisters around the world for many years. In preparation for the day, Reverend Herbert Blair, chairman of the Federal Council of Churches, asked Alice Butts of Pyongyong to make a short outline of the Day of Prayer program available to the churches. When the police examined the program, they discovered a prayer "for the Peace of the World" and charged that such a prayer was a sign of disloyalty to the war effort. Butts was imprisoned for one month, and many Christian leaders were brought to police stations for interrogation.

At this point, the Christian churches in Korea were completely controlled by Japanese politics. A paper prepared by missionaries on November 22, 1949, four years after the end of Japanese rule in Korea, documented that church meetings could not be held without police permission, or without the presence of police representatives at every session. Restrictions imposed upon foreign missionaries were tight, including a restriction against their holding any administrative positions in the church. As Japan progressed toward war, the missionaries were compelled to withdraw from Korea. In October 1940, the U.S. consul-general, Gaylord Marsh, called representatives of the missions and informed them of the State Department order to evacuate all Americans, especially women and children. Marsh urged an early evacuation and arranged to bring the SS *Mariposa* to the Inchon port on November 16. On that day, 219 American citizens, practically all missionaries, were evacuated. Of the further withdrawal of missionaries up to March 31, 1941, the *Japan Christian Year Book* gave these figures:

Of the 108 reported in 1939 by the Methodist Mission, only 3 remain, and they will leave in April. Out of 66 Southern Presbyterians, 5 remain. Of 14 Anglicans, 3 are here, all plan to leave this spring. The Northern Presbyterians, with 118 members in 1939, have 14 now.[13]

With the main body of missionaries out of Korea, it seemed that the church simply became one more organization working for the Japanese cause. A statement adopted by the executive of the Presbyterian church at the General Assembly in November 1940 proclaimed:

> By following the guidance of the Government and adjusting to the national policy based on group organization, we will get rid of the wrong idea of depending on Europe and America, and do our best to readjust and purify Japanese Christianity. At the same time the church members, as loyal subjects of the Emperor, offering public service without selfishness, should go forward bravely to join in establishing the New Order in Asia.[14]

This same outline added, "Like other people, the church members should attend the shrine worship." On December 6, 1940, the Standing Committee of the Korean Presbyterian General Assembly called a meeting to form the Total National Force Union. The meeting was attended by some two hundred twenty delegates from each presbytery as well as by Vice-Governor-General Ohno and other officials of the colonial government. The assembly passed a resolution that "Chosen Presbyterians are resolved to give up the principle of reliance on Europe and America and reform our church as a purely Japanese Christianity."[15] The Methodists in Korea made a similar statement:

> It is both urgent and proper that we Christians should bring to reality the true spirit of our national polity and the underlying principle of Naisen Ittai (Japan Proper and Korea form One body), perform adequately our duties as a people behind the gun, and conform to the new order, therefore we, the General Board of the Korean Methodist Church, hereby take the lead in deciding upon and putting into effect the following:
>
> I.   Right Guidance of Thought
>
> II.   Educational Reform
>
> III. Social Education
>
> IV.   Support of the Army
>
> V.   Unified Control of Organizations[16]

On December 7, 1941, Japan attacked Pearl Harbor with more success than expected, and the Japanese Imperial forces entered into direct confrontation with the United States and the other allied forces in World War II. As the war progressed, the government attempted to force confessions of anti-Japanese activity, and so the remaining missionaries in Korea, including sixty-seven Roman Catholics, were imprisoned. In August 1942, Koiso Kuniaki, chief of staff of the Kwanto Army, became the wartime governor-general of Korea. Under his administration, the foreign bishops of the Roman Catholic dioceses were replaced by Japanese bishops, and the Holiness Church, the Seventh Day Adventists, and Fenwick's East Asian Christian Church (Baptist), were completely suppressed because of their emphasis on the second coming of Christ.

During the war, many churches were without pastors and Christians were forced to work on Sundays. Institutions such as the Christian Literature Society and the British and Foreign Bible Society were closed. Church bells were collected to be melted down for weapons, and the government ordered that the portable Shinto shrines, *kamidana,* be placed in the churches. Many church buildings were used to billet soldiers.

Yet, in spite of the tremendous national effort, bolstered by the broadcasting of distorted war news, Japan was losing. Increased losses by Japanese forces in the battlefield were reflected in the rise and fall of cabinet members. In July 1944, Governor-General Koiso Kuniaki became premier of Japan, succeeding Tojo Hideki; Abe Nobuyuki, another army general, became the new governor-general of Korea.

On July 29, 1945, less than a month before the end of the war, all Protestant churches under Japanese control were ordered to abolish their denominational distinctions and combine into the Nihon Kirisuto-kyo Chosen Kyodan (Korean-Japanese Christian Church). During an organizational meeting for this purpose, a Shinto priest even led the Christian pastors to the Han River for a purification ceremony. Following this forced union, about three thousand Christian leaders were arrested, and fifty of them suffered martyrdom from mistreatment in prison. It was also reported that the Japanese army was planning to massacre a great many more Korean Christians in the middle of August 1945 because of the fear that these Christians might aid the Allied Forces in an invasion of Korea. Dr. Helen Kim wrote:

> Some weeks after the atom bombs were dropped on Hiroshima and Nagasaki, we were told that over ten thousand leaders in Korean society who had been kept on the blacklist of the Japanese police were to have been arrested. In case of eventual Japanese defeat, the authorities thought these Koreans would become leaders and would retaliate against them. They had planned to massacre this group about the fifteenth of August, which proved to be the very day of the Japanese surrender.[17]

Thus, on that memorable day of August 15, 1945, the Korean churches were at last freed from Japanese political control.

9

The Division of the Nation, the Korean War, and the Churches

The end of World War II was a joyous occasion for all Koreans, who, in expectation of independence, began to celebrate their new political and religious freedom from Japanese rule. But the jubilation did not last long. The Korean people soon discovered that their country had been divided in two along the Thirty-eighth Parallel. The expected liberation had not truly come; the national family remained separated. President Harry Truman wrote later in regard to the division of Korea:

> Neither in Stalin's message to me nor in Antonov's to MacArthur nor in any other communication from the Russians was there any comment or question regarding the line of demarcation for the occupation of Korea. The 38th parallel, which was destined to loom so large in later years, was not debated over nor bargained for by either side. Of course there was no thought at the time other than to provide a convenient allocation of responsibility for the acceptance of the Japanese surrender.[1]

Although it was a "convenient allocation of responsibility for the acceptance of the Japanese surrender," the division of the country became the center and cause of conflicts and tragedies in post-World War II Korea. In the hope of establishing an independent Korean government, people's committees, committees to build the nation, and many other indigenous political organizations were formed among all segments of Korean society.

General Order no. 1, declared by the Headquarters Office of General Douglas MacArthur, informed Koreans of the division of the peninsula and stated that "all power of government over the territory of Korea south of the 38th north latitude and the people thereof will be for the present exercised under my authority."[2] Also, when the twenty-fourth Corps of the U.S. Army landed in Inchon to begin the military government in Korea, its commander, General John R. Hodge, ordered Koreans not to engage in political activities, especially any activities in opposition to the U.S. military government. Added to the order was a warning of severe punishment,[3] and on September 9, the office of the U.S. military government declared that English was to be the official language of South Korea.[4]

These orders and declarations were quite harsh, seeking only to fulfill U.S. policies and ignoring Korean interests in creating a united, democratic, independent Korea. In addition, Koreans believed that the United States was using South Korea as a military base and spearhead against the Soviet Union in the cold war, which started at the end of World War II. From the vantage point of the United States, Korea was the most important military base in the North Pacific, because from there, attacks could be made on every target in Northeast Asia. Thus Korea was seen by the United States not as a country to be reconstructed after the oppressive colonial rule, but as a valuable military base against the Communist bloc countries in East Asia.

It is impossible to understand the political situation in post-World War II Korea apart from realizing the importance the United States gave to Korea as an invaluable ally for the U.S. interests in East Asia. In an effort to maintain South Korea as an ally, the United States was eager to establish a strong anti-Communist political base in South Korea. Such a view was already expressed by Dr. Robert T. Oliver, an influential spokesperson for the U.S. policy toward Korea, in a letter to the *New York Times:*

> We should disband our American military government in Korea and set up a genuine Korean government south of the 38th parallel in its place. We should leave troops there, under the command of General John R. Hodge, as a barrier to further Russian aggression against Korea. We should make every effort possible . . . to force Russia to keep her promise of withdrawing from Northern Korea.[5]

Thus, the establishment of a Korean government in the South became the intention of the United States. However, the highest political aspiration of Koreans at this time was to eliminate the Thirty-Eighth Parallel, which divided the country between north and south, and bring about a united and independent country as soon as possible. The two occupying allied forces in Korea could not ignore this strong Korean political sentiment.

Efforts to reunite the country and to establish a united and sovereign government were initiated after occupation by the Allied forces. In December 1945, foreign ministers of the United States, Great Britain, and Russia agreed to hold a joint conference in Moscow in order to discuss means for establishing a provisional government in Korea. There, the representatives agreed to structure such a government under the trusteeship of the United States, Great Britain, the Soviet Union, and China for a period of five years. However, the Korean people opposed this decision. Even Communist party members initially rejected it, although later they came to support it, thinking that the Moscow decision was an effective way to bring about a united country.

To implement the plan, the United States and Soviet Union Joint Commission met in Seoul in 1946 and 1947. However, the differences of national interests between the United States and the Soviet Union were too great, and the joint conferences to bring about a provisional government failed.

In September 1947, the United States brought up the Korean issue in the General Assembly of the United Nations. The General Assembly adopted a resolution to create a UN Temporary Commission on Korea to supervise free elections in both sides of Korea. While this resolution passed the UN Assembly, it did so in the absence of the Soviet Union, who insisted on establishing a provisional Korean government, as was agreed upon in Moscow in 1945. When the U.S. government decided to urge the formation of a UN Commission on Korea to supervise the general election, the United States was probably aware that the Soviet military government in North Korea would not allow the commission to enter the North. The Soviet reasoning for keeping the UN Commission out of the North was their insistence on abiding by the foreign minister's agreement with Moscow in 1945, and North Korea's rejection of interference by an international organization such as the United Nations in the Korean affairs.

In response to the UN-sponsored election, North Korean leader Kim Il Sung called a joint meeting of all political parties and organizations in April 1948. South Korean political leaders such as Kim Ku, a Roman Catholic, and Kim Kyu Sik, a U.S.-educated Protestant leader, supported the proposals of the North Korean leader and went to the North Korean capital, Pyongyang. The political leaders who opposed the UN-sponsored unilateral election in South Korea believed that the election would further divide the country and make eventual unification more difficult to achieve. Along with strong anti-Communist leaders such as Kim Ku and Kim Kyu Sik, 695 political representatives from both sides of Korea participated in the historic conference held in Moranbong Theater in Pyongyang from April 19 through 23, 1948.[6]

In spite of strong opposition, and disturbances to block the election in South Korea, the United States and South Korean political groups led by Syngman Rhee were determined to carry out the election. The result of the unilateral election, held on May 10, 1948, was a victory for the United States and Syngman Rhee. The elected representatives met on May 31, 1948, and drafted a constitution for the new nation. According to the new constitutional provision, the representative assembly elected the first president of the Republic, Syngman Rhee.

The independence of the Republic of Korea was declared on August 15. The establishment of a separate state within a nation having five thousand years of history was a tragedy. Yet, in the eyes of the United States it was a diplomatic victory to establish a firm "democratic" government. The United States could be assured that South Korea would remain a strong ally under the presidency of Dr. Syngman Rhee, who had been educated at Harvard and Princeton universities in the United States. Dr. Rhee was handpicked by the U.S. government, and he remained loyal to the U.S. policy toward Korea.

In response to the establishment of the Republic of Korea in South Korea, North Korea established its own government. According to North Korean sources, 99.97 percent of voters in North Korea participated in the election of people's representatives, and 77.52 percent of the South Korean public participated in secrecy, because of South Korean opposition to elect one of the first representatives to the "People's Congress." In September, the first People's Congress was held in Pyongyang, North Korea, and declared the birth of the Democratic People's Republic of Korea.[7]

Thus in the small peninsula two governments were established with distinctively different political ideologies and economic systems. The division of Korea affected all segments of Korean society, including the Christian churches. However, as far as the political allegiance of the Korean Christians was concerned, they were unquestionably loyal and supportive of U.S. policy in Korea.

Many countries in the third world that were liberated after World War II had been colonies of European Christian nations. However, Korea was colonized by the imperial nation of Japan, which was strongly anti-Christian. During the Japanese occupation of Korea, Christianity was treated harshly and oppressively. When Christian leaders in Korea became aware of the unjust and oppressive nature of the Japanese colonial government, Korean Christians openly opposed the government and some missionaries became sympathetic to the nationalist cause, as we have seen in previous chapters.

As soon as World War II ended, missionaries began to return to Korea with the victorious soldiers and were treated as "liberators" of the people from the yoke of Japanese domination. Korean Christians thanked God for liberation and for the role of the United States in the victory over Japan. Churches held special services of thanksgiving in welcoming missionaries and American soldiers. The Roman Catholic church, for example, celebrated the landing of U.S. forces at Inchon on September 9, 1945, as a sign of God's grace. The day of celebration was observed with a high mass in the Seoul Cathedral, led by the illustrious American Catholic Church statesman Cardinal Spellman of New York.

It seemed that the United States had occupied Korea for the advancement of Christianity in Korea. Korean Christians were totally committed to the support of U.S. policy in Korea. The loyalty of Korean Christians toward the United States was so strong that there seemed to be no possibility of conflict between Christianity and U.S. policies. This was especially true in the Protestant camp. Former Protestant missionaries who had returned to Korea actually participated in the administration of the U.S. military government. Missionaries Harry Rhodes and Archibald Campbell wrote about this close cooperation of missionaries and government:

> Soon after the occupation of South Korea in September, 1945, a number of the members of the mission accepted positions as advisors to the American military government in Korea—Mr. D. N. Lutz in agriculture, Dr. J. D. Bigger and Dr. R. K. Smith as medical advisors, Miss Ella Sharrocks and Miss Edith Myers as nurses, Dr. H. H. Underwood and his son Horace in education, and so on.

> American government officials welcomed the help and enlisted the cooperation of all missionaries in the task of reorganization. Twice, in December, 1946, and in March 1947, the military government called all day conferences with all missionaries, Protestant and Catholic, who could attend. The missionaries were told that since they knew the Koreans, the Korean language and conditions in Korea, their assistance and advice in establishing a stable government in Korea would be welcomed. For some six months until his death in September, 1947, General Lerch, the military Governor, set aside an hour at 10:00 o'clock each Friday morning for a conference with the missionaries. They ate at the Army mess, were allowed to buy at the Army post-exchange and commissary, were furnished with billets in former mission property, technically owned by the Army as spoils of war, using household equipment and provided with transportation facilities, APO mail service, hospitalization and so forth.[8]

Also, many Korean political leaders who returned to Korea after having escaped Japanese persecution and who engaged in the independence movement, were committed Christians. These included Syngman Rhee, Kim Kyu Sik, and many others. The statistics regarding Christian participation in the postwar government are astounding when one realizes that the Christian population was less than 4 percent of the entire population. Rhodes and Campbell wrote this in their documentary history of the Presbyterian mission in Korea:

> In 1946, of fifty Koreans who were in official positions in the Korean government, 35 were professing Christians. Of the ninety members of the Korean Interim Legislative Assembly in 1946, the number of professing Christians was 21, including seven ordained ministers. In the first Korean Legislative Assembly, of 190 members (from August, 1948), the number of Christians is reported to be 38, of whom thirteen were ordained Christian ministers. A Vice-President of the Assembly was Elder Kim Tong Won, who for many years was a prominent Christian layman in the

city of Pyengyang [sic]. In Syngman Rhee's second term, the Rev. Ham
Tai Young, a Presbyterian minister, became Vice President.[9]

Clearly Christianity in Korea was not only in full harmony with U.S. policy,
but actively supported U.S. policies. Christianity in Korea during this time en-
tailed support of the United States and the opposition to the Soviet Union, North
Korea, and communism.

While Christianity was closely identified with U.S. policy in South Korea,
the Christians in North Korea did not fare as well. Soon after World War II, Soviet soldiers occupied North Korea. The Soviets were hostile toward Christians
and confiscated church properties. Conversely, in South Korea, Christians, especially Roman Catholics, made a great impact. Before the end of World War
II, the Roman Catholic church in Korea had projected an image of aloofness
and had separated itself from political involvement in the interests of the Korean people. Faced with new circumstances in the postwar period, an active and
socially conscious Catholic church began to emerge, fostering extensive aid
programs. A benefit of this fresh policy was a period of remarkable growth, and
an increase of about ten thousand new members a year. Among these converts
were such prominent members of Korean society as Hong Chin, chairman of
the Emergency National Assembly; Kim Ku, a noted leader of the nationalist
movement of Korea; and Rev. Chung Chun Su, a prominent pastor in the
Methodist church and one of the thirty-three signatories of the Declaration of
Independence in 1919.

While the Catholic witness now refocused its concern toward the needs
of the people, the Korean Protestants were plagued by internal divisions. The
immediate cause of the strife, especially in the Presbyterian church, was the old
issue of Shinto shrine worship. During the Japanese occupation of Korea some
Christians had participated in the shrine ceremonies, but about seventy church
leaders had refused to do so and were imprisoned for their convictions. Only
twenty of these men survived the torture and deprivations of prison. After their
liberation, they met in Pyongyang to discuss the reconstruction of the Korean
churches, and it was their decision to ask all pastors and church officials who
had participated in the Shinto ceremonies to relinquish their pulpits and administrative duties for a minimum of two months, as a public confession of their
sins.

In November 1945, church leaders from five northern Korean provinces
met at Sonchon to form a united presbytery and to discuss important problems
related to the Soviet occupation. This conference openly criticized the demands
of the so-called liberated saints, who had refused to participate in Shinto rites.
Those who had participated claimed to have obeyed the order to visit Shinto
shrines because of government pressure and not of their own free will. Most
important, they maintained that they had conceded to the government in order

to preserve the church and continue the ministry of the gospel. The participants of Shinto shrine worship further asserted that the sufferings inflicted by the Japanese government on them were just as harsh as the sufferings of those imprisoned leaders.

At a time when a united witness and a vigorous outreach of the gospel were badly needed, these divisions in the church and the nation were unfortunate. In North Korea the pressure of Soviet occupation forces on Christians and the unfriendly attitudes of North Korean authorities toward the churches increased. However, some of the North Korean church leaders supported the regime and they organized the Kiddokkyo Kyodo Yonmmaeng (Korean Christian Federation) in November 1946.

In South Korea, church leaders strove to maintain unity by seeking to establish a single liaison agency for all churches. One such organization was the Chosen Kyodan, which had been formed in the last days of the Japanese occupation. On September 8, 1945, church leaders met in Seoul to discuss the feasibility of continuing the Kyodan, but the effort was in vain. A significant reason for this was that one of the Kyodan's original intentions was to effect greater Japanese control over the Korean churches, a fact which did not endear it to Korean Christians. In addition, Methodist leaders were interested in pursuing their reconstruction activities apart from the Presbyterians and the Kyodan. The meeting to maintain the organization soon broke up, and the Kyodan ceased to exist.

Unfortunately, no other ecumenical church arose to take its place and promote unity in the postwar period. It remained impossible to gain a consensus among church leaders. Some even viewed ecumenism as an "evil" perpetrated by the Japanese. The churches did not rebuild in a spirit of cooperation and reconciliation, but one of competition and bitterness. Many church leaders became obsessed with ecclesiastical power politics, personality conflicts, and regionalism. The number of churches and church members increased during this period, but it is debatable whether these new followers were brought in by the call of the gospel or simply by an urge to increase the numerical strength of competing denominations. In the past, the Christian Church had proven itself a potent influence for good in the political arena. In its fragmented state at the beginning of the postwar era, it failed to make the same contributions to a country sorely in need of unity and reconstruction.

The most tragic consequence of the Japanese occupation was the division of Korea along the Thirty-eighth Parallel. This split of the country created a political atmosphere of distrust, disunity, and even hatred among the Koreans, who had shared the same language and culture for over four thousand years. Along the demarcation line, North and South Korean soldiers were constantly shooting at one another and engaging in guerrilla activities. The division of the country revealed that national order and progress cannot occur unless the unity of the nation is maintained. In Korea's turbulent, conflicted atmosphere the arrest of innocent people by the police, the torture of prisoners of conscience, and the denial of human rights ran rampant. This author, growing up in South Korea as a teenager during this time of Korean history, experienced imprisonment and torture, simply because of his expressions regarding national reunification and the democratization of the nation. Many of his classmates disappeared, to be found dead months later. To avoid such oppression, many youths left their homes and hid in the mountains, engaging in guerrilla activities against the South Korean police and security forces.

Previously, many young Koreans had hoped that the divided country would be unified through peaceful and democratic means. But, as far as the South Korean authorities were concerned, it was unthinkable to sit and negotiate with the Communist "devils" of the North. Anyone who talked about re-unification was considered a North Korean Communist sympathizer and severely punished. The only possibility for the reunification of Korea, according to South Korea, was by a victory over communism, which necessitated military engagement. It is no historical secret that South Korea sent military expeditions into North Korea to destroy military, naval, and even civilian bases. Professor Bruce Cummings of Northwestern University in Chicago wrote regarding the hostile South Korean attitude toward North Korea:

> The Rhee regime also wanted to unify Korea under its rule, by force if necessary. Rhee often referred to a "northern expedition" to "recover the lost territory," and in the summer of 1949 his army provoked the majority of the fighting along the 38th parallel (according to formerly secret American documents), fighting that sometimes took hundreds of lives. This was a prime reason why the United States refused to supply tanks and airplanes to the ROK: it feared that they would be used to attack North Korea. When Acheson delivered his famous speech in January 1950, in which he appeared to place South Korea outside the American defense perimeter in Asia, he was mainly seeking to remind Rhee that he could not count on automatic American backing, regardless of how he behaved.[10]

With Syngman Rhee's policy of Bukjin Tongil (reunification by invasion of the North), one may well argue that South Korea antagonized North Korea, initiating the war. North Korea maintains this position, saying that the Korean War was started by South Korea, with the support of the United States, while North Korea made efforts to reunify the country by peaceful means. It is both immaterial and irrelevant to debate who actually shot first, who initiated military activities. Both sides were constantly firing upon each other and engaging in hostile exchanges even before June 25, 1950. The real cause of the war was the Thirty-eighth Parallel which divided the country. Anyone who is serious about determining the causes of the Korean War should consider the division of Korea as the primary one.

On June 27, two days after the war began, the United States requested that the UN Security Council meet, and it further recommended that UN members provide assistance to restore peace in Korea. President Truman announced that the United States would comply by sending troops into South Korea. Truman stated:

> In Korea the Government forces, which were armed to prevent border raids and to preserve internal security, were attacked by invading forces from North Korea. The Security Council of the United Nations called upon the invading troops to cease hostilities and to withdraw to the 38th parallel. This they have not done, but on the contrary have pressed the attack. The Security Council called upon all members of the United Nations to render every assistance to the United Nations in the execution of this resolution. In these circumstances I have ordered United States air and sea forces to give Korean Government troops cover and support.[11]

American occupation troops stationed in Japan under the command of General Douglas MacArthur began to arrive in South Korea as North Korean soldiers moved steadily southward. The tide of the war turned in mid-September, when the First Marine Division and Seventh Army Infantry Division landed at Inchon behind North Korean lines.

On November 24, 1950, UN forces launched what was to be the final offensive to crush the remaining North Korean forces. This writer was a Republic of Korea soldier working in the Seventh Army Division which was on its way to North Korea. The miliary dispatches confidently predicted that the war would be over by Thanksgiving and that the U.S. troops would be home by Christmas. However, MacArthur had not counted on the possibility of Chinese intervention. When Chinese troops entered the war as "volunteers" to aid North Korea, MacArthur asked Washington for permission to begin bombing supply lines and military posts in China. Granting such a request plainly would have meant extending the war, and on April 2, 1951, President Truman relieved General MacArthur of the command. Meanwhile, the seesaw battles continued, causing heavy casualties on both sides and devastating the land of Korea.

In the midst of the destruction, members of the Christian community engaged in relief work to aid suffering fellow citizens. As Korean Christians received aid from Christians in other countries, especially the United States, church agencies began to seek better ways to distribute relief materials. To create more efficient relief programs, Protestant denominations organized the Korean Christian National Relief Association in July, 1950. Eventually, thirty centers were established throughout the country to bring food and clothing to the needy.

As a result of such cooperative relief work, the impact of Christianity was far greater during the war than before. Communication and projects among the churches increased. Many new Christian schools and colleges were soon established. Outstanding evangelistic and educational work was also begun among members of the armed forces. Practically every Christian denomination in Korea had military chaplains, and Korea was then the only country in Asia to have a chaplains' corps in its armed forces. Many young soldiers were receptive to the gospel. They took its message home with them, influencing others with the Christian call.

In spite of the hardships inflicted by the war, the churches continued their work of relief and evangelism. The suffering people of Korea heard a message of peace, love, and salvation in Christ; the number of Christians increased. Even so, social unrest, political instability, and a residual sense of distrust worked to prevent a full healing of the divisions within the church. Just before the end of the war, the Korean Christians who supported the ecumenical movement and those who opposed it became "enemies" within the fold of Christ. The divisions between them plagued the Christian community. This strife was fed by personal attacks and harsh accusations. Ultraconservative Christians accused moderates who supported ecumenism of being "Communist sympathizers." Such charges were unfounded, and they served to tarnish the image of the church.

10

The Politics of Anticommunism and the Unification Church

The political atmosphere of anti-Communist paranoia along with anti–North Korean propaganda produced a new, unique semi-Christian religious movement in Korea. The Holy Spirit Association for the Unification of World Christianity, commonly known as the Unification church, founded by the self-styled Reverend Moon Sun Myung, is a prime example of such a "Christian movement."

At its roots, the Unification church cannot be considered a true Christian movement, but a religious cult. One distinctive characteristic of any such "new religion" is the amalgamation of different, religious teachings. The Unification church itself acknowledges this aspect, as it describes itself in the following statement: "A new religion, which will serve as the basis for the new civilization, would be the fusion of Christianity and Oriental philosophy."[1]

In advocating this fusion, the teachings of the Unification church reflect yin-yang thought of ancient China in which the deity always works in the activity of creation through a male/positive force and a female/negative force. *Divine Principle,* the official book of Unification church doctrines, describes this work:

> A creation, whatever it may be, cannot come into being unless a reciprocal relationship between positivity and negativity has been achieved, not only within itself but also in relation to other beings. For example, particles, which are the essential components of all matter, have either positivity, or a neutrality which is caused when the positive and negative elements neutralize each other.[2]

According to these teachings, since all things are created and exist through "a reciprocal relationship between positivity and negativity," it is asserted that God created man and woman in the dual harmony expressed in the whole created order. However, this harmony was spoiled when Eve supposedly had illegitimate sexual relations with Satan, and the stain of Satan's blood was transmitted to all descendants of Adam and Eve, placing the human world under dominion of evil.

Now it must be clearly understood that a theological process that promotes dialogue among the various Oriental philosophies is not inherently wrong. It is imperative that Christian theologians in the Orient utilize the traditions of their own cultures in developing an indigenous Christian theology, even as Christian theologians in the West utilized Greek philosophy and culture. The danger of the Unification church, however, rests in its departure from the centrality of Christ in its theology. Moon Sun Myung teaches that the power of the female must be used both in God's redemptive activity and in God's creative activity. According to this theology, Jesus was indeed God's chosen prophet to redeem humankind and restore humanity to its original sinless state. Yet, because Jesus was killed by his enemies without being able to be married and start a family, he failed to leave the descendants necessary to transmit his pure blood to the rest of humanity. Moon wrote:

> When God created man, He placed Adam and Eve, man and woman, in the garden of Eden. They both united with Satan and became sinful, thereby leaving God isolated. In the process of restoration God must restore both Adam and Eve. Jesus came as the sinless Adam, or perfected Adam. His first mission was, therefore, to restore his bride and form the first family of God. Jesus came, but he was crucified. He was not given a chance to restore his bride. And this is why Jesus promised his second coming. Jesus Christ must come again to consummate the mission he left undone, 2,000 years ago.[3]

Since the redemptive work of Jesus remained unfinished, according to Moon, God has now renewed this work through the blood of the "true parents" of humankind, who "ascend from the rising of the sun, with the seal of the living God," as prophesied in the Book of Revelation (7:2ff.). The Unification church identifies the place of "rising sun" as Korea. In 1960, Moon married an eighteen-year-old high-school girl. This is a very young age for a girl to marry, according to Korean standards, especially to a man like Moon, who was forty-one and had been married once before. Their children were claimed to have been born without original sin, and the members of the church belong to the true family of true parents. The emphasis of belonging to the "true family" under the "true parents" of Moon and his wife is a degradation of the actual Holy Family of Jesus Christ. Even more, it is a denial of Christ's merits to say that Christ's mission was unfulfilled because he failed to have a wife and children. Indeed, according to the Unification church, the death of Christ was not only untimely but unnecessary, for "Jesus did not come to die on the cross."[4]

To followers of this new religion, Moon is simply more important than Christ. A professor of sociology in a prominent Korean university, who was a follower of Moon in the early years, summed it up well:

> Moon, therefore, is superior to Jesus Christ, because he fulfilled the mission which Jesus could not accomplish. Jesus is no longer one of the Trinity, the Holy Son, because of his failure in his original mission. But Moon is not only the founder of the Church but also he is the Messiah of the Second Advent, one of the Trinity, a living God.[5]

Obviously, no Christ-centered theologian can seriously consider the Unification church in any way a Christian movement, since it denies the redemptive merit of Jesus Christ. However, the appeal and impact of the Unification church is felt in the political arena because of its commitment to fight communism. An official declaration of the Unification church, published widely in Korean newspapers, stated the following:

> Communism is the enemy of mankind and the enemy of God. The communism that denies the existence of God should be defeated by the Christianity that believes in the existence of God. The principles derived from the teachings of the Reverend Sun Myung Moon prove the truth of the existence of God and the falsehood of the materialism originated by Marx and Lenin. The precious unification thought provides the truth and the confidence of the people of the world for the victory over communism. This is why the communists throughout the world are afraid of the Unification church. The Unification church is playing the leading role in the fight against communism in the free world. This movement is, within the nation (Korea), a movement that directly contributes to the national defense and national survival. Externally it is a movement to save the world and give hope in this world of chaos.[6]

Therefore, the Unification church teaches that the greatest task in which the Christian Church should engage in this world is the struggle against communism:

> Communism is a providential ideology which emerged at the end of the world to take the Cain position of thought in the dispensation of restoration. Human history started with the struggle between good and evil. Cain, who represented Satan, slaughtered Abel, who represented Heaven. Therefore, according to the law of indemnity and separation, God is going to conclude the evil history by separating good and evil worldwide. God (Abel) will subjugate evil (Cain). Communism appeared in this sense as the Cain ideology.[7]

Why does God allow such evil ideology to exist? The Unification people explain that God allowed the trend of thought leading to communism to develop "for the sake of restoring the human environment in the dispensation of restoration." The official source of the Unification church reads:

> God allowed the expansion of the communist ideology as a chastisement to warn the democratic bloc, which is the Abel side, and to direct it toward good. In the Old Testament Age, to awaken the rebellious tribes of Israel, God chastised them through the Gentiles. Today, in order to awaken the Christian nations which stand in the position of the modern Israel, God allowed Communism to emerge in the role of the modern "Gentile."[8]

Now, however, communism is doomed to fail, and the demise of all Communist ideologies including those in North Korea and Cuba will come with the victory of the Unification church. Therefore, the followers of the Unification church go out into the streets and preach against the "evil ideology." The following is a typical example of preaching one might hear in the Unification church:

> In North Korea, school children are required to bow down to statues of North Korean dictator Kim Il-Sung, and are given their choice of praying to the statue or praying to God. If they pray to God, they get no rice for lunch, but if they pray to Kim Il-Sung, they get a full portion. Children who consistently refuse to bow to Kim Il-Sung and call him their "beloved" Father have been shot, along with the entire families, as examples to the "bourgeois and un-proletarianized elements in North Korean society."[9]

The Unification church has many organizational fronts for fighting communism. They include the International Federation for Victory over Communism, the Collegiate Association for the Research of Principles, the Freedom Leadership Foundation, the World Freedom Institute, the American Youth for a Just Peace, the International Cultural Foundation, the One World Crusade, the Project Unity, and the Little Angels Korean Folk Ballet.

Among these the Freedom Leadership Foundation and the One World Crusade are the most vigorous. The Freedom Leadership Foundation sponsors political activities that will oppose communism. The members of the foundation are in the forefront of many campus movements conducting rallies, demonstrations, and prayer vigils. Another active group of the Unification church movement in Korea is the One World Crusade, organized by Moon in 1972. The crusade units travel with groups of young people and conduct rallies, give lectures, and appear on mass media for the cause of anticommunism. The anti-Communist political manuals of the Unification church provide educational materials for anticommunism education in Korea.

The Unification church believes that the United States is God's specially favored nation, chosen to play the leading role in the Unification church movement by opposing communism. In one of his talks to an American audience, Moon asked, "Have you ever thought which nation should be restored first? The leading nation (the United States)! If we restore your nation, one sixth of the globe will be restored."[10]

The Unification church praises America:

> America's existence was according to God's providence. God needed to build one powerful Christian nation on earth for His future work. After all, America belonged to God first, and only after that to the Indians. This is the only interpretation that can justify the position of the Pilgrim settlers.[11] The Unification church further argues officially that

> God has a definite plan for America. He needed to have this nation prosper as one nation under God. God wants to have America as His base, America as His Champion. And America was begun in the sacrificial spirit of pursuing God's purpose. America may consummate her history in the same sacrificial spirit for God's purpose. America will endure forever.[12]

America will endure forever because "America is the center of those God-fearing free-world nations. America has been chosen as the defender of God."[13]

On another occasion Moon told his American audience:

> I know that God sent me here to America. I did not come for the luxurious life in America. Not at all! I came to America not for my own purposes, but because God sent me. . . . The future of the entire world hinges on America. God has a very (big) stake in America.[14]

The effects of this type of preaching were soon evident. A *Newsweek* magazine article of October 15, 1973, reported:

> Dr. Moon has recently shifted his international base of operations from three rented rooms in a poor section of Seoul to a lush 22-acre estate in Tarrytown, N.Y. . . . , which his disciples purchased last year for $850,000. The estate included a luxurious mansion for Moon.

Despite the recognition of the importance of the United States and God's favor upon it, Moon and his followers were aware of the political crisis concerning Watergate. To seek God's help in solving America's Watergate problem, Moon went back to Korea in November 1973, where he spent much time in prayer and meditation, searching for an answer.

God gave Moon an answer. He was "to forgive and love President Richard Nixon." In a statement, "Answer to Watergate," Moon wrote:

> I bend my head and place my ear upon the heartbeat of America. I hear no one seeking the solution from above. We keep on criticizing, and the nation falls even further, deep into greater peril. Now is the time for America to renew the faith expressed in her motto "In God We Trust." This is the founding spirit that makes America great and unique. God blessed America because of this spirit. Furthermore, America is fulfilling a vital role in God's plan for the modern world. God is depending on America today. Therefore, the crisis for America is a crisis for God.

The statement further read:

> I have been praying specifically for President Richard Nixon. I asked God, "What shall we do with the person of Richard Nixon?" The answer did come again. . . . God spoke to me. . . . It is your duty to love him. We must love Richard Nixon. The office of the President of the United States is, therefore, sacred. God inspired a man and then confirmed him as President through the will of the people. He lays his hand on the word of God and is sworn into office. At this time in history God has chosen Richard Nixon to be President of the United States of America.[15]

In support of Nixon, the church sponsored frequent prayer meetings and demonstrations. A headline in the *Washington Post* on December 18, 1973, gives a good indication of this—"Watergate Day of Prayer Asked by the Unification church." Another headline, in the *Minneapolis Star* on December 1, 1973, read "Korean Preacher Urges U.S. Not to Destroy President."

According to Unification church followers, Nixon was the country's greatest president because of his ardent stand against communism. Communist-influenced politicians were responsible for destroying the president. At the national Christmas tree lighting ceremony in 1973, over one thousand followers of the Unification church turned out to "cheer President Nixon," carrying signs such as "God loves Nixon" and "Support the President." Not long after this cheering of the President, Moon was invited to the twenty-second annual National Prayer Breakfast at the Hilton Hotel in Washington, D.C. On the following day the president invited him to an unscheduled meeting.

President Nixon expressed further appreciation for Moon's efforts to support him in a letter from the White House, dated December 11, 1973:

All the words of encouragement I received are deeply heartening to me, and I am particularly grateful for the prayers and good will that you and members of the Unification church have expressed at this time.

I have read news of your efforts, and I share your belief that it is vitally important for this Nation to attain a sense of unity—unity that can come only from sharing our concerns about our common ideals. If we keep faith in ourselves and our faith in God, I am confident that America will remain a great symbol of hope for millions around the globe, a Nation with a rich heritage, and an even more promising future.[16]

President Nixon resigned from office, but the resignation did not weaken or destroy the office of the presidency as the people of the Unification church had predicted. On the contrary, the United States demonstrated to the world the strength of its democratic government and political process.

After the resignation of the president, this writer frequently asked followers of the Unification church about the downfall of President Nixon. The usual answer was: "Our Master, the Reverend Moon, [all members of the Unification church who answered this writer also confessed that they truly believed that Reverend Moon was the Messiah] urged President Nixon to hold onto his office and not resign. But President Nixon was not strong enough and not patient enough to hold his office." In any case, contrary to the hopes and desires of the Unification church movement, the president did leave office.

In spite of such evident contradictions, the Unification church appeals to many frustrated persons in a time of political uncertainty. The leaders of the Unification church strongly argue that the greatest task of Christians is to fight against communism, especially in Korea. The high-ranking officers of this church explained to this writer when he visited the office of the Unification church in Seoul, Korea, that God in his providence divided the peninsula of Korea so that it could be a testing ground for Christianity against communism. After Korea was liberated from Japan, the northern half of Korea was destined to be ruled by the Communist regime and the southern half by "democracy."

Thus South Korea is a special country, not only as the land of the "true parents," but also as the sacred battleground of Christianity in its struggle against communism. In fact, Moon claimed that he would send 1 million Christian soldiers from throughout the world if South Korea were in danger of a Communist takeover. According to the *Christian News:*

Joan Meyer, a former member of the Unification church, said that she was expected to be "willing to go to South Korea to fight, if necessary." One of Mr. Moon's avowed objectives is to unify Korea, "the holy land," and there is fear among those who oppose his movement that he might plunge thousands of the youth into this "holy war" eventually.[17]

Such fears may not be very alarming, but the political involvement of the Unification church does raise serious questions. The *Christian News* also wrote:

Mr. Moon reportedly has said that if necessary he would give the command for hundreds and thousands of his followers to move to certain areas at certain times to effect political and other objectives. Mr. Moon was said to have asserted that even with only 500 fully dedicated workers in each of the States some of the objectives of his theocracy can be put into force.[18]

It should be noted that the political activities of the Unification church are not universally considered ethical or desirable. The *St. Louis Globe Democrat* once reported: "Moon is not above suggesting Watergate tricksterism, such as using beautiful young girls to try to influence senators." Indeed, Rabbi Maurice Davis of New York testified in the United States Senate that "Mr. Moon has said that he wanted 300 good girls for the Senators—so watch out, Senator."[19]

The *St. Louis Post-Dispatch,* together with other major newspapers in the United States, also reported that the Unification church was used by intelligence agents of the South Korean government to manipulate public opinion and "influence U.S. members of Congress." It was further disclosed that even the South Korean Central Intelligence Agency had requested "the fervent demonstrations that followers of evangelist Sun Myung Moon staged in support of Richard M. Nixon in the Watergate scandal."[20] Again, the same newspaper reported:

A New York State audit of the Korean Cultural and Freedom Foundation whose President, Pak Bo Hi, has been identified as another Korean Central Intelligence Agency operative, shows that the foundation transferred $984,218 from its Washington office to Seoul before June 30, 1974. The foundation sent $250,000 that it had obtained in a loan from the Bank of America. An additional $258,000, evidently unconnected with the funds raised in America, went from Japan to Korea through the foundation. Korean sources familiar with the foundation said the money was originally raised, through solicitation, for use in America by adherents of the Reverend Sun Myung Moon. Pak was also Moon's chief aide.[21]

Such evidence of political activities, however sincere the members of the Unification church may be in their opposition to communism, cannot help but reveal the true nature of this movement. Reverend Moon and his followers made great efforts to influence U.S. politics to gain favor toward South Korea. However, Reverend Moon's intentions were not well received by the U.S. government and the public. In 1981, Reverend Moon was charged by the Internal Revenue Service of the United States for failing to report about $112,000 interest earned on a bank deposit of nearly 2 million dollars in the Chase Manhattan Bank in New York. Reverend Moon's lawyers requested a bench trial by a judge without a jury. This request was denied by the government. Apart from Reverend Moon's theological positions, and his political and ideological stands, his trial for tax evasion was somewhat unusual. During the trial and his imprisonment in Danbury, Connecticut, from July 20, 1984, to August 20, 1985, many prominent religious leaders and lawyers spoke out in his defense. They thought that the trial and imprisonment threatened religious freedom in the United States. Dr. Joseph Lowerry, the president of the Southern Christian Leadership Conference expressed a typical sentiment in support of Reverend Moon. He said:

> The Moon case is particularly frightening. Not only is the issue of religious liberty involved but also the issue of racial discrimination. Governments that jail the unpopular to please the crowd will soon jail any crowd it pleases.
>
> We call upon our friend President Reagan to name a task force to investigate the erosion of religious liberty.[22]

After his release from his prison, Reverend Moon visited South Korea more frequently than ever, and in 1989 he returned to Korea permanently. In the same year his church received permission to establish a university south of Seoul. With strong economic backing from his supporters, the Unification church's influence is growing both in Korea's religious life and in its political life.

The influence of the Unification church is also felt in North Korea. On November 30, 1992, Reverend Sun Myung Moon, his wife, and high-ranking officials of the Unification church visited North Korea. While they were in North Korea Reverend Moon visited his hometown and took pictures with his relatives, including his sisters, at the house of his birth. Reverend Moon also met with President Kim Il Sung of North Korea on December 6. The official newspaper of the Unification church reported on the meeting:

> Father and Pres. Kim met in a large room. On one side of the table were Kim Il Sung, Chairman Yoon and Deputy Prime Minister Kim. On the other side of the table were Father, Mother, Dr. Pak and Mrs. Pak. . . . Three times during his talk, Kim Il Sung spontaneously applauded and

said, "Thank you." Father also praised Yoon And Kim in front of Pres. Kim for their hard work.[23]

The subjects of their discussions are not known, although it is suspected that the Unification church wants to develop a tourist business in North Korea, making the birth place of Reverend Moon a sacred place of pilgrimage to be visited by all church members throughout the world. It will help the tourist business of North Korea, and in return the Unification church will extend its influence in North Korean politics, including those of anticommunism.

11

The Military Junta and the Politics of
Conservatism in the Nation and in the Church

After the Korean War, Syngman Rhee continued his policies of conservatism and anticommunism. The country was badly in need of social reform and a creative economic plan that would generate political stability. Rhee's government was not to fulfill these needs. The nation continued to suffer not only from increasing poverty, but also from greater government corruption. Any calls for reform in this status quo regime were typically labeled "Red" or "Communist." In the name of "freedom" and "anticommunism," Korea under Syngman Rhee was deprived of any degree of freedom or democracy, becoming a police state under an iron-handed dictator. Governmental processes were shamelessly manipulated, and legislation that often benefited Syngman Rhee or his Liberal party became official amendments to the nation's constitution. Rhee and his party quickly declined in popularity as they continued their oppressive ways.

In the election of 1960, the Liberal party again nominated unpopular and incapable presidential and vice-presidential candidates with Syngman Rhee and Lee Ki Bong. At the same time, all political rallies by the opposition were prohibited. The Home Ministry of the Rhee administration instructed all police to support the Liberal party and arrest those who refused to do so. Thousands of premarked ballots were distributed and stuffed into ballot boxes on election day. The obvious outcome was victory again for Rhee and his party. This time, however, the people did not accept the election results. A revolt was led by students who organized mass demonstrations on April 19, 1960. After the indiscriminate killing of students by police in a desperate effort to suppress them, Syngman Rhee was forced to resign and leave the country.

During this epoch-making event, known as the "April Student Revolution," the church communities remained silent. Not only did Christians fail to object, but the Christian churches were known to be closely associated with Rhee. No church body or other Christian organization spoke out in support of the student movement at this time. The silence of the Christians earned the distrust of the popular political movement of the time and evoked criticism from the student leaders of the April Revolution. These same students, who brought about the downfall of the Rhee regime, also advocated national reconciliation and reunification. They proposed to meet with the representatives of North Korea at Panmunjom to discuss the matters of student exchanges and travel between North and South. Even on this issue of peace and reconciliation, the church in Korea was silent.

Soon after the fall of Syngman Rhee, an interim government, headed by Huh Chung, conducted elections that gave control of the government to the opposition party of Syngman Rhee, the Democratic party. Under the new constitution, which gave more power to the prime minister than to the president, John M. Chang, leader of the Democratic party and a devout Catholic, was elected to be Prime Minster of the new government. The people had great expectations, but their hopes were met with bitter disappointment. Chang's Democratic party split into factions. He lacked the leadership to create a coalition within the government and unity within the nation. Political unrest and economic instability continued while the people suffered from ever-increasing disorder and poverty. On the morning of May 16, 1961, the military moved into Seoul and overthrew the existing government.

The government of John M. Chang had no chance to prove itself. The military could have supported the existing new government for democratization of the country and helped to maintain order. Instead, it staged a coup d'état! The coup was successful and almost bloodless. Justifying their action, the military generals who led the coup stated that the student demonstrations provided possible opportunities for Communist infiltration and takeover. Paranoia of anticommunism was the main reason for the coup. In the minds of the military, the coup was consistent with the need for a strong anti-Communist rule in South Korea. The legitimacy of the government and its effect upon freedom and democracy were of no great concern to the junta. The new military government selected Park Chung Hee, an army general, as chairman of the Supreme Committee of the Military Revolutionary Council. Park's government rigidly executed anti-Communist and anti–North Korean policies.

The new military government abolished the existing National Assembly and prohibited political activities, especially those directed against the government. In 1963, General Park was inaugurated as president of Korea. In 1967 he was re-elected. The constitution of the Republic of Korea prohibited the president from serving more than two terms in office. In 1968, Park's Democratic Republican party attempted to amend the constitution in order to allow him another term. This political maneuver failed, but in 1970 a national referendum was imposed by the government that approved the amendment. In 1971, President Park was re-elected by a very narrow margin over the opposition candidate Kim Dae Jung. The final tabulation was 49 percent for Park and 46 percent for Kim.

Many university students found the continuation of Park's military government intolerable and detrimental for the development of democracy in Korea. They held demonstrations in opposition to Park and demanded national reunification. Due to this social unrest, the army occupied university campuses in order to suppress student protests. On December 6, 1971, the president declared a state of emergency and prohibited student demonstrations.

During this time, there were strong popular demands for the reunification of Korea. The military government took up some unusual political gestures in response to the popular demands. On July 4, 1972, a joint communiqué was issued by the North and South Korean governments concerning the peaceful reunification of the two. This agreement included a call for an end to hostile accusations and criticism, pledges of noninterference in the internal affairs of each government, agreement that unification would be brought about without the interference of foreign countries or agencies, and the understanding that unification would be achieved by national unity through peaceful means. This communiqué also called for national reconciliation and declared that both governments would work to bring about a speedy reunification. This was a surprising and even shocking development. The people welcomed the announcement. Hopes and dreams of the reunification of the country mounted high.

However, contrary to expectations, the government restricted all such actions that might have led to a peaceful unification of the country. In fall 1972, President Park announced the so-called October Revitalization emergency decree. This decree temporarily closed the universities and colleges. It revoked the power of the National Assembly. All media communications were placed under strict governmental control, and all magazines and newspapers were investigated. At the same time, martial law was imposed restricting the freedom to criticize the government or engage in political activities concerning national reunification.

On November 21, 1972, a national referendum approved an amended constitution, which stipulated that the tenure of the office of president would be six years instead of four. It also allowed unlimited re-election and invested the president with absolute power over all branches of government. In the following months, the newly formed National Committee for Unification unanimously elected Park Chung Hee as president. On March 7, 1973, a new national assembly was organized. One-third of its members were appointed by the president.

In 1974, another series of emergency measures was announced "to consolidate the foundation of constitutional government and ensure national security."[1] On January 8, the president promulgated two emergency measures prohibiting any person from "defaming" the constitution under penalty of imprisonment for up to fifteen years. On April 3, Emergency Measure 4 further restricted dissident activities against government policies, especially by student organizations.

Later emergency measures completely outlawed student organizations, including the Democratic Youth and Student Federation. The government labeled this organization a Communist front used by North Korean agents to plot the overthrow of the South Korean government. This emergency decree provided for the punishment not only of students who belonged to the organization, but also for any one who praised, encouraged, or sympathized with it. The penalty for such actions ranged from imprisonment to the death sentence.

The emergency measures strictly prohibited dissenting voices and activities against the government and provided a basis for the arrest of many intellectuals and students who opposed the government. Soon after the promulgation of Emergency Measure 4 on April 19, a noted poet and a Catholic layman, Kim Chi Ha, was arrested while directing the production of a film. On July 10 the government prosecutor asked for the death sentence to be applied to the poet and six other persons. Fortunately, the death sentences were commuted to life imprisonment. In August, Kang Shin Ok, defense attorney for the Democratic Youth and Student Federation, was arrested. He later received a fifteen-year prison sentence for his criticism of the military court that tried violators of emergency measures.

Despite such harsh government repression, the cry for reform did not die. On October 10, students of the Korea University held a rally and read a Declaration of National Salvation, which asked fellow students and citizens to oppose the government. This statement incited violent clashes with the police. Brutal police tactics led students to issue a Declaration of Conscience that further criticized the government's methods of dealing with demonstrations. The government retaliated by closing the university. However, student demonstrations and rallies took place on other campuses in support of Korea University students and in opposition to the government's treatment of that institution.

The repressive measures of the government peaked in Emergency Measure 9, which was proclaimed on May 13, 1975. This measure was issued soon after the fall of the Saigon government in Vietnam to the Communists. On the issuance of Emergency Measure 9 the government explained:

> The Emergency Measures embody the nation's determination not to allow the Korean peninsula to become the scene of another Indochina catastrophe, a determination prompted by the lesson that the biggest cause of the fall of Khmer Republic and South Vietnam into Communist hands was their failure to achieve national unity and maintain a firm security posture.[2]

The purpose of the government was to maintain a firm security posture against so-called Communists in South Korea who really did not exist. Emergency Measure 9 restricted basic rights of freedom of citizens. Now prohibited were:

> Assemblies, demonstrations or other activities by students which interfere with politics, with the exceptions of (a) classroom or research activities conducted under guidance and supervision of school authorities; (b) activities conducted with prior approval by president or principal of school; or other ordinary, nonpolitical activities.[3]

All violators of this dictatorial legal system were "subject to arrest, detention, search, and seizure, without warrant thereto."[4] The government further explained the necessity of such an emergency decree:

> With the growing danger of a Second Korean War breaking out, as the North Korean Communists believe they now can successfully invade the South on the strength of the outcome of the Indo-Chinese situation, this is the time of great difficulties which the nation should surmount by means of a concerted effort.
>
> Security of a nation is a prerequisite safeguarding its existence as well as to pursuing its stability and prosperity. And the foundation for national security can be laid only upon national solidarity.
>
> Establishment of a firm national unity is required all the more in a situation in which a country, like Korea, is divided into two with one of the halves under the control of bellicose Communists intent upon invading the other side.[5]

According to the government, all curtailments of freedom and all impositions related to the emergency measures were necessary sacrifices by the Korean people to meet the threat of aggression from North Korean Communists. In agreement with this government rationale, conservative Christian churches in Korea supported these policies.

Characteristically, many Christian churches in Korea today are "conservative" and espouse a fundamentalist approach to biblical interpretation. These churches believe it best not to involve themselves in any political or social reform movements, not even in the national reconciliation movement. Conservative church leaders attack ecumenical church organizations, such as the National Council of Churches in Korea, as political tools of liberalism and communism. Conservative leaders are very critical of church leaders who are members of the World Council of Churches. They condemn any statements made by the ecumenical church agencies in regard to peace, justice, and human rights.

In opposition to the National Council of Churches in Korea, which frequently expressed dissatisfaction with the government's repressive policies, a conservative church organization, the Korean Christian Leaders' Association, was begun in 1975. Nineteen conservative church bodies that supported the president's emergency measures became members of this ecclesiastical organization. The leaders of this conservative church organization claimed to represent more Christian communities in Korea than the National Council of Churches. This group, however, was actually formed with the encouragement of the government for the express purpose of supporting governmental ideologies and to replace the National Council of Churches in Korea.

On the occasion of the thirtieth anniversary of Korea's liberation from Japanese rule, the Korean Christian Leaders' Association issued a Declaration of the Korean Churches that supported the anti-Communist politics of President Park Chung Hee. Among other things, the declaration stated:

> In recent years the country has been continually threatened by the North Korean Communists. This is closely related to the national survival. Because of such an insecure political situation, the government proclaimed Presidential Emergency Measures. The Christians of this country have been deeply concerned with this situation.[6]

Such a statement is in perfect agreement with the government's explanation concerning the emergency measures. With full support of the government, the association further declared:

> We recognize that under the present Korean situation the churches in this land cannot exist without the sovereignty of the Republic of Korea, and we regard the defense of our faith and the national security as our first primary task at the present time.

> As Christians as well as citizens of this country we believe that the first principle of our Christian life is to accomplish both of these tasks responsibly.

> If and when the freedom of our faith and mission will be threatened by any pressures, we four million Christians firmly resolve to resist them at the risk of our lives.

> We are deeply concerned with the problems which the entire human race is facing today. Furthermore, we ask that all the churches in the world

give close attention to the threat of Communism which threatens the freedom of Christian faith and denies basic human rights.[7]

While governmental oppression was sanctioned under the emergency decrees, leaders of the Korea Christian Leaders' Association claimed that total freedom of worship was guaranteed and guarded by the state. According to the argument of these church leaders, any restrictions placed upon Christian churches were due to the ecumenical church leaders' involvement in political protests.

Using "national survival" as a key issue, conservative church leaders refused to see government repression or the loss of freedom which the Christian churches were experiencing. In a news release, the Korean Christian Leaders' Association again stated:

> Korea's Christians have every right and freedom now to proclaim the Gospel. But criticism of the government and its leader is prohibited, for that sort of thing is publicized loudly to the world by the Communists in the North and gives the impression that we in the South are prepared to receive them with open arms.[8]

In defense of the government, conservative church leaders rebuked other church leaders who were vocal in their criticism of the government, especially regarding the emergency measures. Such criticism was considered to be unpatriotic.

Conservative churches were in complete harmony with the government of President Park. Both the government and the churches recognized the danger of the political and military power inherent in North Korean communism. Therefore, conservative Christians "could not remain idle speculators" regarding the apparent threat from the north. Strangely, however, conservative Christian groups frequently advocated the strict separation of the church and politics. One such conservative group declared: "It is important to respect the principle of the separation of politics from religion, and that Christian churches cannot neglect their responsibility for national security."[9]

National security was defined by such church groups as opposition to communism. Thus, conservative church groups did not believe in ecclesiastical involvement in political activities, yet they actively engaged in anti-Communist movements. The political journal of the Democratic Republican party reported in 1975: "The Christian Anti-Communist Association sponsored an 'anti-communist lecture' at the Arts Theater in Seoul with some 850 clergymen attending."[10]

According to the conservative churches, such activities were not in violation of the principle of separating "political and religious activities." Yet at the same time, those Christians who criticized the political repression of the government were said to indulge in indiscreet participation in politics.

For too long, churches equated Christianity with anticommunism. Hence, conservative churches served merely as supporters of strict anticommunism under the governments of Syngman Rhee, John M. Chang, and Park Chung Hee. Conservative churches today continue to support the political status quo, often blindly, and fail to pursue their real mission of seeking to effect national reconciliation and unification in a sundered country.

So strong is the church's attachment to its conservative origins and anti-Communist politics, that anyone who promotes an indigenous theology or new methods of Christian ministry or who criticizes the government is likely to be condemned as a heretical Communist sympathizer. Those persons who advocate church involvement in national unification and reconciliation are considered dangerous elements of Korean society both by the government and by the conservative segments of Korean churches. Obviously, Christian churches and governments in Korea are wrong in blaming all the world's ills on communism or on North Korea. Neither can they justify every action and policy of the government and the church simply on the grounds that they are anti-Communist.

12

CHRISTIAN OPPOSITION TO
PRESIDENT PARK CHUNG HEE

It is true that the majority of Korean Christian churches are of a conservative nature and that they closely identify Christian faith with support of anti-Communist governments. However, political involvement and dissent by Korean Christian churches, in opposition to injustice and political repression, are not lacking in the history of Christianity in Korea.

During the time of the Japanese absorption of Korea, Korean church leaders and missionaries officially decided to accept the foreign rule in Korea as "inevitable." Yet, when it was discovered that the Japanese government was oppressive, unjust, and cruel toward Koreans, some Christians did not hesitate to engage in political dissension. Even foreign missionaries who lived in Korea, who considered themselves political neutrals could not "sit silent." Sammel Moffet, a distinguished second-generation missionary, wrote in reference to the missionary involvement in the independence uprising in 1919:

> Though the basic stance of the foreign missionaries was political neutrality, it was too much to expect that missionaries representing the Gospel of Christ should sit silent when inhuman atrocities are being inflicted upon a helpless and unresisting people as was declared in an official paper issued by the Northern Presbyterian, the then largest Protestant mission in Korea.[1]

As the missionaries "representing the Gospel of Christ" did not "sit silent" in opposition to "inhuman atrocities" inflicted upon the people, neither did Korean Christians. Christians who were concerned with the welfare of the total person, the spiritual and physical realms of life, protested the injustice, oppression, and cruelty of the government.

Under the regime of Park Chung Hee and his Democratic Republican party, many Korean Christians definitely felt that they were oppressed and denied basic human rights. Some Christian leaders even questioned the legitimacy of the military coup of 1961 and criticized the military takeover of the government as "usurpation of power" by illicit means. Also, the government of Park was considered too pro-Japanese, having allowed the Japanese economy to encroach upon Korea with its dangerously polluting chemical industry. Thus, many Christians joined Korean students in their opposition to the normalization of Korea-Japan relations in 1964 and 1965.

However, the most serious political dissent of the Christian churches, with far-reaching impact both at home and abroad, emerged after 1968 when the Democratic Republican party attempted to change the existing constitution to allow the president of the Republic of Korea to serve the third term. Christians opposed the change in the constitution and the third term for President Park which it would permit, fearing the death of democracy in the country. Distinguished Christian leaders such as Rev. Kim Chai Choon, Rev. Park Hyung Kyu, Rev. Moon Ik Hwan, and others organized a Committee to Oppose the Change of the Constitution and Prevent the Third Term of the Presidency.

The gap between the government and the Christian community widened when the government, ignoring opposition, pushed a national referendum in 1970 to effect the constitutional change. In response, Christian leaders such as Ŏm Myong Ki and Ham Sŏk Hŏn organized the National Council for the Preservation of the Democracy, and actively engaged in dissenting activities against President Park's government.

As Christian dissent became more active and vocal, the government of President Park responded harshly. The government authorities put Christian churches under surveillance, examined records dealing with church finances, and checked the sermons of ministers. Such government activities were clearly in contradiction to the provision that guaranteed freedom of religious worship in the country. Continuous surveillance of churches by government authorities was documented in 1975 by Amnesty International, an organization that went to Korea to investigate the situation:

> KCIA [Korean Central Intelligence Agency] surveillance of church sermons and prayer meetings to see whether "political matters" such as civil rights are mentioned is commonplace. Interrogation and detention of churchmen who have actively involved themselves in community work for the poor and underprivileged is frequent.[2]

In the latter part of 1972, the government increased the pressures on Christian dissidents. In July of that year, the police arrested Cho Seung Hyuk, general secretary of the Ecumenical Modern Mission Committee. Ŏm Myong Ki was arrested in December on charges of instigating people to oppose the government. Pastor Ŏm was arrested at his church while he was conducting an evening prayer meeting. Since the situation had grown so alarming that a Christian pastor could be arrested in the midst of a church service, the Presbyterian church in the Republic of Korea, in which Pastor Ŏm held his membership, called a meeting of its General Assembly. The assembly issued a petition to President Park, the Ministry of Justice, and the director of the KCIA to reconsider such arrests.

Political dissent by Christians was not limited to opposition to the prolonged administration of President Park and his dictatorial rule. It was also extended into the area of the economic policies of the government. A Christian organization, the Urban Industrial Mission was especially active in trying to bring about a just economic policy and to improve the working conditions of laborers. The organization was seriously concerned about the low wages of laborers and the denial of their human rights. The Industrial Mission demanded improvement of poor labor conditions and asked for better wages for laborers. The government considered such demands dangerous both to the security of the country and to the economic progress of the people. In February 1973, the government arrested two pastors, Presbyterian Cho Ji Sŏng and Kim Kyung Nak of the Methodist church. These two leaders of the Urban Industrial Mission were asked by the police to stop their activities among the industrial laborers.

Government intimidation and prohibition of Christian mission work among the laborers violated the principle of religious freedom. In these serious circumstances, one of the important theological documents of this century, Theological Declaration of Korean Christians, 1973, was issued May 20, 1973. The declaration was formulated in secrecy by Christian scholars and church leaders, smuggled out of Korea, and published in different languages abroad. The declaration stated, among other things:

1. The present dictatorship in Korea is destroying rule by law and persuasion; it now rules by force and threat alone. Community is above being turned into jungle. In fact no one is the law except God; worldly power is entrusted by God to civil authority to keep justice and order in human society. If any people pose themselves above the law and betray the divine mandate for justice, they are in rebellion against God.
2. The regime in Korea is destroying freedom of conscience and freedom of religious belief. There is freedom neither of expression nor of silence. There is interference by the regime in Christian churches' worship, prayer, gathering, content of sermons, and teaching of the Bible.
3. The dictatorship in Korea is using systematic deception, manipulation, and indoctrination to control the people. The mass media has been turned into the regime's propaganda machine to tell the people half-truths and outright lies, and to control and manipulate information to deceive people. We believe that Christians are witnesses to truth, always struggling to break any system of deception and manipulation, for to tell the truth is the ultimate power that sets people free for God's Messianic Kingdom.[3]

This statement further accused the government of being "sinister and inhuman and at the same time ruthlessly efficient" in destroying political opponents and Christian dissidents. The document also criticized the government's economic policy through "which the powerful dominate the poor." The declaration then called upon the people for action and support to withdraw any form of recognition of the laws that have been wrought since October 17, 1972, and to the Christians in Korea to prepare for martyrdom. Although the theological declaration was not openly publicized, it circulated among church leaders and young people in Korea and boosted the morale of dissenting Christians. The declaration also provided a theoretical basis for justifying Christian political dissent against the dictatorial rule of a government.

In response to the theological declaration and other Christian activities of dissent, the government escalated pressures upon the Christian community. In June 1973, the government arrested Park Hyung Kyu, a prominent Presbyterian pastor educated at Union Theological Seminary in New York, who had served as editor of the leading Christian journal in Korea, *Christian Thought*. At the time of his arrest, he was pastor of the First Presbyterian Church in Seoul and chairman of the policy-making subcommittee of the Church and Society Committee of the National Council of Churches in Korea. At about the same time that Pastor Park was arrested, others were also taken into custody, including Kwon Ho Kyung, then a lay evangelist of Pastor Park's church, and Kim Kong Whan, a Methodist evangelist. A few days later, in early July, Na Sang Ki, chairman of the Korean Student Christian Federation, Chŭng Myung Ki, an active member of the student federation, and Sŭ Chang Sŭk, the vice-chairman of the Christian Student Federation, were also arrested. They were all brought in "on suspicion of planning an insurrection" by using persons who had gathered for the Sunrise Easter Service on Namsan mountain, in April of that year. At that Easter service, placards that read "Politicians Repent," "The Resurrection of Democracy Is the Liberation of the People," and "Lord, show thy mercy to the ignorant king," had been displayed. Government authorities interpreted the statements on the placards as statements of accusation and insult against the government of President Park, in effect, attempts to overthrow the government.

The arrests spurred more active Christian dissent against the government. The Women's Committee of the Presbyterian church in the Republic of Korea sent a letter of appeal to President Park and Prime Minister Kim Jong Pil. Christian journals and church organizations made public statements and petitioned the government to release the arrested persons as quickly as possible. The National Council of Churches in Korea held an executive committee meeting on July 10 in which they decided to meet with the minister of justice in order to inquire about the arrest of the church leaders. The same committee met again ten days later and established an ad hoc committee to investigate the events surrounding the arrests of church leaders and to protest to the government. Many

Christian churches joined the First Presbyterian Church, holding prayer meetings, making public statements of concern, and asking the government to release the arrested persons.

On August 1, a group of eminent Christian leaders—Dr. George Paik, former minister of education in Syngman Rhee's government and president emeritus of Yonsei University; Dr. Kim Ok Gill, president of Ewha University; and Rev. Han Kyong Jik, pastor of the largest Presbyterian church in Korea—visited with Prime Minister Kim Jong Pil. In that meeting, the Christian leaders inquired about the true nature of the arrests of the church workers and expressed their concern about the relation of church and government in Korea.

The Presbyterian Church in the Republic of Korea issued a statement on August 7, 1973, expressing support for and solidarity with its arrested colleagues. Many churches in major cities of the country held vigils and prayer meetings to protest against the government actions and to petition for the speedy release of imprisoned church leaders. Church Women United organized nationwide meetings for prayers and raised funds to support the families of arrested church members and to pay their legal fees.

While tensions mounted in Korean domestic politics, in the capital city of the neighboring country of Japan, Kim Dae Jung, the South Korean opposition leader and former presidential candidate, was kidnapped from his hotel. He was smuggled out of Japan by boat and five days later was brought to Seoul. This abduction of a prominent political leader aroused both domestic and international disapproval toward the Park regime. South Korean authorities announced that North Korean cigarettes were found in Kim's room, suggesting that the kidnapping had been a North Korean conspiracy. However, the world soon found out that it was a South Korean act.

Meanwhile, in Korea, students demonstrated for academic freedom and the release of imprisoned professors and students. Christians representing different denominations joined to hold "save the nation" prayer meetings in Seoul. In the last month of 1973, a year marked by tremendous Christian dissent, fifteen senior religious leaders, including Cardinal Stephen Kim of the Roman Catholic church, Reverend Kim Kwan Suk, general secretary of the National Council of Churches; and Yun Po Sun, former president of the Republic of Korea and a prominent Christian layman, issued a statement calling for a restoration of full democracy in South Korea and demanding the restoration of the National Assembly. Also, toward the end of the year, a campaign was initiated by Christian leaders to amend the constitution of President Park's government. To stop this movement, which was spreading throughout the country, President Park declared his emergency measures on January 8, 1974. (These emergency measures were discussed in the previous chapter.)

On January 17, some Christian activists, including Kim Kyung Nak, Lee Hae Hak, Kim Chink Hong, and Park Hun Soo, visited major church office buildings and solicited signatures for a petition to amend the constitution to bring about democracy in Korea. Consequently, six Christian activists were arrested. On February 7 they were tried by a military court and sentenced to ten to fifteen years' imprisonment, with the suspension of their civil rights.

In all these actions of Christian dissent against the government of President Park, the participation of Roman Catholics was very slight. Even at the time of the abduction of Kim Dae Jung, a prominent Roman Catholic layman, Catholics as a group did not actively engage in political dissension movements. Father James Sinnott, a very vocal critic of the Park regime, who was subsequently expelled from Korea, spoke about Roman Catholic participation in the dissension movement: "The people were already terrorized, and only a handful, students mostly, still dared to resist. Some few brave Christian ministers too had spoken out and were jailed, but my church was silent. And through June of 1974, I was very frustrated and discouraged."[4]

However, this picture of Roman Catholic political inaction drastically changed in summer 1974. On July 6, Bishop Daniel Chi returned to Korea from Europe and was arrested at the airport by government authorities. This event awoke the Roman Catholic church community in Korea. Father Sinnott described the change of events in this way:

> All Catholics automatically became involved. Every grandmother felt she had a grievance against the regime and during the seven months the Bishop was in jail, we got much educating done at the almost biweekly prayer meetings. In church is where most Koreans learned a little truth about their government, and because this truth was being taught, the Church became a high priority enemy of the regime.[5]

Four days after the arrest of Bishop Chi, a special mass was held in the Seoul Cathedral. Then on July 23, Bishop Chi issued his famous Declaration of Conscience. In the declaration the Bishop bitterly criticized the government of President Park:

> The so-called Revitalizing Reforms Constitution is invalid and contrary to truth. It has been forged by violence, intimidation, and fraud. It is said to have been passed by referendum, but in fact it has no true relationship with the opinion of the people. It was imposed on the people shortly after the arbitrary suspension and betrayal of the true Constitution on October 17, 1972.
>
> This so-called Revitalizing Reforms Constitution is in violation of the most basic and essential rights of the people. The so-called Emergency Decree gives all power to one man whenever he wishes to declare

such an emergency. This is a law in violation of fundamental human dignity. Under such a law the sphere of human conscience in the affairs is eliminated.

The so-called Presidential Emergency Decrees Nos. 1 and 4 which I am accused of violating are, in fact, a cruel violation of the Natural Law. These two decrees forbid any petition or expression of opinion to reform the Revitalizing Reforms Constitution. No communication or opinion on this matter is permitted. Any expression of disagreement or complaint against the Emergency Decree is punishable by life imprisonment or death.[6]

Three days after the announcement of this declaration by Bishop Chi, a conference of bishops was called to discuss the grave situation of the church in Korea. After the conference, a special mass was offered on behalf of the arrested bishop. The concern and dissent of Roman Catholics in Korea greatly increased. New Catholic organizations were developed whose objective was to increase careful planning and efficiency among movement participants. On August 26, 1974, the Korean Association of Priests for the Realization of Justice was formed, and under the leadership of this organization, many prayer meetings and masses were held. One such prayer meeting was held at Seoul Cathedral on September 11, with over fifteen hundred Korean Catholics attending the meeting. On that occasion the Association of Priests issued a petition for the freedom of Bishop Chi and other arrested church leaders.

On September 26, Catholics held street demonstrations, asking for the restoration of a democratic constitution and the abolishment of the Revitalization Constitution; the release of all arrested church leaders and students; the guarantee of freedom of assembly, speech, and basic human rights; and the provision for the basic welfare of the people with a minimum standard of living. All fourteen dioceses of Roman Catholic churches in Korea held prayer meetings on November 11 for the restoration of human rights.

Among the Catholic dissenters, the most vocal and colorful figure making a significant international impact was the young popular poet, Kim Chi Ha. Poet Kim had once been an assistant to Bishop Chi and had worked closely with the bishop in the diocese office in Wonju. In 1964 he had been a student activist, one of the leaders in the student movement against the normalization of relations between Korea and Japan. Due to his active opposition to the Korea-Japan treaty, he had been arrested and imprisoned and had been in and out of prison ever since.

Kim continued to write poems of political dissent and satire against the government of President Park. In March 1972, while he was out of prison, he published a long satirical poem called "Groundless Rumors," which accused the government bureaucracy of corruption. As a result of writing this poem, he was imprisoned again, this time as a violator of the anti-Communist law of South Korea, a crime punishable by death. However, because of the pressures of the Catholic Christians and because the charge that he was a Communist was unfounded, Kim was later released.

In spring 1974, he was arrested in connection with the National Association of Students and Youths for Democracy case. The government had labeled this student organization an agent of the Communists and charged that the poet Kim Chi Ha was connected with the organization. He was sentenced to death, but because of international opinion and support, he was freed from prison on February 15, 1975, by a special presidential order.

Less than a month later, on March 13, 1975, Kim was imprisoned again, once more accused of being a Communist. From his prison cell he smuggled out a twelve-thousand-word Declaration of Conscience. It read in part:

> The Park regime has imprisoned me under the allegation that I am a Communist who has infiltrated the Catholic Church. Worse, this conspiracy is not only against me as an individual, but is against the entire movement for the restoration of democracy and against both the Protestant and Catholic churches that have taken up the struggle for establishing social justice.[7]

Then he vigorously defended himself against the charges:

> I have never thought of myself as a communist. That continues to be true now. I am not a communist. Although the KCIA has been spreading propaganda that I am, by publishing my confession in my own handwriting, that statement was not written out of my own free will.[8]

Evidently government authorities had intimidated the poet during confinement, pressuring him to confess that he was a Communist, forcing him to sign a statement. The poet himself testified in trials that were held in Seoul District Criminal Court that the Korean Central Intelligence Agency had forced him to sign a document that was later distributed publicly with the intention of proving that he was a "self-confessed Communist." This charge has been consistently denied at court trials.

As Korean Christians were actively involved in the dissension movement, certain missionaries were also critical of the government and its oppression. Rev. George Ogle and Father James Sinnott were two of the most vocal critics of the government. Both criticized the government's handling of the case of the so-called People's Revolutionary party. Missionary Ogle and Father Sinnott believed that the case of the People's Revolutionary party was a fabrication by the government. The missionaries made their own investigation of the case and met with the families of the accused. As a result, they were expelled from the country. This government action against the missionaries became an important item of world news. A prominent Midwestern newspaper in the United States, the *St. Louis Post Dispatch,* reported on Dr. Ogle's forced departure from Korea on December 15, 1974:

> The Rev. George Ogle, 45 years old, was placed on a Korean Air Lines flight to Los Angeles, immigration authorities reported. A group of Christians conducted a brief demonstration at his home as the missionary was taken away by immigration officials. The Ministry of Justice ordered the deportation on the ground that the missionary had participated in illegal political agitation and demonstration through his preaching and public speeches. In a telephone interview, the Rev. Mr. Ogle said he had not violated Korean laws against political activity but had protested out of Christian conscience to restore human rights and freedom suppressed by the Korean Central Intelligence Agency.[9]

Although missionaries in Korea were there as "guests," such involvement in political dissent was inevitable. Missionaries who wanted to identify with the suffering people of Korea could not ignore the peoples' suffering under government oppression and injustice. Missionary involvement in political dissent was an integral part of the Christian community in Korea and its expression of Christian conscience. The article in the *St. Louis Post Dispatch* eloquently demonstrates why some missionaries have been, and still are, so involved in political opposition in South Korea:

> The missionaries justify their open opposition to political restrictions with a variety of arguments, the most common being that their Korean friends are being hurt. "I don't care a fig about politics," said a priest. "It's the people involved. I've seen my people beaten and tortured and raped and kidnapped. One whole family had disappeared. What am I supposed to do—close my eyes and go tiddly beads?"[10]

While the missionaries attempted, on the one hand, to justify their involvement in political protests, the government in turn charged that missionaries involved in such political activities were not doing "God's work." Mr. Kim Jong Pil, the premier, publicly stated that "the missionaries were allowed into Korea to preach, and have enjoyed complete freedom to do so. He has said that they are guests and their activities have amounted to foreign interference in domestic politics."[11] The government expected the missionaries to support its rule in South Korea as ordained and instituted by God. Yet some missionaries and Korean Christian leaders continued to involve themselves in political opposition against the government in order to protect the rights of their fellow Christians in Korea. The Christian community matured as a formidable political pressure group in the politics of Korea.

13

THE CHRISTIAN MOVEMENTS FOR DEMOCRACY AND THE ASSASSINATION OF THE PRESIDENT

As Christian political dissent continued against the dictatorial rule of the military government, the Christian movements became increasingly ecumenical, especially between the Protestants and the Roman Catholics. The ecumenical movement in Korea as a whole had been weak, despite the presence of outstanding ecumenical church leaders such as Reverend Kim Kwan Suk, Reverend Moon Ik Hwan, Reverend Kang Won Yong, Reverend Park Hyung Kyu and others. Ecumenical relations between Protestants and Catholics had been particularly poor. These two communities had eyed each other with distrust, as if they were strangers believing in different gods.

But the active participation of church leaders from both communions in the areas of justice and human rights and democracy movements altered this picture. As Christian protest movements escalated, the Protestants and the Catholics often held joint prayer meetings and church services. The Monday night meetings of the Protestant Missionary Fellowship and the Thursday prayer meetings of Protestant Christians were attended by Catholic Christians. In return, Protestant Christians attended masses and meetings sponsored by the Catholics. Catholics and Protestants in Korea joined in meaningful dialogue and worked together on the common cause for political freedom and economic justice.

The year 1975 was marked by excellent cooperation between Protestants and Catholics in nationwide movements opposing oppressive governmental policies. On the first day of the new year, the Association of Catholic Priests for the Realization of Justice placed a five-column advertisement in *Dong A Ilbo,* a newspaper that was under attack by the government. The notice made an appeal for freedom of the press. On January 9, 1975, church leaders met and announced a campaign to collect 1 million signatures opposing the "Revitalization Constitution" and in support of restoring the democratic constitution. The campaign was moving along successfully; then police confiscated the signature lists. The government declared a national emergency and put the military on alert. On January 22, the government announced that it would hold a

National Referendum in mid-February. The announcement of the National Referendum was a shrewd move on the government's part to discredit the movement of Christian leaders who were engaged in the signature campaign. This was an effort to silence the voice of dissent and to improve world opinion in favor of the regime.

The government announced that the referendum would take place on February 12, one day after the New Year holiday in the lunar calendar. Strong opposition voices urged a boycott of the referendum, but the government threatened police punishment of those who supported it. The movement to oppose the referendum was restricted. The government's strategies were carefully directed to bring large numbers of persons to the voting booths. On the day of the referendum, the voter turnout was 80 percent of the entire population. Among these, 73 percent of the votes cast were affirmative and 25 percent negative.

Celebrating the victory three days after the national referendum, President Park announced that he would suspend prison terms and release those who had been imprisoned under Emergency Measures 1 and 4. Some prisoners of conscience were released from prison. Then, on March 19, 1975, the Ministry of Education demanded the resignation of Dr. Park Tae Sun, president of Yonsei University, a prestigious Christian university. Christians protested against government interference in the affairs of the university, and Yonsei University students held emergency rallies in support of Dr. Park Tae Sun, who wanted to reinstate professors and students.

However, because of strong government pressure, the university president resigned on April 3. Virtually the entire student body of Yonsei University participated in a rally on that day to protest against the government. President Park Tae Sun stated:

> In order to put an end to the problem of reinstating the released faculty and students, . . . I completed the procedures for reinstating the students, and with the cooperation of the United Board for Christian Higher Education in Asia have appointed Professors Kim Chan-Kook and Kim Dong-Gil as research professors for the time being and will pay them from research funds. Consequently, judging that the great private institution, Yonsei, should suffer no further disturbance or trouble, and for love of Yonsei subduing my distress at leaving, I have submitted my resignation to Board Chairman Lee Chun-Whan as of today.[1]

A year later, the former president circulated a printed letter to his friends abroad, expressing his profound love of Yonsei University and justifying his actions. He wrote:

During my ten years and seven months as president of Yonsei University, the oldest and one of the largest and most famous universities in Korea, I have tried to do my best in developing the university and upholding its academic freedom.

Last year in February, I exerted my rights as president of the University and reinstated two professors and fifteen students who had been released from prison. The Ministry of Education had ordered me not to do so, but I went against them and so was forced to resign and so leave my beloved Yonsei.[2]

Then Dr. Park added this statement that explained so well the state of Christianity in Korea under the regime of Park Chung Hee:

The United Board for Christian Higher Education in Korea in New York and the Union Theological Seminary invited my wife and me for a year's stay in the States, but our government has given orders not to let me go out of the country. For over a year now the order has not been lifted and I have spent the time quietly in reading, meditation, and prayers, but we are hoping the way will be opened for us to meet our friends and thank them personally for all the spiritual and material support they have given us.[3]

Another momentous event took place the day Dr. Park resigned from his university presidency. Government agents raided the offices of the National Council of Churches in Korea, and papers dealing with financial accounts were confiscated. Church officials, including Reverend Kim Kwan Suk, the general secretary of the National Council of Churches, were arrested. They were charged with embezzling about eighty thousand dollars given by the German branch of Bread for the World. From that fund, twelve thousand dollars had been used to cover the expenses of the lawyers and twenty-two thousand to support the families of those imprisoned on charges of violating the presidential emergency decrees during 1974. However, these uses of the funds were in agreement with the policies of the Bread for the World agency, and church officials had previously written to the agency and obtained approval to use the funds as they did.

After the arrest of Reverend Kim Kwan Suk, the Seoul Metropolitan Community Organization, which worked closely with the National Council of Churches in Korea, made a statement charging that the arrest of Reverend Kim was an "attack against the Christian community" by the government. The statement said:

This raid (the arrest of Reverend Kwan Suk Kim and raid on the NCC offices) is the result of a confrontation between the movement for the realization of justice, and the suppression by the authorities. Reverend Kim Kwan Suk was selected by the authorities as a target in their attack against the movement for the realization of justice in the Christian community. He has become a victim, and is deprived of his integrity. It is clear that the authorities only want to obtain the effects of the propaganda that Kim Kwan Suk is being investigated on charges of embezzlement. This irresponsible defamation by the authorities, which did not take into consideration what the result of their acts would be, is also a grave violation of human rights. We see it as a form of revenge against KNCC and the General Secretary, both of whom have supported the movement for the recovery of human rights internationally.[4]

There were some government attempts to prove the alleged crime of Reverend Kim, but the charges were never substantiated. The director of Bread for the World defended Reverend Kim and the use of agency funds as having been authorized by the agency. The agency further announced it would renew such grants in 1975 and 1976.

The government unremittingly escalated its attacks on the Christian community. On April 11, Moon Dong Hwan, professor at the Hanguk Theological Seminary and the secretary designate of the National Council for the Restoration of Democracy, was arrested. In addition, church leaders Reverend Kim Song Sŏn and Reverend Lee Hae Dong, leaders of the Seoul Thursday morning prayer meeting, were interrogated along with other church leaders. Participants in the Thursday prayer meeting were forbidden to attend, but members of the Korean Central Intelligence Agency turned up at these meetings to observe them.[5] When Ham Sŏk Hŏn, the elderly and eminent Quaker leader, presided at an antigovernment assembly with Kim Dae Jung on April 19, the KCIA arrested him.

Then, on May 8, 1975, about one hundred church leaders, representing six member denominations of the National Council of Churches in Korea, met at Academy House in Seoul to discuss the state of the church and to formulate a policy for the protection of the rights of the churches and their mission activities. The leaders agreed that the arrest of Reverend Kim Kwan Suk and other church leaders was an "unpardonable violation of freedom of religion, and an illegal intervention of the authorities on mission activities."[6]

While domestic political opposition to the government of President Park Chung Hee became stronger, on the international scene, the war in Southeast Asia ended with the victory of the Vietnamese. May 2, 1975, the government outlawed all antigovernment activities and attempted to silence all voices of dissent. But the voice of dissent did not die out, especially the voice of conscience expressed by Christian communities.

In early 1976, there was a joint Catholic-Protestant prayer meeting in Wonju, diocesan headquarters of Bishop Chi. Seven hundred faithful people attended the gathering and issued a declaration demanding the restoration of justice and democracy in Korea. Then the most eventful and climactic demonstration of all Christian political dissent under the Park regime took place on March 1, 1976, when the Declaration for National Salvation and Democracy was proclaimed at the joint Catholic-Protestant service held at the Roman Catholic Cathedral in Seoul. The service was held to commemorate the fifty-seventh anniversary of the independence movement of 1919. The declaration asked President Park to resign from his office! It was read by Lee Oo Jung, president of Korean Church Women United. She was arrested immediately after the service. Within a week the total number of arrested church leaders had reached twenty-seven.

On March 10 the government formally charged that the March First Incident was a plot to overthrow the government. Kim Dae Jŭng and Reverend Moon Ik Hwan were accused by the government of being the chief instigators of the alleged plot. In recognition of the seriousness of such charges against church leaders and in response to the arrest of several Roman Catholic priests, Cardinal Kim Su Hwan led a prayer meeting on behalf of the arrested persons on March 15, 1976. Eight bishops, two hundred priests, and approximately twenty-three hundred Catholic Christians attended, along with many Protestant Christians. In addition to prayers, the cardinal read a statement that defended the arrested priests, saying that the priests had only engaged in works of religion and had been concerned with the protection of the civil rights of the people. Never, he argued, had they any intention of overthrowing the government.

The March 1 incident of 1976 focused international attention on the affairs of Christianity vis-à-vis the Korean government. In the first part of May and early June, while attention on Korea was heightening, the Seoul Metropolitan Police arrested eighteen church leaders who were associated with the Seoul Metropolitan Community Organization. This organization had been formed by Christian pastors and evangelists in 1971 to do mission work among the poverty-stricken people in the slum areas of Seoul. The organization clearly stated its purpose:

> We believe that Jesus came to the poor to preach the good news of the Kingdom of God; we believe that God has created humanity according to his image and he works in the midst of history to restore that image of humanity. Upon the call of God, we missioners [sic] entered into slum areas to help the people as they struggle to overcome poverty and hopelessness, believing that the people in the poor areas are clean, righteous and wise people.[7]

To carry out this mission, the workers of the Metropolitan Organization had closely identified themselves with the poor, even living with the poor in slum areas. They had also helped to organize the community in order to protect the rights of the poor and to gain for the impoverished the right to participate in decision-making processes. Many Christian university students joined the labor forces and supported the Metropolitan Organization's mission works. The work of the Metropolitan Community Organization was also supported by the National Council of Churches in Korea, the Christian Conference of Asia, and the World Council of Churches. Under the auspices of such national and international Christian organizations, the works of the Metropolitan Organization endeavored to bring Christ's love in word and deed to the urban-industrial poor.

Regrettably, the government considered the purposes and activities of the Metropolitan Organization to be dangerous and subversive, even communistic. The government tried to prove the connection between so-called Communist activities and the Metropolitan Organization, but it never succeeded.

Attempts to repress Christian groups such as the Seoul Metropolitan Community Organization typified the nature of the conflicts between the government and the Christian community. The government could not actually prove that any Christian community organization such as the Metropolitan Organization was connected with Communist activities. In fact, the government was always aware that the spiritual force of Christianity in Korea was the best defense the country had against communism. The government simply disliked Christian criticism of the governmental affairs and became more dictatorial than ever. Against this dictatorial government, Christians spearheaded the democratic movement in Korea.

With hope for the democratization of the government and the protection of human rights of laborers, Christian dissension against the government continued throughout the late 1970s. One of the Christian engagements in the protection of human rights for laborers was its involvement in the closure of the Y.H. Trading Company. On April 3, 1979, the company closed its factory without provision of compensation for its five hundred workers. The workers assembled to protest the closing of the company. When riot police invaded the factory two hundred workers were injured. On April 18, the Y.H. Trading Company consented to remain open, but later the owner absconded with the company's profits and the company was compelled to close due to the lack of financial resources. Once again the workers, especially the young women, protested and asked for compensation.

The Y.H. factory demonstrations were strongly prohibited by the government. On August 11, the oppressed women workers went to the office of the New Democratic party, the opposition party, since it supported the right of the laborers to hold sit-in demonstrations. Two hundred and fifty young women workers were attacked by one thousand riot police. One worker died. In these demonstrations, the Reverend Moon Dong Hwan, former professor at the Hanguk Presbyterian Seminary, presently a member of the National Parliament, was active in the support of the workers.

After the incident of August 11, the National Council of Churches in Korea protested police brutality and asked the government to provide subsistence rights for industrial workers. Some churches, such as Hanbit Presbyterian Church in Seoul, sponsored a sit-in demonstration in support of the women workers on August 15. On August 20, Cardinal Kim Soo Hwan conducted a mass for over ten thousand persons at the Myong-dong Catholic Cathedral in Seoul in support of the industrial labors and for the peaceful solution of the crisis in Korean society.

Demonstrations by Christians, both Catholic and Protestant, and by students, for the release of eight persons arrested in the Y.H. incident, along with protests against the government oppression of church groups, began to take place more frequently and intensely. There were uncontrollable, bloody street demonstrations, especially in the southern cities of Masan and Busan. Between October 16 and 19, demonstrations were held by thousands of students, supported by the citizens. On October 24, students of the Hanguk Presbyterian Seminary in Seoul declared a Confession of Faith that urged fellow students and Christians to oppose the oppression and injustice of the government. The students shaved their heads as a symbolic act of dissent and determination in their struggle against the political oppression.

Tension mounted. On the evening of October 26, 1979, President Park was shot by General Kim Jae Kyu, director of the Korean Central Intelligence Agency, at their dinner table. General Kim and others who participated in the shooting were arrested, and General Kim was executed. With President Park's death, tension between the government and the Christian communities eased. It seemed that Christian movements for the democratization of the nation had prevailed. Many imprisoned Christian leaders were freed, and ousted Christian professors were able to return to their former teaching positions. The future of Korea appeared bright. However, military generals who wanted to control the country in the name of national defense and anticommunism continued to hold power, and the discord between the government and Christian communities continued.

Stressful relationships between the dictatorial military government and Christian communities existed because Christian communities represented the democratic segments of Korean society. Politically, Christians were champions of democracy, freedom, and human rights. Dictatorial government was threatened by such a force in Korean society. Christian efforts to organize the poor in slum areas, to encourage the people to participate in the political process of the community, to educate the young to read and write, to make efforts to have a better life, and to assert the dignity and the individual worth of every human being before God challenged the authoritarian military government.

14

DEMOCRATIZATION AND THE ANTI-AMERICAN MOVEMENT DURING THE RULE OF GENERAL CHUN DOO HWAN

After the death of Park Chung Hee, Prime Minister Choi Kyu Ha assumed the leadership of the government as acting president. The people of Korea welcomed the change of government from the military dictatorship to a civilian government. The people hoped that a liberal democratic government would be established under which they would enjoy a certain degree of freedom and human rights. In the beginning of his administration, President Choi seemed to make efforts to bring about such democratization. The president ordered his cabinet "to investigate the possible release of political prisoners held under Emergency Decree 9 and the reinstatement of imprisoned and expelled students."[1] The infamous Emergency Decree 9 itself was revoked by the president on December 7, 1979. Sixty-eight political prisoners were released, including Kim Dae Jung, who was under house arrest at the time.

But real political power was in the hands of those military generals associated with the former dictator, General Park. Under the influence of the military, the government extended martial law, which had been declared upon the death of President Park. General Chun Doo Hwan, the Defense Security commander, was appointed to investigate President Park's death.

Among the military ranks the struggle for political hegemony continued. They were determined not to allow democratization to take place in the country. The military leaders did not want to hand over governmental power to the political opponents of Park. On the night of December 12, 1979, Major General Chun Doo Hwan and General Roh Tae Woo, strong supporters of Park's military government, took over the government by coup d'état. The political leaders who were inclined toward political reform and democratization were ousted from their positions or imprisoned. As his power solidified, General Chun promised that there would be no change in South Korea's anti–North Korean posture and that strong relations with the United States would be maintained.

This policy set off renewed demonstrations by university students and Christian political leaders, especially those opposing the new military government's strong ties with the United States. Students and Christian leaders such as Reverend Moon Ik Hwan, Professor Han Wan Sang, Professor Ahn Byong Mu, and the Roman Catholic political leader Kim Dae Jung demanded that the military take its hands off politics, and that the United States withdraw its support of the military government.

Early in 1980, economic conditions in Korea began to stagnate. Small businesses closed. The labor situation deteriorated. There were eight hundred labor strikes in the first three months of 1980.[2] Labor unrest and political demonstrations by students increased in April and May. Citizens and students assembled in Seoul railroad station on May 15, demanding liberalization and democratic reform in the country. Three days later the government responded by enforcing nationwide martial law, ordering all colleges and universities to close. Student demonstrations spread to different cities throughout the country, all demanding democracy for the nation.

In the city of Kwangju, the largest student demonstrations took place. On May 16, representatives of nine area universities, numbering more than twenty thousand students, demonstrated with torchlights. Another torchlight parade, urging the end of martial law, was held the next day.

The students indicated that they were willing to stop the demonstrations if the government would lift martial law and make promises for democratization. The government was unwilling to do either. Instead it increased oppression against the students and civilians. The night of May 17, the military force arrested hundreds of citizens, including Roman Catholic priests, Protestant ministers, professors, and students. Catholic Christian political leader Kim Dae Jung was arrested again, this time with his son. When news of his arrest reached the city of Kwangju, located in his home province, citizens there arose in great numbers, protesting against the government of the military generals.

On May 18, paratroopers from the Seventh Special Combat Unit of the Korean army were called in to stop the demonstrations. The paratroopers, who had been in the Kwangju area since May 10, shot at demonstrators indiscriminately. A report of the Kwangju incident stated:

> Many demonstrators were beaten or bayonetted to death, and there were bludgeoned corpses. Some corpses of female demonstrators had their breasts cut off. Corroborated eyewitness accounts state that a pregnant woman had her womb cut open with a bayonet and her fetus cut out. Enraged by such unspeakable savagery the people of Kwangju spontaneously joined the demonstrators to fight the military forces. What started out as a student demonstration rapidly expanded in number and scope. Labor-

ers, merchants, high school students, office workers and the city's poor all joined the demonstrators calling for the demise of Chun and martial law forces.[3]

On May 21, the government cut all communication lines in the city of Kwangju. More atrocities were committed by the troops. In reaction to the brutality of the government forces, citizens of Kwangju armed themselves and took over government buildings.

The final confrontation between the soldiers and the citizens of the city took place in the early morning of May 27. Although the citizens fought bravely, the soldiers quickly overran them. The soldiers, armed with helicopters and tanks, attacked the civilian positions with intensity and brutality. The government announced that only 190 persons died in the violence. However, ecumenical Protestant church organizations, Roman Catholics, and even members of the National Assembly challenged the government figure. Eyewitnesses estimate that more than two thousand people were killed.[4] This ended what demonstrators had called the "spring of democratization."

After the bloody repression of demonstrators, the military leaders organized the Special Committee for National Security. This committee was created on May 27, 1980, to administer the enforcement of martial law. General Chun Doo Hwan became the chairman of the Standing Committee of the newly established organization. The organization soon imposed an election, which resulted in Chun becoming the eleventh president of the Republic of Korea. Two months later, on October 27, his government promulgated the new constitution. The "new constitution" was not necessarily new, but it did provide a restriction limiting the president to a single term of seven years. On the occasion of the announcement of the new constitution, the president declared:

> As you all know, we introduced, for the first time in this land, a modern democratic constitution in founding the Republic of Korea in 1948. But, in the course of the following 30-odd years, we have failed to achieve a peaceful change of government by a free choice of the people, even though this should be the touchstone of a democratic constitution. Instead, we have witnessed repeated arbitrary revisions of the constitution designed to permit the chief executive to hold onto power for a prolonged period, thereby virtually precluding a peaceful change of government.[5]

The constitution also paid some attention to human rights issues, and expressed the desire to guarantee the basic rights of citizens. In connection with this concern, the president went on to say:

When a gap develops between the consciousness of the people and their country's institutions in the course of its political history, that gap must, without fail, be closed as quickly as possible. The constitution of the Fifth Republic is intended to meet just such a requirement.[6]

However, shortly before the declaration of this constitution, the South Korean military court imposed the death sentence on Kim Dae Jung, finding him guilty of sedition for supposedly starting the demonstrations. This harsh treatment of a political leader, along with the denial of human rights of citizens, caused reaction among many leading newspapers. The U.S. House of Representatives also heard reactions from the Honorable Don Bonker of the state of Washington. He said:

Mr. Speaker, on September 17, a South Korean military court imposed the death sentence on Kim Dae Jung, who has dedicated his life to the task of restoring freedom and democracy in Korea. Since then the hue and cry on the national and international level, against that unjust decision has been phenomenal and profound.[7]

Under the presidency of Chun Doo Hwan, the human rights situation in Korea did not improve. Church leaders such as Reverend Moon Ik Hwan remained in prison, and Christians who were engaged in advocacy for justice and peace were arrested and imprisoned.

While the repression continued and democratization was stalled, the newly inaugurated president of the United States, Ronald Reagan, invited President Chun to visit Washington, D.C. As Chun left Seoul for an eleven-day visit to the United States, the following was announced:

At the invitation of President Ronald Reagan, President Chun Doo Hwan will visit Washington on February 2, 1981. The official visit will afford the two presidents the opportunity to discuss bilateral political, economic and security aspects of the United States of America and the Republic of Korea as well as regional issues affecting Northeast Asia.[8]

The two presidents met in the White House as scheduled and reaffirmed "a mutually vital alliance and friendship" between the two nations. This strong support of a military general, who did not implement the promises of democratization nor guarantee human rights, by the president of the United States, was considered an insult to the aspirations of Koreans who struggled for democracy in their own country.

Student leaders and representatives of Christian communities demanded that the government investigate the Kwangju uprising and apologize for the brutal killings of civilians. Christian leaders also began to question the involvement of the United States and the role of the U.S. military in the Kwangju incident. The question was how Korean special forces, who were under the command of a U.S. military officer, could have been moved to the city of Kwangju without the knowledge or consent of the U.S. command in Korea, or even the U.S. government. Many Christians concluded that this was not possible and that the United States at least had known about the military engagement in the civilian demonstration at Kwangju.

Based on this conclusion, dissenting Christian leaders began to blame the United States for the incident at Kwangju, and the opposition movement against General Chun's government became an increasingly anti-American movement. A Korean specialist and former U.S. State Department official, who served in Korea, explained the increasing anti-American movements in Korea and the possible involvement of the U.S. Army in the Kwangju incident:

> As commander in chief of the Joint U.S.–South Korean command, a four-star American general must give permission whenever a normal Korean combat unit is moved. Coups, which always involve such shifts, either defy the command structure, as in 1961 and 1979, or when U.S. permission is sought and given, involve American command consent in the bloody suppression of forces seeking democracy, as in 1980 Kwangju. Even when, as in October 1972, the use of troops to enforce authoritarian constitutional changes was too minor to involve command permission, suspicion of implied command assent remains.
>
> American command (however qualified) over South Korean armed forces that are deeply implicated in internal Korean politics tarnishes the American name. Attempts to formalize the position only increases the dangers of "commanding" without control. Many Korean students thus perceive the United States as the mid-wife of the Chun regime's 1979–80 takeover of power and as the continued backer of this "puppet" of our "imperialism." To us as well as to Chun is increasingly ascribed a quarter of a century of repression of democracy within a highly educated nation aspiring to greater freedom.[9]

With such conclusions, anti-Americanism became an intense reality of Korean dissension, and "Yankee go home" was now frequently heard in Korea, where such a voice had seldom been heard before.

One of the most shocking anti-American incidents involving Christians was an act of arson at the American Cultural Center in the second largest city in Korea, Pusan. On March 18, 1982, a conservative Presbyterian seminarian, Moon Bu Shik, and his friend, Kim Hyun Jang, put fire bombs in the library of the Cultural Center and set them ablaze. The ground floor of the building was gutted, and a student who was studying in the library was trapped and died. A seminarian and sixteen others, including a Roman Catholic priest, Choi Ki Shik, who provided shelter to the accused, were arrested. The trial of the defendant took place in August 1982. Death sentences were given to Moon Bu Shik and Kim Hyun Jang. Moon's wife was sentenced to life imprisonment. Father Choi Ki Shik received a sentence of three years.

During summer 1982, anti-American demonstrations intensified. U.S. flags were burned amid shouts of political slogans such as "Yankee go home." In response, the government increased its pressures on Christian youth activities. In Taejon, a major city south of Seoul, a Presbyterian church was operating a night school which educated young people who had no other educational opportunities. During May 1983, a deacon of the church and several teachers of the night school were arrested by the security agency of the government. The homes of the teachers and the students were searched. All suspicious books and materials, including those of antigovernment and anti-American sentiment, were confiscated. The arrested church leaders were interrogated and forced to confess that they were Communists.

The Christian students of the Seoul District Youth Association of the Presbyterian church held a meeting on June 3, 1983, in connection with the anniversary of the normalization of Korean-Japanese relations. It was a meeting of lectures and Christian reflection. Riot police surrounded the church building, and at the end of the meeting used tear gas. Many young people were beaten, and church property was damaged.

Another church in Seoul, Hyungje Church, also operated a night school for young laborers who could not attend school otherwise. Called "Street Learning Place," this school too was harassed due to suspicions of anti-American activities. A teacher was arrested in June 1983, and students and church members suffered detention, arrests without warrants, and imprisonment.

As violations of human rights became even more frequent during the regime of General Chun, Christian dissidents accused the United States of supporting the dictatorial military government. They demanded that the United States not interfere in Korean internal politics. However, the United States continued to support General Chun. Early in summer 1983, the U.S. government announced that President Reagan was to visit South Korea in November.

As announced, President Reagan visited Korea on November 12 through 14, 1983. Before the president left Washington, D.C., he praised President Chun for the "increased respect for human rights" in Korea. With such a statement, the United States demonstrated that it was interested neither in improving human rights nor in developing democracy in Korea. Instead, the United States showed that its only concern was to protect its own interests. Unequivocal U.S. support for the defense of the government of General Chun Doo Hwan was promised to continue.

During the visit of President Reagan, the Korean government extended its political arrests. There were 480 political prisoners at that time, a total greater than the number which President Park's administration held at any one time. The government also arrested several hundred students during the same period. The office of the North American Coalition for Human Rights in Korea, located in Washington, D.C., issued this report:

> The Korean National Council of Churches Human Rights Committee's initial report said that between November 9–13, 145 persons were picked up and detained for three to five days, 135 were placed under house arrest and 3 were accompanied everywhere they went by security agents. These figures had to be revised upward as the Human Rights Committee's investigation continued. Korean authorities were quoted as saying that more than 1,200 churchmen, students and former politicians were detained or placed under house arrest; church and human rights sources now believe that the figure may have been as high as 3,000.[10]

Increasing anti-American sentiment was also prompted by U.S. attempts to open up Korean markets to American farm products. When the United States demanded the opening of Korean markets, to products including tobacco and liquor, Korean Christians strongly reacted. On March 29, 1985, the Catholic Farmers Federation asked the Korean government to protect Korean farmers by not allowing the indiscriminate importation of U.S. farm products. The unrestricted importation of American beef and other meats caused bankruptcy among Korean farmers, as they were unable to sell their products at reasonable prices.

While President Chun was meeting with President Reagan in the United States once again in April 1985, the Korean Christian Farmers Federation demonstrated against the importation of American agricultural products in front of the U.S. embassy in Seoul. On the following day, April 26, ten members of the federation entered the embassy yard, distributed leaflets, and shouted anti-American slogans. They were arrested and beaten so severely that they required hospitalization.

From May 23 through 26 of the same year, students staged sit-in demonstrations at the U.S. Information Service office in Seoul. Then, on November 4, fourteen students took over the office of the U.S. Chamber of Commerce in the Chosun Hotel, demanding that the United States stop pressuring Korea to open its markets to U.S. goods. Koreans especially resisted the importation of U.S. cigarettes and opposed the operation of American insurance companies in Korea. The Korean insurance companies had not been operating long and were financially weak in comparison to the U.S. companies. Permitting U.S.

firms to operate in Korea certainly would have meant the takeover of all Korean insurance businesses.

The number of anti-American demonstrations and attacks against U.S. offices increased throughout 1985, especially in the city of Kwangju. On December 2, 1985, students in the city threw gasoline bombs at the U.S. Cultural Center. Continuing attacks were so frequent that the United States closed the Cultural Center.

In spring 1986, the anti-American movement intensified, as did demonstrations for the democratization of the nation. On April 23, two students protested against "U.S. imperialism," attempting to kill themselves by self-immolation. One student, Kim Se Jin, died, while the other Lee Jae Ho, survived.

In spite of violations of human rights, the secretary of state of the United States, George Shultz, praised President Chun Doo Hwan for his efforts to bring about democracy in Korea. Speaking on May 7, 1986, during his visit to Seoul, the secretary of state also severely criticized the political opponents of Chun. Contrary to Shultz's praise of Chun Doo Hwan, the National Council of Churches in Korea issued a report in July indicating that the number of political prisoners had increased from 1,108 in May to 1,147 in July of that year.[11]

In October, a woman student, Kwon In Sook, was arrested and sexually tortured by a policeman in Puchon. On the last day of October, 1,274 students were arrested in one day at Konkuk University as they were holding meetings. Church groups were not exempted from arrest and torture. On November 18, 1986, 80 Protestant pastors were holding a prayer meeting asking for religious freedom. Police broke in and physically attacked the ministers, leaving several unconscious.

On January 14, 1987, a Seoul National University student, Pak Chong Chul, died after being tortured by the National Police in the Seoul police station. The National Police explained that he had died from strangulation when his neck was pressed against the edge of a tub while he was held under water during interrogation. While this was bad enough, a doctor who performed an autopsy on Pak said that Pak had died from blood clots induced by electric torture. Thousands of citizens wore black armbands to express their sympathy to the Pak family, and to protest the prison torture. On February 7, a memorial service was held for him and church bells were rung.

The death of Pak Chong Chul mobilized practically the entire nation to oppose the existing government. Demands were made to change the constitution and to hold direct, popular, presidential elections. On April 13, 1987, President Chun publicly announced that he would nominate his successor and hold an election under the existing constitution. Demonstrations broke out throughout cities and college campuses, demanding constitutional change and popular elections. Christian church leaders also demanded constitutional change. On April 21, fifteen Roman Catholic priests began meetings of prayers and fasting.

Soon, prayer meetings spread throughout the country as people said prayers for the nation. Over six hundred Roman Catholic priests and fifteen hundred Protestant pastors shaved their heads to show their support for democratic reforms and for a general election to choose a new president with a new constitution. Unmoved, General Chun insisted that he would nominate his successor. On June 10, 1987, President Chun held the nominating convention of his ruling party. The convention accepted Roh Tae Woo, another military general, as Chun's successor.

Spontaneous demonstrations took place nationwide opposing the current constitution and the nomination of another general to follow President Chun. The day before President Chun nominated Roh Tae Woo, a Yonsei University student, Lee Han Yol, was struck by a police tear gas canister and later died. Hundreds of thousands of people assembled in the cities to hold protest rallies demanding constitutional reform in the government. Unable to control these demonstrations, the government was forced to respond to the people's demands.

On June 29, the presidential nominee, now occupying the chair of the ruling Democratic Justice party, vowed to bring about changes in the country. To accomplish these changes, he announced eight points of reform:

A new system of government based on direct presidential elections. Revisions in election laws to "ensure maximum fairness and justness" to allow unrestricted campaigns and honest voting. Release of people arrested for taking part in opposition protests, unless they are guilty of treason or serious criminal offenses, and restoration of opposition leader Kim Dae-jung's full political rights. A guarantee of basic rights for all citizens, an end to all human rights abuses, and major extension of habeas corpus. Press freedom and an end to existing restrictions such as not allowing newspapers to have bureaus in provinces and requiring journalists to have government press cards. Local government autonomy and "freedom and self-regulation" for all sectors, including universities and colleges. This is to end the central government's strict control over many aspects of life. Freedom for political parties. Roh also issued a plea to all parties to behave responsibly and settle differences through peaceful politics. Broad reforms to curb crime and corruption.[12]

To implement the reform demands, the National Assembly discussed and adopted a set of new constitutional amendments, providing for the direct election of the president by the people. After approval of the amendments by national referendum on October 27, an election was scheduled for December 16, 1987.

Opposition party members, students, and Christians suggested that only one political opponent run against Roh Tae Woo in order to guarantee victory in the election. However, neither Kim Yong Sam nor Kim Dae Jung, the opposition leaders, conceded. As a result, Roh Tae Woo won the presidency with only 35.9 percent of the popular vote. Kim Yong Sam received 28 percent, and Kim Dae Jung received 27 percent. Had the two Kims not run against each other, Roh's opponent would have won at least 55 percent of the vote and ended the military dictatorship through the constitutional provision of direct presidential election. The Korean people felt dismayed and betrayed. On February 24, 1988, the day before the inauguration of the new president, a group of students invaded and occupied the U.S. Information Service Library in Seoul. The students threw homemade bombs, demanding the "end of U.S. imperialism." The election of the new president did not end anti-American demonstrations. It only served to intensify them.

15

CHRISTIANITY AND THE POLITICS OF REUNIFICATION

"The day when freedom and human rights could be slighted in the name of economic growth and national security has ended. The day when repressive force and torture in secret chambers were tolerated is over."[1] Thus spoke the new president, General Roh Tae Woo, in his inaugural speech, given February 25, 1988. The government, attempting to demonstrate a gesture of amnesty and reconciliation, released 125 political prisoners on the following day. However, these released prisoners comprised only 10 percent of the thirteen hundred political prisoners that were still being held, none of whom were serious political leaders, and all of whom had only a short time remaining in their prison terms. The gesture of amnesty and reconciliation did not go far enough. People throughout the country continued to demonstrate against the new president.

Three days before the inauguration, the National Coalition for Democracy issued an opposition statement against General Roh, refusing to recognize the legitimacy of his place in office. This refusal was not based on the fact that Roh had received only about 36 percent of the popular vote in the December 16, 1987 election. Instead, the coalition cited election irregularities and human rights violations as reasons for their opposition.[2] In addition, President Roh was another army general who was thought to be involved in the suppression of the Kwangju Uprising in May 1980. Koreans were determined not to trust another military general who had suddenly become a professional politician. Above all, dissidents refused to recognize Roh's presidency because he was strongly supported by the United States. Indeed, thoughtful Koreans began to believe that the policy makers of the United States had too great an influence over the destiny of Korea. It was with the support of the United States, the people believed, that the division of the country and the cycle of military dictatorship continued. Koreans began to exert a greater sense of self-determination to free themselves from the United States, determined to achieve the national reconciliation and reunification of divided Korea.

Continuing military rule and oppression under the anti-Communist security law were considered by the common mass of Korean people to be the results of the division of their country. Thus, political movements against the government in Korea became the movements of national reconciliation and re-unification in the late 1980s and early 1990s.

Christian organizations emerged as the most powerful force toward the achievement of the highest aspiration of all Korean people, the reunification of their homeland. Four days after the inauguration of President Roh, the National Council of Churches in Korea issued a "Declaration of the Churches of Korea on National Reunification and Peace." The declaration stated, among other things:

> We the Churches of Korea believe that all Christians have now been called to work as apostles of peace (Colossians 3:15); that we are com-manded by God to overcome today's reality of confrontation between our divided people—who share the same blood but who are separated into south and north; and that our mission is to work for the realization of uni-fication and peace.[3]

This historic document was first drafted at the Fourth Conference on National Reunification, sponsored by the National Council of Churches in Korea, in January of 1988. After careful consultation with member churches of the National Council, the declaration was issued on February 29. This doc-ument covers a wide range of political issues related to reunification. How-ever, of even greater significance is the theological idea of Jubilee called for in the declaration:

> Based upon this confession, the National Council of Churches in Korea, in order to fulfill its mission for peace and reconciliation, to share in the suffering division has caused, and to respond to the historical de-mand to overcome the division, now in a spirit of repentance and prayer announces plans to initiate a movement for a Jubilee Year for Peace and reunification, as follows.

> 1. The National Council of Churches in Korea proclaims the year 1995 to be the "Year of Jubilee for Peace and Reunification." . . . The "jubilee year" is the fiftieth year following the completion of a cycle of seven sabbatical years totaling 49 years (Leviticus 25:8–10). The year of jubilee is a "year of liberation." The proclamation of the year of jubilee is an act of God's people which reveals their com-plete trust in God's sovereignty over history and their faithfulness in keeping God's covenant. The jubilee year is the overcoming of all social and economic conflicts caused by the repressive and ab-solutist political powers, internal and external: the enslaved are lib-erated, the indebted have their debts forgiven, sold land is returned

to its original tillers, and seized houses are returned to their original inhabitants (Leviticus 25:11–55); the united covenant community of peace is restored through the establishment of *shalom* based on God's justice. The Korean churches proclaim 1995, the fiftieth year after Liberation, as a Jubilee Year.[4]

The words of the declaration renewed the vision of a Korea in which tragic national divisions had ended. These divisions promoted military confrontations, served to waste national resources, and severed 10 million families, barring them from all contact, even by phone or mail. This document, courageously voicing the Christian witness of love and peace, opened the discussion of reunification throughout all segments of Korean society. Previously, those who suggested national reconciliation through dialogue or reunification talks with North Korea were considered "Communists" or "Reds." In reality, however, patriotic Koreans have never given up the hope of reunification since the time of the country's division. It was only after the Korean War of 1950 through 1953 that discussions of reunification, especially peaceful reunification with North Korea, became taboo in South Korea.

Still national aspirations to reunite a divided Korea never fully died out among the people. Suppression of reunification discussions among the people by the government was the main reason for the downfall of Syngman Rhee's regime. In the early 1970s, under President Park, popular demands for national reunification were so strong that the government simply could no longer ignore them. The government response came out as shocking news on July 4, 1972: the governments of North and South Korea announced that Lee Hu Rak, the director of the South Korean Central Intelligence Agency, and Kim Young Joo, his North Korean counterpart, secretly met and agreed on three principles for Korean reunification. They were:

> First, unification shall be achieved through independent Korean efforts without being subject to external imposition or interference. Second, unification shall be achieved through peaceful means, and not through the use of force against each other. Third, as a homogeneous people, a great national unity shall be sought above all, transcending differences in ideas, ideologies, and systems.[5]

As a result of such serious agreements, there were some significant government contacts between officials of South and North Korea. In these meetings, South Korea approached the reunification issue by first recognizing the reality of two Koreas and then proposed that reunification be achieved by a gradual process. However, North Korea wanted to ease the military tension, by moving from the cease-fire treaty of 1953 toward a peace treaty which would include the withdrawal of U.S. forces from Korea. North Korea also wanted to invite representatives from all political parties and social organizations, including representatives of Koreans living outside of Korea. However, South Korea insisted that talks be limited to only "one window," namely that of the governments. With such different ways of approaching the unification issue, there was not much progress. However, the July Fourth Joint Communiqué aroused much excitement and raised expectations that the tragic division could be ended. South Korean students and political opponents insisted on their rights to participate in reunification discussions. In fact, the students constantly demanded to meet their counterparts at Panmunjom. Demonstrations and government repression in South Korea increased.

After the death of President Park, expectations for the achievement of reunification heightened. General Chun Doo Hwan, who succeeded General Park as president, made various proposals for reunification. In January and again in June 1981, he proposed visits between the heads of North and South Korea. However, he was more concerned with strengthening the defense agreement between the United States and South Korea than with increasing military preparations against "the aggression from North Korea." Consequently, the people of Korea questioned the ability and sincerity of President Chun to engage in serious reunification discussions. Many dissidents even thought President Chun only spoke for U.S. interests and was not concerned about achieving Korea's highest national goal: reunification. The people even concluded that close U.S.–Korean cooperation, including annual military exercises, was an obstacle to Korea's reunification. Gregory Henderson wrote: "As anti-militarist sentiment rises, moreover, the annual joint U.S.–South Korean 'Team Spirit Exercises' become seen as 'the training of military hoodlums' or, more soberly but dangerously, as the chief roadblock in North-South Korean unification talks."[6]

Although President Chun made some important proposals for reunification, the people did not take him seriously, for the issue of democratization in South Korea continued to be ignored, while human rights violations increased. North Korea, too, was reluctant to treat President Chun as a serious partner in the South-North reunification negotiations.

While South Korea's posture toward North Korea and reunification basically had not changed, North Korea presented a new plan in October 1980. This plan proposed the achievement of reunification by recognizing the existence of the two governmental systems while agreeing on their confederation, participating in all international sports events as one Korean team, and reducing the size of the military. President Kim Il Sung of North Korea suggested that this new reunited nation be called the "Democratic Confederal Republic of Korea."

This North Korean proposal to establish a confederation of the two Koreas earned considerable attention and support among the Christian groups within

Korea and abroad. In particular, a group of Korean Christian scholars and church leaders, who later formed the Theological Society for the Reunification of Korea, were attracted to this proposal as one possible means to achieve the difficult task of reunification. This Korean Christian group abroad contacted the Korean Christian Federation of North Korea, which had been in existence since 1946. The representatives of the North Koreans and of the South Koreans living abroad met in November 1981 at the Albert Schweitzer House in Vienna, Austria. This was the first face to face meeting of North Korean representatives, including Presbyterian pastors, with Korean Christian leaders living abroad. *Christian Century* reported on this historic event:

> At a landmark meeting in Vienna, Austria, November 3–6, Christian delegates from North Korea and South Koreans living in Europe and North America discussed the 36-year separation between the two nations and passed resolutions to underline their determination to achieve reconciliation. South Korea opposed the meeting and did not send any delegates.

> The following resolutions were adopted:

> Korea must be reunited and the right of self-determination must be realized in both countries. U.S. troops must withdraw from South Korea and stop all interference in Korean politics. "We oppose the proposal of 'bilateral U.N. membership' since this would legalize the permanent division of Korea."

> Korea must be reunited peacefully and the cease-fire agreement of 1953 must be changed to a permanent peace treaty. The Korean peninsula must be free from nuclear weapons.

> The suppression of human rights must be stopped and all political prisoners released immediately.

> There must be a dedication "to the sacred task of national reunification."

> Pastor Ki Joon Koh of North Korea reported that there are about 5,000 practicing Christians in the country and about 500 house churches worshiping regularly. The Federation of Korean Christians has a three-year theological education program in Pyoungyang to train pastors.[7]

Since this "landmark meeting," the groups have gathered almost every year, meeting on most occasions either in Vienna or in Helsinki. The latest meeting was January 9, 1991, at the Evangelical Academy in Arnoldsheim near Frankfurt, Germany. Such contacts between Korean Christians abroad and North

Korean Christian leaders, after so many years without communication, were indeed welcome events and aroused much interest from Christians everywhere. Significantly, the meetings also raised the visibility of the efforts of Korean Christians for reunification.

Within South Korea the National Council of Churches in Korea organized an executive committee to establish the Institute of National Unification in 1983, and attempted to hold conferences in May and June of that year to discuss issues of reunification. Both meetings were blocked by the South Korean police. In response, the National Council of Churches released a statement strongly protesting the actions of the police. Then, from October 29 to November 2, 1984, in Tozanso, Japan, the World Council of Churches and the Christian Conference of Asia held a consultation on peace and justice in northeast Asia. At this meeting, the Korean reunification issue received much attention. Among other things, it was decided at the conference to "support Korean attempts to bring about peace, reconciliation and unity, including reunification of the Peninsula" and to establish a "constructive relationship with Christians and with the government" of North Korea.[8]

To implement the "Tozanso Process," two delegates of the World Council of Churches visited North Korea in November 1985 and met with the officials of the Korean Christian Federation. Under such efforts, Christian leaders both from South and from North Korea held an ecumenical Bible study seminar on peacemaking in Glion, Switzerland, in September 1986. There they shared the Lord's Supper for the first time since the country had been divided. In the latter part of 1986, the National Council of Churches of Christ in the United States issued a statement asking the United States to alter its policy of confrontation and make efforts toward Korea's reunification. In 1987, the National Council of Churches in the United States sent delegates to visit North Korea, while in the same year, the National Christian Council of Japan sent Japanese Christian delegates to Pyongyang.

As the 1980s moved along, a growing number of Korean Christians within the country were inspired by the work done for Korean reunification by Christians outside Korea. Christians in South Korea undertook serious efforts for reconciliation, seeing North Koreans as brothers and sisters who were victims of the same tragedy: the division of their nation. Dorothy L. Ogle, a Methodist missionary to Korea, correctly expressed Korean Christian sentiment in her testimony to the subcommittee on Asian and Pacific Affairs, Committee on Foreign Affairs of the U.S. House of Representatives, in May 1988:

> From the Christian church in Korea which suffered greatly during the years of the power struggle they are hearing a message of reconciliation. They are seeing a church which is examining itself and confessing the sin of having turned anti-communist ideology into a virtual idol. They

are seeing a church which is beginning to think of their North Korean brothers and sisters as co-sufferers in the division, power struggle, and war. They are seeing a church which through a series of consultations beginning in 1984 has been deeply involved in a movement for reunification, and has recently published a document with principles for reunification and proposals for reconciliation.[9]

A significant development in the reunification movement has been the participation of Christian women. A month after the publication of the National Council of Churches in Korea declaration on national reunification in 1988, the Korean Association of Women Theologians, meeting in Seoul, stated in its own declaration:

> We have come to the realization that the overcoming of our national division and the achievement of the reunification of the Korean people is a question of our national survival. We see reunification as the most important mission task of the Korean church, and furthermore we believe it is the way to resolve the sufferings of women in Korean society.[10]

Active women theologians and church leaders held a women's forum in conjunction with the International Consultation on Justice and Peace, meeting in Inchon. The forum, which brought together more than one hundred women from seventeen countries, affirmed the Declaration of Korean Women Theologians on the Peace and Unification of the Korean People. The forum also proposed:

1. to urge a special emphasis on the Korean unification issue during the Ecumenical Women's Decade;

2. to establish a monthly 'hour of prayer' or 'day of prayer' for reunification;

3. to hold a meeting of north and south Korean women in a neutral third country, through the help of ecumenical church bodies, perhaps the WCC; and

4. to urge our governments to move positively to support peace and reunification in Korea.[11]

The April 1988 meeting of the International Christian Consultation on Justice and Peace proved to be a watershed event of Christian participation in the Korean reunification movement. This consultation, co-sponsored by the World Council of Churches, included over three hundred church leaders from seventeen countries. Dr. Emilio Castro, general secretary of the World

Council of Churches, and Park Sang Jung, general secretary of the Christian Conference of Asia, who had also been responsible for organizing the Tozanso consultation, were important participants. The government of South Korea attempted to disrupt the meeting by various means. It refused to issue entry visas to participants from eastern Europe, to four participants from Japan, including key-note speakers Professor Sumiya Mikio and Dr. Peggy Billings of the United States.

Several major papers were presented at the consultation. Dr. Suh Kwang Sun, professor of theology and then director of the graduate school at Ewha Women's University presented "The Theology of Reunification: A Korean Theology of the Cross and Resurrection." Patricia Patterson, from the United States, presented her work, "Liberation Bound Together: U.S. Responsibility and the Work of the Churches in Relation to Korea." "Human Consequences of the Inter-Korean Impasse: A Christian Perspective," was presented by Dr. Park Han Shik, professor of political science at the University of Georgia. Dr. Wolfgang Huber, professor at Heidelberg University in Germany, presented his paper, "What Kind of Peace? Confidence Building in the East-West Conflict and the Tasks for the Churches." Besides discussing these papers, this historic conference adopted the Message of the International Christian Consultation for Justice and Peace in Korea. This message reaffirmed the Declaration of the National Council of Churches of Korea on National Reunification and Peace and asked the churches of the National Council:

1. to encourage their congregations to study and act upon its recommendations;

2. to widen their dialogue to Christian churches in Korea which are presently outside the ecumenical movement . . . as a means toward the development of a common Christian stance on peace and reunification;

3. to further broaden the dialogue with people of other faiths and with the movement of the minjung;

4. to engage the people's deeply felt desire to participate in decisions regarding the reunification of the Korean nation, and to build relationships of trust and confidence between people in North and South;

5. to confront the enmities . . . , seeking to replace the idolatry of enemy images with the concept of love for neighbor, which is at the centre of the Christian Gospel.[12]

In response to the Christian call for national reunification efforts, student movements renewed their focus on issues of reunification. The May 10, 1988, a student rally served as a good example. On that day, thousands of students held a rally on the campus of Korea University and inaugurated a campaign to move President Roh Tae Woo and his administration to actualize concrete steps toward national reconciliation. One of the steps which the students proposed was a plan to hold the Summer Olympic Games, scheduled to begin on September 17, 1988, jointly with North Korea. Five days later, when the government failed to show much support for this proposal, a student leader, Cho Sung Man, killed himself in protest. Eleven days later, on May 26, another student, Choi Duk Soo, from Danguk University, committed suicide, demanding that the government support the student efforts for national reunification. These student protests brought national and international attention to the student demands. They compelled the South Korean government to work more seriously to improve relationships with North Korea. The *Washington Post* reported:

> Following a violent confrontation with students seeking to open a dialogue with North Korea on the emotionally charged issue of reunification of the two Koreas, conservative President Roh Tae Woo faces the complex task of proving to skeptical South Koreans that he genuinely wants to warm relations with the communist North, according to politicians and diplomats here.

> If Roh fails to show good faith on the reunification issue, the president is likely to face continued challenges from radical students, who are small in number but capable of making trouble for the Seoul Summer Olympics and of stirring up the general population as they did a year ago.

> "The student action has brought the reunification question into the foreground," said a western diplomat. "It hits on a certain nerve, which is a general feeling in the population that the government hasn't done as much as it could. It has created a problem that the government has to face."[13]

On June 10, 1988, a mass rally of students representing practically every university in South Korea attempted to approach Panmunjom, the point of demarcation between North and South Korea. The students did not succeed, but their fervor for unification created much social unrest. In response to the explosion of unrest, the government was forced to abandon its policy of confrontation. It tried to appease the people by responding to some of their demands. On July 7, 1988, President Roh issued a special conciliatory declaration permitting free discussions of reunification issues. The president announced, "Today, I am going to enunciate the policy of the Sixth Republic to achieve the peaceful unification of our homeland, a long-standing goal dear to the hearts of the entire Korean people." He then outlined his unification policies in six points:

1. We will actively promote exchange of visits between the people of South and North Korea, including politicians, businessmen, journalists, religious leaders, cultural leaders, academics and students, and will make necessary arrangements to ensure that Koreans residing overseas can freely visit both Koreas.

2. Even before the successful conclusion of the South-North Red Cross talks, we will promote and actively support, from a humanitarian viewpoint, all measures which can assist dispersed families in their efforts to find out whether their family members in the other parts of the peninsula are still alive and their whereabouts, and will also promote exchanges of correspondence and visits between them.

3. We will open doors of trade between South and North Korea, which will be regarded as internal trade within the national community.

4. We hope to achieve a balanced development of the national economy with a view to enhancing the quality of life for all Koreans in both the South and the North, and will not oppose nations friendly with us trading non-military goods with North Korea.

5. We hope to bring to an end wasteful diplomacy characterized by competition and confrontation between the South and North, and to cooperate in ensuring that North Korea makes a positive contribution to the international community. We also hope that representatives of South and North Korea will contact each other freely in international forums and will cooperate to pursue the common interest of the whole Korean nation.

6. To create an atmosphere conducive to durable peace on the Korean peninsula, we are willing to cooperate with North Korea in its efforts to improve relations with countries friendly to us including the United States and Japan, and in parallel with this, we will continue to seek improved relations with the Soviet Union, China, and other socialist countries.[14]

This declaration included the most positive policies of the South Korean government toward North Korea since the division of the country. Encouraged by this forward-looking policy statement, two important Christian meetings took place during the latter part of 1988. The first meeting was held on November 23 through 25 in Glion, Switzerland. This was the second gathering of Christian delegates from North and South Korea to be organized by the Commission of Churches on International Affairs of the World Council of Churches. The forty delegates at the meeting reaffirmed their commitment to work for national reconciliation and agreed on the three principles of reunification adopted by the two governments in 1972. On the last day of the meeting, the delegates unanimously adopted the Glion Declaration on Peace and the Reunification of Korea. Among other things, the declaration made the following recommendations:

1. We support the decision of churches in both North and South Korea to observe 1995 as the year of Jubilee for Unification, and to observe the Sunday before 15 August each year as a Common Day of Prayer for Peace, for which we have adopted a common prayer text. We request the WCC to recommend to its member churches to join in prayer with the Korean churches by observing this Sunday.

2. We reaffirm the three guiding principles for the "unification of the Motherland," agreed between the North and South Korean governments in 1972, namely "independence, peaceful reunification and great national unity." We also confirm that the reunification process must honour and guarantee two existing systems in the spirit of peaceful coexistence, with the objective of building up one reunified country.

3. We affirm that the subject of the Korean reunification process is the people (minjung) themselves, in both parts of the peninsula. Any foreign forces which have been involved in the division are therefore considered as stumbling blocks for peaceful reunification and should be removed. We also affirm that reunification should be carried out through a process of democratic participation by all members of the Korean nation.

4. In order to build peace in North-East Asia, including the Korean peninsula, it is necessary to achieve the reunification of Korea. We therefore oppose any attempt to legitimize the status quo of division. We believe those attempts to be a quasi-peace; we therefore oppose any proposed alternatives or measures that fix the division as a matter of fact.

5. We believe that for the sake of the peaceful reunification of Korea, it is imperative to build confidence between North and South, which have been separated for several decades. We therefore recommend to the churches of both North and South to engage in special efforts to overcome hostility and hatred, thereby creating an atmosphere of forgiveness and reconciliation. We request, furthermore, that the worldwide Christian community help to build confidence through a variety of approaches, including the enlisting of cooperation by international organizations such as the United Nations, keeping firmly to the guidelines established in the Tozanso Consultation regarding ecumenical coordination of contacts.[15]

The second major meeting that took place during the last part of 1988 was the Suwon Conference, held at the Academy House in the city of Suwon, south of Seoul. Delegates to this meeting included South Korean Christians and Christian leaders living in Europe and North America who were actively involved in the reunification of Korea. In conjunction with the Suwon Conference, a new theological association, the Theological Society for Korean Reunification, was organized within South Korea. This society took upon itself the task of devoting theological energy to the issues of peace, reconciliation, and the reunification of Korea. Dr. Hong Kun Soo, who was in prison at the time of this writing, became its first president. Reverend Moon Ik Hwan, the leading Christian advocate for Korean reunification, and Park Hyung Kyu were elected to the advisory board of the society. In the meeting, many pastors engaged in the ministry of minjung churches participated together with the noted woman theologian Dr. Park Soon Kyung.

The year 1989 was especially eventful for Christian participation in the reunification movement. In late March, Rev. Moon Ik Hwan, a Presbyterian pastor and poet, visited the capital city of North Korea and discussed the issue of reunification. While he was in North Korea, he attended a Protestant church service in Pyongyang on Easter Sunday. In spite of the July 7, 1988, declaration of President Roh, the peace mission of Reverend Moon was perceived by the South Korean government as a grave violation of the security law. Moon was arrested even before he stepped off his plane at the Kimpo International Airport. Security officers forced the doors of the plane open and arrested the pastor. Some eleven thousand police surrounded the Seoul airport at the arrival of this seventy-one-year-old minister, preventing anyone from approaching or welcoming him, including his ninety-five-year-old mother. On September 20, 1990, while Moon was serving a seven-year prison sentence, his mother died. Under rising pressure, the government released Reverend Moon from prison in October 1990, but he was reimprisoned soon after.

Despite heavy-handed government reactions, efforts by Christians to bring about the reunification of Korea intensified. Not only are the National Council of Churches in Korea and its affiliated church bodies speaking out, but also practically every Christian organization, student group, youth group, and women's organization is now speaking out in support of the reunification of its country.

The courage and determination of Korean Christians were reflected in the Conference on Peace and Reunification, sponsored by the National Council of Churches in the U.S.A. held at the National 4-H Center in Chevy Chase, Maryland, on April 23 through 24, 1989. The primary aim of the gathering was to implement and support the annual Common Day of Prayer for Peace, and the 1995 year of jubilee for Korea. Four Christian delegates from the Korean Christian Federation in North Korea participated in the meeting. This was the first such meeting of North Korean Christians within the United States. The North Korean delegates affirmed their solidarity with Christians everywhere, working together for God's cause of peace and the reconciliation of Korea.

Above all, the most powerful witness of the Christian cause of reunification was the visit of a Roman Catholic woman student, Im Soo Kyung, to the Thirteenth International Youth-Student Festival held in Pyongyang and her return to South Korea through the cease-fire village of Panmunjom in the summer of 1989. While she was in North Korea, Ms. Im participated in the International March for Peace and the Reunification of Korea. The march started at Mount Baekdu, on the Chinese-Korean border, and ended in Panmunjom. Over four hundred people from thirty countries participated in the seven-day march, which began on July 20, 1989. The marchers from North Korea were to join with those from South Korea, who were to begin at Mount Halla in Korea's southern most Cheju Island, at Panmunjom, but South Korean authorities prohibited the march and arrested the participants. Under these circumstances the significance of Ms. Im's participation as the South Korean student representative in the North Korean march was greatly heightened.

On the final day of the march, July 27, the thirty-sixth anniversary of the Korean armistice, Ms. Im wanted to cross the Demilitarized Zone in Panmunjom and return to South Korea. However, the U.S. military stationed there, along with the South Korean authorities, did not allow her to go home. Im Soo Kyung and over one hundred participants of the march then engaged in a hunger strike. On the sixth day of the strike, Ms. Im announced that she would cross the demarcation line in Panmunjom and return to Seoul.

Before crossing the Demilitarized Zone and entering South Korea, on August 15, the anniversary date of Korea's liberation from Japan, Im Soo Kyung and her priest, Father Moon Kyu Hyun, who had accompanied Ms.Im during her visit to North Korea, denounced the presence of the forty-three thousand U.S. troops stationed in South Korea and asked for their withdrawal. They stated that the peaceful reunification of the country was impossible as long as U.S. soldiers remained in Korea. They then crossed the demarcation line, saying their own prayers and the famous prayer of St. Francis of Assisi, "Lord, make me an instrument of your peace." The event was a powerful Christian witness of love and peace to the world.

As soon as they arrived in the southern zone, they were arrested and indicted on charges of violating the National Security Law. Im received a ten-year prison term, with the sentence later being reduced to five years. Father Moon first received eight years but also had his term reduced to five years. What a betrayal of confidence to imprison a twenty-one-year-old college student and a priest because of their effort to bring about national reconciliation!

However, the Christian witness of peace and reunification continued within Korea and abroad. In the summer of 1990, the Association of Korean Christian Scholars in North America met in Beijing, China, to discuss the issues of Christian concerns over reunification. At the two-day meeting, they were joined by delegates from North Korea, including a woman student from a North Korean seminary in Pyongyang, three North Korean pastors, and one social scientist from Kim Il Sung University. After the meeting, the Korean Christians from North America traveled to Pyongyang. There they participated in the Pan-Korea rally for peace and the reunification of Korea, held on August 15, on the North Korean side of Panmunjom. These delegates also worshipped in Bong Soo Protestant Church in Pyongyang and held dinner meetings with North Korean pastors.

The movement for national reunification among Christians in Korea is spreading like wildfire. No one can quench this fire, kindled for peace, coming from the Spirit of God. It is a historical reality that Korean Christians are determined to make significant contributions to end the tragic division of their homeland. The latest example is provided by the visit of Reverend Kwon Ho Kyung, the general secretary of the National Council of Churches in South Korea, to North Korea. During his visit from January 7 to 13 in 1991, he met with high government officials, including President Kim Il Sung, and church officials of North Korea. The Christian leaders on both sides agreed to meet regularly and worship and pray together to achieve the highest national goal of the Korean people, reunification. It was the Korean Christian commitment to achieve the year of jubilee of reunification in 1995, the fiftieth anniversary of the end of World War II and the division of Korea.

16

THE CHRISTIAN PRESIDENT AND THE POLITICS OF REFORM

This author arrived in Seoul on August 12, 1993, to attend academic conferences. As I was riding toward the city from the airport, I asked the taxi driver, "What is happening in Korea these days?" "A revolution is happening," the driver answered. I asked him. "What revolution?" He told me that an economic revolution was taking place.

It was on that day that President Kim Young Sam announced a special economic reform called "the real-name financial transaction system." This meant that people had to use only real personal names, rather than aliases or other people's names in financial transactions. This economic reform measure was enacted to wipe out corruption among the officials in the government who embezzled public money and received large amounts of bribes then transacted the money with pseudonyms or in other people's names. President Kim announced this economic reform as his major political reform in the new civilian government to bring about justice. He announced: "Unless the real-name financial transaction system is introduced, corruption cannot be eliminated and collusive links between politicians and businessmen cannot be severed."[1]

With the announcement, the president ordered all government officials, including military officers and members of the congress, to disclose their financial holdings. In November 1993, when President Kim attended the Conference of the AsiaPacific Economic Council, which met in Seattle, Washington, he made the following remarks on his politics of reform:

> Since assuming office last February, I have pursued the eradication of misconduct and corruption as the highest priority of our reform tasks. As President, I was the first to publicly disclose my assets. Other ranking public officials followed suit. Those who were found to have amassed illicit fortunes were made to resign. . . . To establish clean politics and honest government, we have enacted legislation requiring ranking public officials to publicly disclose their assets and have banned false-name or anonymous financial accounts to abolish havens for "dirty money."[2]

President Kim Young Sam was elected on December 18, 1992. The election was a democratic and free election in which President Kim received about 42 percent of the votes, 10 percent more than his opponent, Kim Dae Jung. It was a decisive victory for Kim Young Sam, who struggled for many years to bring about a democratic and nonmilitary government in South Korea. His election to the presidency ended the thirty-two years of military rule in South Korea. On January 4, 1993, the president elect appointed fifteen men to a transition team led by Chung Won Shik, former prime minister, and announced that his administration would enact reforms in all segments of Korean society.

On February 25, 1993, when the new president was inaugurated, he promised the nation that his administration would be a government of "clean and honest politics." During the first year of this administration, President Kim restructured the government agencies, creating a small but efficient government, and providing effective services. During this time of restructuring, the president transferred more than ten thousand government officers to other positions, abolished one hundred fifteen divisions, and one thousand two hundred officers were fired from their government jobs.[3]

With the special aim of eliminating political corruption, President Kim urged the National Assembly to pass the "Political Party Act" in December 1993 and the political reform bills of March 1994. These bills were not only to eliminate corruption among the politicians, but also to bring a higher standard of democratic life to Korean society. These bills included the prevention of electoral irregularities and allowed local autonomy through election of local government officials directly by the people of the locality. These new political reforms prohibited the long-standing practice of buying votes.

President Kim also made efforts to heal wounds of the Korean people, especially the people of Kwangju, who had suffered under the military rule. On May 13, President Kim made a televised speech promising that "his government will take various steps to help Kwangju citizens retrieve their honor and heal the scars they suffered during the May 1980 uprising."[4] Then the government allowed a memorial service to be observed in Kwangju on May 18, 1993, to commemorate the thirteenth anniversary of the 1980 Kwangju incident. The government officials themselves joined with more than one hundred thousand people in the memorial service.

For the first time the government also condemned the participation of the military in the political life of the country. The incident of December 12, 1979, through which General Chun Doo Hwan was able to take power and consequently become the president of the republic was condemned as an incident having "the nature of a military coup d' état in which lower ranking military officers revolted against their seniors."[5]

With such a courageous stand against the military and sweeping reforms, the president seemed to demonstrate his Christian morality. He became a popular president among the common mass of people, especially among the Christians. Some Christians supported President Kim's reforms as "coming from the Bible" and praised his politics. A Christian journal stated:

> Pres. Kim Young Sam's basic principles of reform come from the Bible. An elder at Choong Hyun Presbyterian Church, he has been having Sunday services at his residence, the Blue House, since his inauguration. . . . For the first time in 32 years hymns and prayers have been heard there, in worship led by Pastors Chang In Kim and Sung Jong Shin, pastors of Choong Hyun Presbyterian Church. Christians find new meaning in the fact that their president is an elder and his way of administering the country is based on his faith.[6]

However, the political popularity of the civilian president dwindled quickly, especially after a series of major accidents in the country. On March 28, 1993, a train derailed outside of Pusan. Seventy-nine people died, and one hundred-five people were injured in the derailment. On June 10 at a Korean army artillery range, an explosion occurred while solders were assembling a 155mm caliber shell. In the explosion, nineteen soldiers died. On October 10, 1993, Korea's worst maritime accident occurred when a ferry boat capsized in the west coast of North Cholla Province. In this accident, nearly three hundred persons perished. Another terrible accident was reported throughout the world a year later on October 21, 1994. The Songsu Bridge in the heart of Seoul, which is a major Han River bridge, collapsed during rush-hour traffic. A section of the bridge fell into the river with six vehicles, killing thirty-two people. Before the end of the year, yet another accident took place when a gas explosion occurred in a residential area of Ahyon-dong in Seoul. Twelve people were killed and sixty-five were injured.

This tragic series of accidents overwhelmed the Korean people with a sense of uneasiness and insecurity. The citizens blamed the government's negligence in inspecting public facilities such as bridges and gas pipes and condemned the government for not protecting citizens' safety. In his efforts to maintain his initial popularity, President Kim seemed to modify his reform movements and not to push ahead for the actualization of the reforms. His politics became more conservative, and he appeared to be leaning toward the conservative politics of previous administrations. In fact, from the beginning of President Kim's administration, his political party, the Democratic Liberal party had connections with conservatives and authoritarian elements of previous military rules. Kim's Democratic Liberal party was a product of a coalition of a previous ruling party controlled by its military leaders. Before the national election, Kim Young Sam shrewdly joined with the ruling party to extend his political power basis. With this coalition of political powers he won the election. Consequently, President Kim's polices and reforms had limitations. They failed to give a clear vision of the future and appeased conservative elements of Korean society. A prominent professor of public administration at Korea University criticized President Kim's methods of carrying out reforms:

> President Kim's reform methodology doesn't allow for debate. Neglect of Democratic processes and procedures is linked to this problem. . . . President Kim is leading the policy-making process with paternalistic authority and the charisma of a saint-king. Reform has become a sacrosanct ideology. Thus, representative politics, national participation and public discussion are skipped.[7]

Because of such "neglect of democratic processes" in his politics, the people labeled him "a civilian dictator" as if President Kim's administration was not any different from previous military dictatorships.

President Kim's conservative politics and certain retreat from his policies of reform were more evident in his dealings with North Korea. Less than a month after his inauguration, the joint U.S.–South Korean military exercise Team Spirit, 1993 was launched on March 7. In the previous year, under President Roh Tae Woo, a military general, the annual exercise was suspended for the gesture of peaceful relations with North Korea. Instead of pursuing continued peaceful relations with North Korea, President Kim revived the annual military exercise. This event was considered the largest military maneuver of the world in peace time, with nuclear weapons and Stealth bombers.

The North Korean government quickly responded to the revived Team Spirit military exercise. On March 12, the Pyongyang government issued the following statement:

> A grave situation has been created today in our country, which threatens its national sovereignty and security of our state. The United States and South Korean authorities have defiantly resumed the "Team Spirit" joint military exercise, a nuclear war rehearsal against the Democratic People's Republic of Korea. . . . The resumption of the "Team Spirit" joint military maneuvers, . . . compelled our country to enter a semi-war state. . . . The Government of the Democratic People's Republic of Korea and the Korean people are convinced that the Governments and peoples of the countries of the world that value peace and justice will pay a profound attention to the serious situation in the Korean peninsula and extend their support and solidarity to the self-defensive measure of the Government of the Democratic People's Republic of Korea.[8]

On the same day, North Korea withdrew from the Nuclear Non-Proliferation Treaty.

Reacting to the resumption of the Team Spirit military exercise, the National Council of Churches of Christ in the United States called upon the United States government "to stop permanently the Team Spirit Exercises, ending a practice that has been perceived by North Korea as directly threatening its security and removing the risk of incident leading to military engagement."[9]

Also the National Council of Churches in Korea issued a similar statement:

> We feel keenly that the present tension and crisis are derived from, first, the violation of the principle of independence and peace as the highest priority in the South-North Korean relationship. Second, this crisis has been caused by certain actions going against the people's will to overcome division and confrontation and to realize peace and the reunified motherland.[10]

In spite of the Christian plea for peace and to avoid escalation of confrontation with North Korea, President Kim added tension when he ordered his cabinet members responsible for national security "to prepare for possible provocation by North Korea" on April 6, 1993.

What was the issue that caused the situation to escalate into such tension between nations? It was "the nuclear issue of North Korea" as far as President Kim was concerned. President Kim held a press conference on June 2, celebrating the first one hundred days of his presidency. On that occasion he said: "We cannot embrace them (North Korea) as long as they possess nuclear weapons,"[11] although the possession of nuclear weapons in North Korea was never proved. North Korea always stated that its nuclear program was for peaceful purposes only, to produce electricity, and that it did not have the intention or the ability to produce nuclear weapons.

The nuclear issue propelled South Korea to attempt to isolate North Korea from the world community. South Korea and the United States sought UN sanctions against North Korea. Politicians in both countries threatened North Korea with possible military attack on nuclear facilities that could certainly bring about another Korean war. In this stressful situation, the Reunification Committee of the National Council of Churches in Korea issued the following statement:

> It is our hope that the International Atomic Energy Agency (IAEA) and the United Nations Security Council will not employ the method of forced inspections or economic and military sanctions in the process of their attempt to clear up suspicions of North Korean nuclear weapons development, since such methods would violate the peace and security of the Korean peninsula. For the sake of the lives and sovereignty of our

nation, we firmly oppose the use of any such resolution or method, which could bring about a second "Gulf War" on the Korean peninsula.[12]

While the tensions in Korea were heightening, a remarkable meeting took place between the United States and the Democratic Republic of Korea from June 5 to 11 in New York. In that meeting, North Korea agreed to remain and honor the Nuclear Non-Proliferation Treaty. Another goodwill gesture to lessen the tension came from North Korea. On July 12, 1993, with proper military protocol North Korea handed over the remains of seventeen U.S. solders who were killed at Panmunjour during the Korean War. Then on August 3, North Korea allowed three inspectors of the International Atomic Energy Agency to enter North Korea for the inspection of suspected nuclear sites. Again on August 31, five members of the International Atomic Energy Agency under the leadership of Brund Pellard, the deputy director, were allowed to meet with North Korean officials for five days in Psongyang.

To further the cause of peace, Christian churches within South Korea organized a series of activities, especially during the month of August 1993. Among them the most notable were the Christian Convention for Peace and Reunification Toward the Jubilee Year 1995, held in Seoul on August 12 to 14; a prayer vigil, held near the Demilitarized Zone at Imjingak on August 13 to 14; and the Human Chain Movement, held on August 15. In the Human Chain Movement, sixty-five thousand people participated, linking hands from the Independence Gate in Seoul to Imjingak near Panumunjom. August 15 happened to be the Sunday of worship. This author preached at a Presbyterian church in Seoul, and after the service I met with volunteers who were going to participate in the human chain event in the afternoon. They all expressed their desire to have a speedy reconciliation and peaceful reunification with North Korea. Their expressions witnessed to the love of Christ and justice of God. The Christians who participated in the event sang Christian hymns and prayed for the reunification of Korea.

On the same day of celebrating Korea's liberation from Japanese colonial rule and division of Korea, the South Korean government announced the Three-Stage Reunification Plan as the blueprint of reunification. The government document stated among other matters:

> The first step is the "reconciliation and cooperation" stage, in which hostilities and distrust are ended and the ground is opened for mutual cooperation. In this stage North and South Korea will activate exchanges and cooperation in various fields.
>
> The second stage is that of "South-North confederation," in which autonomous exchanges and cooperation will continue and peace will be

systematically assured. In this stage North and South Korea will establish an order of coexistence and co-prosperity and recover and develop the national community.

The third stage will bring to completion "one-people, one nation reunification, simultaneously with the recovery of the national community." In this stage, north and south Korea will establish political reunification, uniting the people and the state into one.[13]

However, the demand and pressure of the International Atomic Energy Agency for further inspection of North Korean nuclear sites, which included military sites near Yongbyon, continued. North Korean authorities responded that those military sites were unrelated to nuclear activities and such demand from the outside was an encroachment on sovereignty and interference in internal affairs of their country. On this basis, North Korea rejected any new inspections of nuclear facilities by the agency on September 27, 1993. On the same day, President Bill Clinton of the United States asked North Korea to open North Korean nuclear sites for full inspection. The International Atomic Energy Agency in Vienna also urged North Korea to prove that it was not engaged in a nuclear weapons program through inspections by the agency. Then on October 12, North Korea announced that it would no longer deal with the International Atomic Energy Agency and demanded direct negotiations with the United States of America.

As the end of 1993 approached, the pressure on North Korea increased. On November 1, the UN General Assembly adopted a resolution to urge North Korea to open up nuclear facilities for international inspection. Four days after the UN resolution, Warren Christopher, the U.S. secretary of state, announced that the United States would seek a UN sanction against North Korea if the International Atomic Energy Agency's inspections were not allowed. The stern warning came from President Clinton, who said that North Korea "cannot be allowed to develop a nuclear bomb" and that "an attack on South Korea would be considered an attack on the United States."[14] President Clinton's warning was repeated by Secretary of State Warren Christopher a week later on November 17, in Seattle, Washington.

As the new year of 1994 dawned, President Kim's government decided to promote a Visit Korea Year 1994 campaign and encourage tourists from abroad to visit Korea. However, the tension surrounding the nuclear issue did not subside. The United States and South Korea continued to pressure North Korea through the International Atomic Energy Agency to open up all suspected nuclear facilities, including two military bases near Yŏngbyŏn, for inspections. To add to the mounting tensions, the South Korean government announced, on March 21, the deployment of Patriot missiles in South Korea and also resumed the Team Spirit military exercise. The following day the president held a luncheon meeting with high-ranking military officers at the presidential palace and instructed Korean armed forces to be ready for defense of the country.

On June first, President Kim Young Sam met with Russian President Boris Yeltin when he visited Russia. In the meeting, they agreed that if North Korea continued to refuse to accept inspections of nuclear sites by the International Atomic Energy Agency, the international community would impose sanctions against North Korea. On June 6, North Korea notified the International Atomic Energy Agency that it would not allow the inspection of two nuclear waste sites which the agency deemed necessary to inspect in order to determine whether North Korea did develop nuclear weapons or not. As soon as President Kim Young Sam returned to Korea, he called a meeting of the National Security Council on June 6, as if war were imminent. To make the situation worse, North Korea threatened to withdraw from the International Atomic Energy Agency altogether, refusing any further international inspections. On June 13, the Pyongyang government also announced that UN sanctions against North Korea "will be regarded as a declaration of war."[15] To avoid conflicts in Korea, Christians called a public rally consisting of prayers for peace. Some seven hundred thousand Christians assembled at the Youido Plaza in Seoul on June 25, 1994, the fourth anniversary date of the outbreak of the Korean War. For four hours, the Christians prayed for the peace of Korea in the midst of pouring rain.

Other peace efforts were made from this side of the Pacific in the United States. Former President of the United States Jimmy Carter courageously arranged to visit North Korea to break the stalemate. Carter wrote about the background of his trip:

> About an hour before President Clinton departed for Europe to participate in the Normandy landing ceremonies, I called to tell him how concerned I was about the developing crisis with North Korea. We agreed that I would receive a definitive briefing, which later resulted in Assistant Secretary Robert Gallucci's visit to my home. I was impressed with the seriousness of the situation and the apparent lack of an avenue of communication with the top leader of North Korea, who was the only one who could make the decisions to alleviate the crisis and avoid another Korean war.

> The following day the North Koreans reconfirmed my standing invitation to visit Pyongyang, with assurances that it was from President Kim Il Sung. I called Vice President Al Gore and informed him of my strong inclination to accept. The next morning he called back to report that President Clinton and his top advisers approved my visit.[16]

With this approval, but not as an official representative of the U.S. government, former President and Mrs. Carter, with two assistants and an interpreter, left home on June 12 and arrived in Seoul on the following day. While they were in Seoul they met with President Kim Young Sam, government officials, and the U.S. commander of military forces in Korea, General Luck. Carter reported:

> While in Seoul, we had talks with President Kim Young Sam and his top advisers. They seemed somewhat troubled about our planned visit to Pyongyang. Minister Lee, in charge of reunification talks, was more positive and helpful, and seemed to have more objective views toward North Korea. U.S. General Luck, Commander of all military forces in South Korea, was deeply concerned about the consequences of a Korean war. He estimated that the costs would far exceed those of the 1950's.[17]

To avoid another Korean war, of which "the costs would far exceed those of the 1950's," Carter made a timely visit to North Korea, arriving in its capital on June 15. Within a few days of his stay in Pyongyang, unthinkable things did happen. North Korea agreed to allow two inspectors of the International Atomic Energy Agency to continue to stay in North Korea and inspect nuclear sites, and the United States announced it would not seek international sanctions against North Korea. Carter also communicated to President Kim Il-Sung that the United States would hold the third round of high-level meetings with North Korea to solve nuclear issues.

Carter's most important achievement, during his four-day stay in Pyongyang, was to arrange the summit meeting of President Kim Il-Sung of North Korea and President Kim Young-Sam of South Korea without any preconditions. As Carter communicated this message to President Kim Young-Sam, South Korea quickly accepted the proposal. On June 20, 1994, two days after Carter returned to Seoul, Prime Minister Lee Yung Duk telephoned North Korean officials to meet on June 28 to arrange the details of the summit meeting.

On that same day, the representatives of the two Koreas met at Panmunjom and agreed to hold the historic summit meeting on July 25 through 27 at the North Korean capital.

Along with Koreans within Korea, the whole world was excited and rejoiced over this development. Alas! Seventeen days before the scheduled summit, President Kim Il-Sung died! It was understandable that all of Korea felt a shock wave of sadness. This time of sorrow and expression of condolences could be a period to work for further reconciliation for South Korea with North Korea. However, instead of using this opportunity for reconciliation, President Kim Young Sam held emergency meetings of the National Security Council and cabinet. The South Korean government ordered all of South Korea on military alert against North Korea. Practically all world leaders dispatched words of condolences to North Korea, including President Clinton. However, Kim Young Sam's government arrested those South Koreans who wanted to express their condolences for the death of Kim Il-Sung. Prime Minister Lee Hon-Ku called a meeting of cabinet members on July 18 and announced that the South Korean government would not permit the expression of condolences or pay tribute to the deceased North Korean president. Such an attitude on the part of South Korea appeared to Christians as loveless and betrayed the spirit of Christian reconciliation.

With the death of the president of North Korea, a new spirit of McCarthyism emerged in South Korea. It reinforced Korean political anticommunism, and persons labeled "Communists" were hunted even after the fall of so-called Communist countries. Soon after the death of Kim Il-Sung, authoritarian repression and the infamous National Security Law were reinforced to suppress the citizens' freedom of expression and assembly. The emergence of this new McCarthyism coincided with the announcement of Park Hong, the president of So-Gang University, a Roman Catholic Jesuit institution, who accused radical student groups and labor organizations in South Korea of being manipulated by the new North Korean leader, Kim Jong Il. The government increased its activities, arresting and harassing students and labor leaders. There was initially no response to Father Park Hong and the emergence of new McCarthyism. The Roman Catholic Association of the Clergy for the Realization of Justice issued a statement on July 21, 1994, asking Father Park to be responsible for his statement and prove allegations that North Korea had contacts with student and labor leaders.

Despite the storm of McCarthyism sweeping South Korea, constructive meetings between the delegates of North Korea and the United States were held in New York, Beijing, and Geneva in the latter half of 1994. Through this new series of meetings, the conflicts in Korea were drastically reduced. The meeting held in Geneva, Switzerland, on August 5 to 12, 1994, was very constructive. In the meeting, the U.S. delegation was headed by Assistant Secretary of State for Political-Military Affairs Robert L. Gallucci, and the North Korean delegation was led by First Vice-Minister of Foreign Affairs Kang Sok Ju of the Democratic People's Republic of Korea. They agreed on four major points, and the agreed-upon statement was announced on August 12, in Geneva. The four points of agreement were:

1.   The DPRK is prepared to replace its graphite-moderated reactors and related facilities with light water reactor (LWR) power plants, and the U.S. is prepared to make arrangements for the provision of LWRs of approximately 2,000 MW(e) and 200 MW(e) reactors, forego reprocess-

ing, and seal the Radiochemical Laboratory, to be monitored by the IAEA.

2. The U.S. and the DPRK are prepared to establish diplomatic representation in each other's capitals and to reduce barriers to trade and investment, as a move toward full normalization of political and economic relations.

3. To help achieve peace and security on a nuclear-free Korean Peninsula, the U.S. is prepared to provide the DPRK with assurances against threat or use of nuclear weapons by the U.S., and the DPRK remains prepared to implement the North-South Joint Declaration on the Denuclearization of the Korean Peninsula.

4. The DPRK is prepared to remain a party to the Treaty on the Non-Proliferation of Nuclear Weapons and to allow implementation of its safeguards agreement under the Treaty.[18]

After this agreement, nuclear technology experts and delegates of the U.S. government visited Pyongyang and held a series of meetings, discussing ways to implement the August agreement, especially establishing liaison offices in the two countries. Among the various contacts and meetings between the officials of North Korea and the United States, the meeting held in Geneva from September 23 to October 17 was crucial. Among the agreements of the October meeting were that North Korea would suspend nuclear activities immediately, dismantle nuclear-related facilities, and transfer fuel rods to a third country. This agreement solved not only the nuclear issue of North Korea but also moved toward the establishment of a diplomatic and trade relationship between the United States and the Democratic People's Republic of Korea. The agreed-upon document, signed by Kang Sok Ju of North Korea and Robert Gallucci of the United States on October 21, 1994, stated:

1. Within three months of the date of this Document, both sides will reduce barriers to trade and investment, including restrictions on telecommunications services and financial transactions.

2. Each side will open a liaison office in the other's capital following the resolution of consular and other technical issues through expert-level discussions.

3. As progress is made on issues of concern to each side, the US and DPRK will upgrade bilateral relations to the Ambassadorial level.[19]

The Geneva agreement was truly a monumental achievement of diplomacy, liberating all Korean people from the fear of another Korean war that possibly could be a nuclear war. Christian churches celebrated the prospect of peace with prayers of thanksgiving, and church organizations made statements to support the Geneva agreement.

The Geneva agreement brought special joy and encouragement to Christian communities working to make 1995 the year of jubilee with the purpose of realizing some form of reconciliation and reunification between the hostile and divided parts of Korea. The National Council of Churches developed a worship resource to be used for the commemoration of the fiftieth year of the division of Korea. The worship resource contained a "Prayer for the Reunification of Korea":

O God, source of all life,

you promised that justice would flow like a river, that debts would be cancelled, slaves released and land restored.

Forgive the sins which divide Korea, separating North from South, Koreans from Koreans, Koreans from Americans.

Govern the hearts and minds of those in authority, that your holy will of reconciliation, peace and unity will come to Korea and to the whole world. Amen.

With this prayer to realize the "holy will of reconciliation, peace and unity" Korean Christians would continue to advocate for political justice, witness to the love of God, and share the gospel of peace in the political arena of Korea.

President Kim Young Sam announced his New Year policy statement on January 6, 1995. The top priority would be the politics of globalization: "The basic concept behind this was to build on the policies of internationalizing the nation and enhancing its competitiveness . . . and preparing the nation for the emerging borderless global economy being bolstered by the birth of the World Trade Organization (WTO)."[20]

The idea of globalization announced by President Kim was congenial with Christian ideals to bring the world to Korea and to relate Korea to the world. However, such high ideals of globalization could remain a mere political slogan unless the government were to become more serious about the initial "politics of Reform" which President Kim so strongly identified with his new administration. Consistent with the initial enthusiasm of the politics of reform, the relationship within divided Korea should be improved. The conservative influence of elements of President Kim's administration and the active influence of McCarthyism might jeopardize the Geneva agreements of October 21, 1995. Kim's politics could be labeled as "status quo" or "reactionary." Korean Christians certainly would not retreat from opposing reactionary politics but would continue to fulfill God-given responsibilities to be the light and salt of the world in all the politics of Korea, especially to bring about reconciliation and peace in Korea.

CONCLUSION

CHRISTIANITY IN NORTH KOREA AND ITS FUTURE IN RELATION TO CHRISTIANITY AND THE POLITICS OF SOUTH KOREA

The influence and success of the Christian missionary work in North Korea were far greater than in the South before the division of Korea took place in 1945. The reasons may be that southern Korea had a stronger influence of Confucianism that vehemently rejected Western teachings and ideologies. Northern Korea was more open to accepting foreign ideologies and had greater access to different ideas and religious beliefs because of easy geographical access to China and Russia. Northern Koreans were also far more interested in modern education, which Christian missionaries introduced, especially for women.

Among the mission work in northern Korea, the Protestant work, especially that by the Presbyterians, was most successful. Even before the arrival of resident missionaries, there were Korean Christians who were converted by Scottish Presbyterian missionaries such as John Ross and John McIntyre, who labored in northeastern China, near the Korean border. Beginning in 1873, Ross and McIntyre preached the Christian message to the Koreans living in northeastern China. These early Korean converts established the first Protestant churches in Uiju, Sonchon, and Sorai in the northern part of Korea, without any financial support from missionary agencies.

The success of Christian outreach, especially in Pyongan and Hwanghae Provinces in northwestern North Korea, was great, and the number of converts rapidly increased. To meet the needs of the increasing number of Christian churches, a theological seminary was established in Pyongyang at the turn of the century. Six years later, Soongsil College, whose English name was Union Christian College, was established in the city to train lay leaders.

The Christian impact in northern Korea was so strong that many whole villages were converted. Pyongyang was called "the Jerusalem of Korea." According to the last available statistics before the liberation of Korea, North Pyongan Province had 29,129 Presbyterian communicant members. Kyunggi Province, where Seoul is located, and north Choongchung Province combined had 5,714 communicant members.[1] It is estimated that altogether there were about 300,000 Christians, including about 50,000 Roman Catholic, and about 2,000 church buildings in North Korea at the end of the World War II.[2]

Alas! The many years of faithful witness of the Christian churches had to halt in North Korea with the division of the country and the eventual establishment of a government which was hostile to Christianity. The Soviet military government with its Marxist-Leninist ideology naturally suppressed Christian activities, although the military office first announced the guarantee of "the freedom of religious worship." As in many other socialist countries in former East Europe, church activities were restricted by government officials and outright persecutions took place.

In opposition to the Soviet political ideology of materialism, Christian-nationalist leaders such as Yun Ha Young and Han Kyung Jik, both prominent Presbyterian pastors, organized a political party, the Christian-Social-Democratic party, on September 9, 1945, in Shinuiju. This was the first Korean political party organized in the Korean peninsula after the liberation of Korea from Japan. The party's organizational purpose was to establish a new independent Korea on the basis of Christian ideals. Soon after the formation of the party, "Christian" was dropped to increase appeal to all segments of North Korean society. The party became the Korean Social-Democratic party, and it made a strong impact in northwestern Korea. However, with the pressure of the Soviet government against the party, and with the departure of Reverend Han Kyong Jik in October from North Korea to South Korea, the party was absorbed into Choson Minju-Dang, or the Korea Democratic party.

The Korea Democratic party was led by another Christian leader, Cho Man Shik, who was an elder in the Presbyterian church and a prominent nationalist leader. On November 13, 1945, this party was organized in Pyongyang with thirty-three members of the central executive committee and Cho Man Shik as its party chief. The growth of the party was phenomenal. Within three months of its inaugural meeting, membership reached five hundred thousand and the party had branch offices in all North Korean provinces.

Many party officers were Christian pastors and lay leaders. Under the growing influence of Christian involvement in the politics of North Korea, there was the Shinuiju student demonstration against Communist influence in North Korea on November 23, 1945. This powerful student uprising was led by Christian student leaders, one of whom, Chang Do Young, became a South Korean army general. According to General Chang, the students armed themselves and attacked Communist party headquarters.[3] Then in December 1945, Christians demonstrated again in opposition to North Korean support of the Moscow agreement of foreign ministers from the United Kingdom, the Soviet Union, and the United States to place Korea under five years of "trusteeship."

As 1946 dawned, the first full year of Korea's liberation from Japan, the North Korean government initiated land reforms.[4] In March, a land reform law was announced, and a month later the reform was practically completed. In that reform, all church-related properties and land were confiscated by the government and distributed to the peasants. Christian dissent and confrontations against the government increased. Two major confrontations between Christian communities and the North Korean government in 1946 included the March 1 incident and the Christian boycott movement against the election of North Korean governmental officials in November.

The March 1 incident was in commemoration of the twenty-seventh anniversary of the March 1, 1919, independence movement. The new North Korean government wanted to use the occasion to rally its people to support the Communist government. Therefore, the military government decreed that all North Koreans must participate in the government-sponsored rallies. The Christians, however, boycotted the rallies and held separate Christian rallies in major cities throughout the country.

Another serious confrontation against the government by the Christians was in opposition to the provincial, county, and city elections of "people's representatives" on November 3, 1946. November 3 was a Sunday. To Christians, it was the Sabbath, and they wanted to keep it holy for the worship of God. The Christians believed that participating in the election was a violation of their observance of the Sabbath law. They not only boycotted the election, but they also protested that the North Korean authorities were anti-Christian. The Christians also issued a declaration saying that

1.   Christians shall not participate in any activities other than church-related activities on Sundays,

2.   Christian churches are holy places, and therefore the church buildings should be used only for church activities, and

3.   those church workers who were political candidates should resign from the membership of the church.[5]

In response to such alarming and strong Christian protests against the government, some Christians, sympathetic to the North Korean "peoples' government," formed the Chosen Christian Federation shortly before the election. This federation had the encouragement of the government. Its leader was Kang Yang Ok, maternal uncle of the late North Korean President Kim Il Sung. Kang Yang Ok had graduated from Pyongyang Theological Seminary and at the time of Korea's liberation was serving as an ordained pastor in a Presbyterian church in Pyongyang. He often was a political candidate and was elected to high offices of peoples' committees and served as the general secretary of the Supreme

People's Committee, equivalent to Congress or Parliament in other countries. Under the leadership of Pastor Kang, the Korean Christian Federation made a declaration in November 1946 saying:

1. We support the government of Kim Il Sung.

2. We do not recognize the government of South Korea.

3. We shall be the leaders of the people (Min Jung).

4. Therefore, we actively participate in the governmental elections.[6]

Meanwhile, the North Korean authorities arrested and imprisoned those Christian leaders who did not join the Christian Federation. As a result, many North Korean Christians fled to South Korea and some went underground. When the Korean War started in 1950, many Christian leaders remaining in North Korea were arrested and executed. Among them was Cho Man Shik, the elder of the Presbyterian church and a lay leader. The North Korean persecution extended also into South Korea when the North Korean army took over most of the South in summer 1950. The invading Communist soldiers confiscated the church buildings for their military and governmental purposes. Every church denomination suffered under the Communist rule.

In the early years of the war, Methodist Bishop Yang Ju Sam was abducted and taken to North Korea where he died. He had been educated in the U.S. universities of Vanderbilt, Yale, and Columbia. He had been the first Korean Methodist bishop and had served as president of the Korean Red Cross. He had been an outstanding church leader, theological educator, and theologian and had published a journal, *Sinhak Segye* (theological world).

During the Korean War, about 150 Roman Catholic church workers, including 95 missionary priests and 52 Korean priests, were arrested throughout the country. Many of them suffered martyrdom. A heroic account of suffering and martyrdom was reported in a biography of Bishop Patrick James Byrne, the apostolic delegate to the Republic of Korea, by his friend, the Most Reverend Raymond A. Lane, the superior general of Maryknoll. Bishop Byrne was arrested in Seoul on July 11, 1950, and he was interrogated. Bishop Byrne's biographer wrote of the interrogation and the conditions of the prison:

> Bishop Byrne, Father Booth, and Father Riou were taken to the heart of Seoul, to a commercial building that had been transformed into a huge jail. They were led immediately to the foul-smelling, fly-ridden basement, where under a bare electric-light bulb Communist officers were questioning Korean civilians. The basement was like a Turkish bath, and the Communist interrogators were wet with perspiration. The new prisoners

were herded into a dark corner of the room to a space about fifteen by twenty feet in which other foreigners were huddled. They were to spend the next eight days in this fetid hole, allowed to stir from it only once in the morning and once at night to go to the washroom. Twice a day they were served a ball of barley and a bit of rice on a piece of dirty newspaper, and given a small cup of water.[7]

When the UN force fought back to retake Seoul and advanced to the North, the prisoners, including Father Byrne, were taken to North Korea and marched in the death march in winter 1950. The biography of Bishop Byrne included this information about the march:

> The Death March was made in winter weather. It took us eight days to travel a hundred miles through the mountains. It was a procession of suffering that cannot even be imagined. Part of the time it snowed, and always the weather was freezing. The wind screamed around our heads. Always at our side was a North Korean guard, his rifle ready to be used on anyone who fell out of line.

> Picture the procession of misery. There were 700 G.I.'s, many of them wounded, all of them weak, some with bare feet. Then we civilians—men, women, and children. All of us starving, practically all of us racked by dysentery. The fillings were falling from our teeth because of malnutrition. We were skin and bones, having lost on an average of fifty pounds each. I did not even weigh a hundred pounds.[8]

> Bishop Byrne died on November 25, 1950, and was buried outside of a small village called Ha Chang Ri, near the Korea and China border across the Yalu River.[9]

Even though Christians suffered such harsh treatment by North Korean authorities, some remained in North Korea. During the war, this author was able to see Christian church buildings in Bukchong, Poongsan, and Kapsan, in the northeastern part of North Korea during the winter of 1950 when the UN force invaded North Korea. While we were in the North, I met North Korean Christians and participated in Sunday worship services. Also while in North Korea, some of my Korean friends and I occasionally brought G.I. C-rations (canned food) to the North Koreans and in exchange were able to taste Korean food with Kimchi. I was serving in the Seventh U.S. Army Division as an interpreter. I and a few other Koreans attached to the American unit did not like the American food and were always hungry for Korean food.

One evening in late November 1950, when light snow was falling, we visited a Korean family who happened to be Christian. An elderly mother prepared a Korean supper. After the meal I asked many questions about Christian life in North Korea. She told me that North Korean authorities were not openly prohibiting church attendance or preventing participation in church activities in her town. But at the time of Sunday worship, there were many government-sponsored programs to attend, such as sports activities, music events, or public works of construction of streets or bridges, which discouraged attending church worship services.

As we were leaving, she told us that her son went to war as a soldier of the "Peoples' Army": "My son is only seventeen years old, a couple years younger than you are," she said. "When you engage in a battle against the 'Peoples' Army,' call the name of my son with a loud voice. His family name is the same as yours. And find my son and bring him back safely to me." Then she prayerfully grasped my hands, and her two daughters who were sitting nearby softly began to sing "Silent Night."

In late November 1950, Chinese soldiers entered the Korean War to aid North Korea. The UN forces began to retreat from the North. In the retreat, near the Chosin Reservoir, Chinese soldiers surrounded the Korean soldiers and Allied forces. Many were killed. As the UN forces left North Korea, many civilians also fled. Some fled to escape the fires of war and some to seek political freedom in South Korea. The majority of the refugees, however, were Christians who left their homes in search of religious freedom. Regardless of the reasons for leaving, none of the 10 million separated family members thought their separation would last, much less continue even to this day—forty-five years later.

After the war, Christian churches in North Korea disappeared. North Korean authorities often listed two reasons for the demise of churches:

1.   the mass exodus of Christians to the South and

2.   bombings of U.S. Air Force planes which destroyed practically all existing church buildings.

Christians everywhere, however, have survived under all kinds of governments, surroundings, and difficulties. In two thousand years of Christian tradition, Christians have lived under the Roman Empire, the Ottoman Empire, Hitler's government, the Japanese colonial government, and the Communist governments of the former Soviet Union and Eastern European countries. They all survived. The survival of Christians in North Korea will not be an exception. The Korean Christians also will survive!

In fact, there were Christians in North Korea. In November 1981, when this author participated in the Christian Dialogue between North and South Korean Christians Abroad for the Peace and Reunification of Korea, in Wien, Austria, I met such Christians. In the meeting, Christian pastors from North Korea reported that there were about 5,000 Christians and about two hundred house churches in North Korea.

In winter 1987, this author was in the northeastern part of China and met Korean Christians living in China near the Korean border along the Tuman River. One Korean woman living in China told me that she volunteered one summer to work in Pyongyang doing construction work. While praying before a noon meal one day, a North Korean woman came and asked her if she was a Christian because she prayed before the meal. She answered, "Yes." Thereafter, the two often prayed together before meals.

Every year since 1981, overseas Christians have met with North Korean Christians in Wien and Helsinki. The overseas Korean Christians often requested the North Korean delegates to build Christian church buildings as visible evidence of the Christian presence there. Finally, the North Korean authorities granted the building of two Protestant churches—Bong Soo Christian Church and Jangchoon Catholic Church—in Pyongyang, which have been open for public worship since 1988.

In 1993, Chilgol Christian Church was opened. This is said to be the church the late President Kim attended as a young lad with his mother. He wrote about his experience of attending Christian churches in his biography:

> When my mother was so tired by chores of the house, she went to Christian church. . . . In the vicinity of Namri there were many Christians . . . when the elders went to church, we young children accompanied them and participated in worship. . . . Once I asked my mother, "Do you believe in God?" My mother shook her head with a smile and said, "I do not go to church for God or heaven, but I go there to rest."[10]

In honor of Kim's mother, this new church is called "Ban Suk Church," taking the given name of Kim's mother; the name means "foundation stone."

Now it is said that there are about ten thousand Christians in North Korea, twice as many as was first reported in 1981. Also reported were about five hundred house churches. North Korean Christian delegates who visited the United States in summer 1995 reported that another church is to be built in Rajin-Sunbong's Free Economic Zone in the near future. There is also a theological seminary located adjacent to Bongsu Protestant Church in Pyongyang.

North Korea shows some evidence of appreciating Christian values and tries to use Christianity as a point of contact with South Korea. The delegates who participated in international dialogues often reported that Christianity and the North Korean political philosophy of *"juche* idea" share some common ground in that they both emphasize human value, service, and love for neighbors. North Korea claims that its "Juche idea has been perfected as the guiding idea of revolution in our age in the practice of the Korean revolution."[11] This "guiding idea" of North Korean politics, however, basically contradicts the theocentric or christocentric world view of Christianity. An official booklet on the *Juche* idea, published by the North Korean government states:

> The Juche idea raised the fundamental question of philosophy by regarding man as the main factor, and elucidated the philosophical principle that man is the master of everything and decides everything.
>
> That man is the master of everything means that he is the master of the world and of his own destiny; that man decides everything means that he plays the decisive role in transforming the world and in shaping his destiny.
>
> The philosophical principle of the Juche idea is the principle of man-centered philosophy which explains man's position and role in the world.[12]

This anthropocentric political philosophy is an arrogant philosophy of humanism, placing human beings as the center and basis of all the judgment of human life and the world. Christian idealism does not not have a place in that kind of godless materialism. However, Christians do take human justice and justification seriously. The value of human life, human well-being, and love of humanity are essences of Christ's message included in the teaching of the apostles, Erasmus, Luther, and many other theologians. It was Christ himself who broke the Sabbath law of the Old Testament for the well-being of humanity, saying, "The Sabbath was made for humankind and not humankind for the Sabbath" (Mark's Gospel 2:27).

Humanism has occupied an important place in Korea's philosophical tradition. In the establishment of the first Chosŏn Kingdom, the founder, Tankun, placed the idea of *honqik inkan* (broad benefits for humanity) as the ideological basis of his rule. During the dominance of Buddhism in the Shilla and Koryo periods, the idea of *hoguk bulkyo* (Buddhism for the protection and benefit of the nation) was a strong element of Korean Buddhism. Then during the Yi dynasty, Confucian humanism dominated Korean thought. At the end of the nineteenth century, when the indigenous religion of Chondogyo emerged, its basic philosophical idea was *in nae chon* (heaven is in humanity). Shamanism, the influential spiritual force among the Korean people, always emphasized this worldly practical and utilitarian benefit of everyday life of the people. In this strong humanistic tradition of Korean ethos, the *juche* idea is not too far apart from the Korean philosophical tradition.

For a future relationship of North Korea with South Korea, the latter must take this humanistic tradition seriously. North Korea must also take Christianity seriously as a spiritual force that has powerful influence to transform an individual as well as a collective society. The North Korean Christians and some of the overseas and South Korean theologians have attempted to find common ground between Christian humanism and *juche* thought. Recently, some important books have been published in Korean languages on the subject. They are *Juche Idea and Christianity,* by Sunoo Hakwon and Hong Dong Kun; *Juche Idea in Christian Perspective,* edited by Seoul Presbytery of the Korea Christ Presbyterian Church; *Christianity and South-North Reunification,* edited by Hong Kun Soo; and *Christian Dialogue with Juche Ideas,* edited by the Association of Korean Christian Scholars in North America.

Whether or not there is common ground between Christianity and the *juche* idea is an academic question. It is certain that the two thoughts are contradictory. However, Korean national interest is at stake due to the division and confrontation between the North and the South. To solve this conflict, Christians on both sides shall play significant roles as forces of reconciliation and peace. Prolonged division of the national body may bring the death of the nation, as this author wrote more than twenty years ago in an article in *Christian Century:*

> Now, an assembly of Christians is often called a "church body," just as an assembly of a country's like-minded citizens is called a "national body." But if a "body" is to survive, blood must circulate through it freely. Prolonged separation of one part of the "national body" from the whole will eventually lead tothe death of the nation. The small country of Korea is like a home where husband and wife are divided. In such a situation it is difficult to maintain peace, security or economic stability. Both sides boast of progress and prosperity, but such boasts aremeaningless. Unless Korea's unity is achieved,whatever progress and tranquillity either side claims to have won will not last, and in the end a bloody conflict will be joined. Therefore, the reunification of the nation is historically imperative.[13]

On this historical imperative of reconciliation and reunification, there is a future for Christians on both sides of Korea!

Appendix A

The North-South Peace Agreement of July 4th, 1972

The three main points of the Communique read as follows:

The two sides have agreed to the following three principles for unification of the fatherland:

First, unification shall be achieved through independent Korean efforts without being subject to external imposition or interference. Second, unification shall be achieved through peaceful means, and not through the use of force against each other.

Third, as a homogeneous people, a great national unity shall be sought above all, transcending differences in ideas, ideologies, and systems.

The Communique further agreed upon these points and ended as follows:

1. In order to ease tensions and foster an atmosphere of mutual trust between the south and the north, the two sides have agreed not to slander or defame each other, not to undertake armed provocations, whether on a large or small scale, and to take positive measures to prevent inadvertent military incidents.
2. The two sides, in order to restore severed national ties, to promote mutual understanding, and to expedite independent peaceful unification, have agreed to carry out various exchanges in many fields.
3. The two sides have agreed to cooperate positively with each other to seek an early success of the South-North Red Cross talks, which are underway, with the fervent expectations of the entire people.
4. The two sides, in order to prevent the outbreak of unexpected military incidents and to deal directly, promptly and accurately with problems arising between the south and north, have agreed to install direct telephone lines between Seoul and P'yŏngyang.

5. The two sides, in order to implement the aforementioned agreed items, solve various problems existing between the south and north, and to settle the unification problem on the basis of the agreed principles for unification of the Fatherland, have agreed to establish and operate a South-North Coordinating Committee co-chaired by Director Fu Rak Lee and Director Young Joo Kim.

6. The two sides, firmly convinced that the aforementioned agreed items correspond with the common aspirations of the entire people, who are anxious to see an early unification of the Fatherland, hereby solemnly pledge before the entire Korean people that they will faithfully carry out these agreed items.

This Communique signed by:

Lee Fu-rak
Director, South Korean Central Intelligence Agency

Kim Young-joo
Director, North Korean Organization and Guidance
Department of the Workers Party

July 4, 1972

APPENDIX B

THEOLOGICAL STATEMENT OF KOREAN CHRISTIANS

I. *Motive* – We are facing a serious situation in which:

1. The regime identifies the government with the state and thereby suppresses any speech and any action which is critical of government policies, by force.
2. In the name of the threat from North Korean communists, and preservation of freedom, a *controlled harmony* is imposed upon us, and the rights of survival of workers and poor people are violated.
3. In the name of the so-called "limit of religion," and "separation of church and state," the church is under surveillance; *the content of sermons is interfered with;* and proclamations for justice on the basis of conscience of faith are all suppressed. This means the restriction, suppression, or control of the fundamental posture of religion. Especially the recent statement by the Prime Minister, arbitrarily quoting Biblical passages, is a sign of absolutization of power. The Prime Minister speaks as though the present government is the representative of God, and says that any mission activities which are critical of government policies will be the object of judgment. This situation is very serious, causing us to clarify our position as the Christian Church, and thus we make a theological statement as follows:

II. The State and Religion

"All powers that be come from god." (Romans 13) This passage of the Bible expresses the limits of the political power before it speaks of obedience to it. The political ruler is commissioned to preserve life, property, and freedom, which are fundamental human rights, and the exercise of political power should be within this limit. *The political power that violates the life and the freedom of man, his fundamental human rights, is in rebellion against God.* Christianity understands that if the relative thing is absolutized it is called an *idol*. Traditionally Christianity fights against such an idol. Therefore, when absolutized power violates human rights, the church has no choice but to struggle against it. Common survival and mutual help are necessary for people to create meaningful and fruitful lives. Christians are fighters against the power of evil which prevents the possibility of such common survival. Thus the church is commanded to fight suppression, on the side of the poor and the oppressed, to liberate them and to restore their human rights. The church is not an organization which intends to take political power, but in order to carry out its mission, the church sometimes is positioned in conflict with a political power.

III. Human Rights

Human rights are given by God, and it is the Christian faith that human rights belong to God. Man is created according to the image of God, and man is created by God. (Genesis 1: 27) Man is the image of God, and therefore he is a precious being. This means that men cannot be used as instruments. Institutions and the law are permissible so long as they serve to guarantee human rights. Institutions and the law are for men, not men for them. In this sense Jesus said man does not exist for the Sabbath; on the contrary, the Sabbath exists for man. (Mark 27: 28)

IV. The Mission of the Church

The core of Christian mission is in the Word of salvation and liberation. "The Lord has anointed me to preach the gospel to the poor, preach freedom to the imprisoned, give sight to the blind, liberate the oppressed, and to spread the grace of the Lord." (Luke 4: 18) Man is not only soul, but also body. Man is not only an individual existence, but also a social being. Therefore, the salvation of man is total and it must be accomplished in a comprehensive sense. Thus the mission of the church in the modern world is the liberation of man, the socialization of mankind, humanization of institutions, establishment of social justice and peace in the world, and reconciliation between man and nature. We cannot stop mission activities under any circumstances, because we believe in the coming of the Kingdom of God and we have a firm hope in the Resurrection.

V. Statements by the Korean Church on the Present Situation

Various recent statements of the Korean Church, domestically and internationally, about the current situation are a continual expression of conscience of faith and an expression of our loyalty to our people. These statements are the communication of the Word of God; they represent the voice of the people; and we hereby enumerate some representative examples in the following, to reaffirm them:

1. Theological Declaration of Korean Christians, 1973, by Christian leaders and ministers.
2. Human Rights Declaration, by the Human Rights Conference of Korean National Christian Council, 1973.
3. Declaration of Conscience, by Bishop Chi, Wonju Diocese of Korean Catholic Church, 1974.
4. Statement of Determination, by National Catholic Priests for the Realization of Justice, and the National Laymen's Conference of the Catholic Church, 1974.
5. Our Statement—Catholic-Protestant United Prayer Meeting for the Imprisoned, 1974.
6. Declaration by the Republic of Korea Presbyterian Church, 95th General Assembly, 1974.
7. Assembly's Statement on the Current Situation, by Jesus Presbyterian Church Assembly, 59th Assembly, 1974.
8. Statement on Current Situation, by Korean Methodist Church, 12th Assembly, 1974.

These statements criticize the absolutization of power, the oppression of power, corruption of the privileged class, and economic invasion by foreign countries; and they demand the immediate democratization of the political system. We support these statements wholeheartedly, realizing that they are the expressions of the church that carries mission in the modern world.

November, 1974

APPENDIX C

DECLARATION OF THE CHURCHES OF KOREA ON NATIONAL REUNIFICATION AND PEACE

We first offer praise and thanks for the grace and love of God, who has sent the Gospel of Christ to the Korean peninsula, making known to us the death of Christ on the Cross and his resurrection, and enabling us, through our faith in Christ, to be accepted as God's children and granted salvation. We also give thanks for the presence of the Holy Spirit in the history of the Korean peninsula and in the lives of all of our brothers and sisters in faith, filling us with the mission commitment that will unify the whole church in our efforts for the liberation and salvation of our nation.

We trust in one God, the Creator of the heavens and the earth (Genesis 1:1), and we believe that all people are invited to become the children of God (Romans 8:14–17; Galatians 3:26, 4:7).

Jesus Christ came to this land as the "Servant of Peace" (Ephesians 2:13–19), proclaiming God's kingdom of peace, reconciliation and liberation to a world torn by division, conflict and oppression (Luke 4:18; John 14:27). To reconcile humanity to God, to overcome divisions and conflicts, and to liberate all people and make us one, Jesus Christ suffered, died upon the Cross, was buried and rose again in the Resurrection (Acts 10:36–40). Jesus blessed the peace makers, declaring their acceptance as children of God (Matthew 5:9). We believe that the Holy Spirit will reveal to us the eschatological future of history, will unite us, and will make us partners in God's mission (John 14:18–21; 16:13–14; 17:11).

We the churches of Korea believe that all Christians have now been called to work as apostles of peace (Colossians 3:15); that we are commanded by God to overcome today's reality of confrontation between our divided people—who share the same blood but who are separated into south and north; and that our mission task is to work for the realization of unification and peace (Matthew 5:23–24).

Based on this confession of our faith, the National Council of Churches in Korea hereby declares before the churches of Korea and the world ecumenical community, our position on national unification and peace. At the same time our appeal is directed in a spirit of prayer to all our Korean compatriots and to the leaders of government in both south and north.

The Mission Tradition of the Korean Churches for Justice and Peace

It has been more than a century since Protestants first preached the Gospel in this land, and during this period the churches have committed many errors before the Korean people. And yet, through the proclamation of God's Kingdom, Korean Christians have made great efforts to realize the true hopes of our people for liberation and independence. Our forebears in the faith, strengthened by the Holy Spirit and guided by the Scriptures (Luke 4:18–19), preached the Gospel to the poor, planted the hope of liberty and independence among our oppressed people, and pursued the mission of national liberation arid independence as they shared the suffering of the whole Korean people under the slavery of the Japanese imperial rule.

In the time both preceding and following the Korean Conflict, Christians of north Korea who confronted the north Korean communist regime endured suffering and death, while hundreds of thousands of Christians from the north left their home communities and churches and underwent the hardships of refugee life as they fled to the south. During the Korean War a considerable number of south Korean Christians were kidnapped or subjected to cruel, tragic executions. Communist sympathizers became victims of ideological warfare and were ostracized from society as "traitors."

The Korean peninsula, reduced to ashes by the war, continued to be entangled in the international political conflict of the east-west Cold War structure, mutual vilification, distrust and hostility between the north and the south. Peace on the peninsula was destroyed, and the general belief grew that national reconciliation would be impossible.

With the hardening of the "armistice line"—originally intended as a temporary measure following the signing of the Armistice in 1953—into a "dividing line," the wall between north and south loomed ever higher, and in this context of separation and confrontation the two systems in the north and south became ever more hostile and aggressive toward one another. The mutual military rivalry has been accelerated to a state of armed readiness that counts 840,000 troops in the north and 600,000 in the south, for a total of some 1,500,000 troops on the peninsula; and the nuclear weapons now deployed here or targeted upon the peninsula constitute a destructive force more than sufficient to obliterate the whole Korean people.

The prolongation of the division has led to violations of human rights under both systems, in the name of security and ideology; thus we have seen repression of the freedoms of speech, press, assembly and association. And the complete suspension by both sides of postal service, travel, visitation and communication has turned the two halves of Korea into the two most distant and different countries on earth. The education and propaganda activities of north and south share the goal of mutual vilification, each perceiving the other as the most hated enemy to be weakened and eliminated through the competition of the two systems. As a result the people of both north and south are not only ignorant of the life and culture of their fellow Koreans, but have been trained to believe they *must not* know about one another. Both systems are teaching their people to see their blood brothers and sisters as their most feared enemy.

Dialogue between north and south was begun in 1972, and the July 4th Joint Communique of that year raised hopes for an opening that would lead to further dialogue, cooperation and exchanges. The Red Cross talks between north and south were reopened in 1985, and although some separated families were able to visit their home communities, their numbers were extremely limited, and dialogue and negotiations remain fruitless.

Up to the early 1980s, south Korean Christians were unable even to verify the existence of a church or Christian believers in the north; and their long-standing, deep-seated mistrust and enmity toward the communist regime—intensified and hardened as the division itself became hardened—kept Christians blindly attached to an anti-communist ideology.

Korean Christians, however, could not find the true meaning of peace in the complacency and security of a life bowed down in obedient slavery. Peace had to be the fruit of justice (Isaiah 32:17), and a peace without national independence or human liberty was only a false peace (Jeremiah 6:13–14). The peace movement of the Korean churches during the Japanese imperialist rule over our land was necessarily a movement for national independence which shared the pain of our enslaved people—a national liberation movement which proclaimed the Kingdom of God and strived to realize this faith within history.

The Christians of Korea stood in the forefront of the March First Independence Movement of 1919, resisted the policy of national annihilation by the Japanese imperialists, and shed martyrs' blood for their defiance of the enforcement of Shinto worship, a deification of Japanese nationalism.

After the division of Korea in 1945, the Christians of south Korea cared for the refugees, orphans and victims of war who were suffering under the reality of national separation. The churches received into their midst the members of churches and of separated families who had fled from the north, offering them love and support.

As the division became a fixed reality, dictatorial military regimes emerged to repress human rights in the name of security and to oppress laborers and farmers under the logic of economic growth; but the churches of Korea mounted resistance to such oppression, through a faith which sought justice and peace. The human rights and democratization movement of the Korean churches in the 1970s and 1980s is direct heir to this mission movement tradition for justice and peace.

The Reality of a Divided People

The division of the Korean peninsula is the sinful fruit of the present world political structure and existing ideological systems. The Korean people have suffered as a sacrificial lamb caught in the midst of the military and ideological confrontations and conflicts of the world's superpowers.

In 1945, at the end of the Second World War, the Korean people were liberated from their slavery under the Japanese imperial colonial rule, but were again shackled by the new fetters of the division into north and south. The line of division which was established in the name of disarming the aggressive Japanese imperialist forces became fixed by the Cold War structure of the Soviet Union and the United States. The northern and southern parts of Korea separately established different governments, and over the last forty years their military, political and ideological antagonism and conflict has become ever more severe.

The Korean Conflict which began on June 25, 1950, brought about the tragedy of internecine war and intensified the international conflict. The quantity of bombs dropped on Korea during this conflict exceeded the amount dropped on the whole of Europe during World War II; the entire peninsula was reduced to ashes. This war resulted in 220,000 south Korean, over 600,000 north Korean, 1,000,000 Chinese, 140,000 American, and over 16,000 United Nations military casualties, and if the number who died from disease during the war is included, a total of 2,500,000 soldiers' lives were sacrificed. If the 500,000 south Korean and 3,000,000 north Korean civilian casualties are added to this total, the blood of six million persons was spilled upon the earth of this land (statistics from the *Encyclopedia Britannica,* 1970 edition). In addition, three million refugees and ten million separated family members were produced by this conflict.

A Confession of the Sins of Division and Hatred

As we Christians of Korea proclaim this declaration for peace and reunification, we confess before God and our people that we have sinned: we have long harbored a deep hatred and hostility toward the other side within the structure of division.

1. The division of the Korean people is the result of the structural evil reflected in the world's superpowers in their east-west Cold War system, and this

reality has also been the root cause of the structural evil present within the societies of both north and south Korea. Due to the division we have been guilty of the sin of violating God's commandment, "You shall love your neighbor as yourself" (Matthew 22:37–40).

Because of the division of our homeland, we have hated, deceived and murdered our compatriots of the same blood, and have justified that sin by the political and ideological rationalization of our deeds. Division has led to war, yet we Christians have committed the sin of supporting rearmament with the newest and most powerful weapons, plus reinforcement of troops and expenditures, in the name of preventing another war (Psalm 33:16–20; 44:6–7).

In this process the Korean peninsula has become dependent upon outside powers, not only militarily but politically, economically and in other ways as well: it has been incorporated into the east-west Cold War structure and subjugated under that structure. We Christians confess that we have sinned during the course of this subjugation by abandoning our national pride and by betraying our people through the forfeit of our spirit of national independence (Romans 9:3).

2. We confess that throughout the history of our national division the churches of Korea have not only remained silent and continuously ignored the ongoing stream of movement for autonomous reunification of our people, but have further sinned by trying to justify the division. The Christians of both north and south have made absolute idols of the ideologies enforced by their respective systems. This is a betrayal of the ultimate sovereignty of God (Exodus 20:3–5), and is a sin, for the church must follow the will of God rather than the will of any political regime (Acts 4:19).

We confess that the Christians of the south especially have sinned by turning the anti-communist ideology into a virtual religious idol, and have thus not been content to treat just the communist regime in the north as the enemy, but have further damned our northern compatriots and others whose ideologies differ from our own (John 13:14–15; 4:20–21). This is not only a violation of the commandments, but is also a sin of indifference toward our neighbors who have suffered and continue to suffer under the national division; it is, moreover, a sin of failure to ameliorate their suffering through the love of Christ (John 13:17).

The Basic Principles of the Churches of Korea for National Reunification

So that God's Kingdom of justice and peace may come, we Christians must practice the Gospel of peace and reconciliation (Ephesians 2:14–17) by sharing in the life of suffering of our own people. It is only through such sharing that national reconciliation and reunification can be accomplished; thus we recognize that our concern and efforts for unification are an issue of faith. By overcoming the division which threatens the life of the Korean people and endangers world peace, reunification becomes the path leading us from conflict and confrontation to reconciliation and coexistence, and finally to one peaceful national community.

Through a series of consultations beginning in 1984, the National Council of Churches in Korea has established the following basic principles of the churches toward national reunification.

The National Council of Churches in Korea believes that the three broad principles articulated in the first north-south negotiated Joint Communique of July 4, 1972, namely 1) independence, 2) peace, and 3) great national unity transcending the differences in ideas, ideologies and systems, should provide the guiding spirit for our nation's reconciliation and reunification. In addition to these, we Christians believe that the following two principles also should be honored in all dialogue, negotiation and action for reunification.

1. Reunification must bring about not only the common good and benefit of the people and the nation, but must provide the maximum protection of human freedom and dignity. Since both nation and people exist to guarantee human freedom and welfare, while ideologies and systems also exist for the sake of the people, primary consideration must always be given to humanitarian concerns and measures, which must never be withheld for any reason.

2. In every step of the discussion process to plan for reunification, the full democratic participation of all the people must be guaranteed. Most importantly, participation must be guaranteed for the minjung (common people), who not only have suffered the most under the division, but who—despite the fact that they constitute the majority of the population—have consistently been alienated and excluded from the decision-making processes in society.

The Proposals of the Churches of Korea to the Governments of South and North

Based upon the above principles, the National Council of Churches in Korea urges the responsible authorities in the governments of both north and south to exert their utmost efforts for dialogue so that the following may be accomplished as soon as possible.

1. For the healing of the wounds caused by division
   a. First of all, the separated families, who—as the victims of the division—have endured all sorts of suffering during the past 40 some years,

must be reunited and allowed to live together, and must be guaranteed the right to move freely to whatever place they choose to live.

    b.   Even before reunification is achieved, all persons living in separation from family members in north or south must be freely permitted to visit their relatives and home areas for definite periods, on an annual basis (perhaps at Chusok* or some other holiday season).

    c.   The unjust social discrimination which still prevails against some persons because of their momentary errors or the past records of their families or relatives, problems which inevitably arose during the solidifying of the national division, must be ended at once.

2.   For the promotion of the people's genuine participation to overcome the division

    a.   Neither government, north or south, may exercise a monopoly over information about the other side, nor monopolize the discussion on reunification. Freedom of speech must be guaranteed so that the people of both north and south may participate fully and freely in the process of discussing and establishing policies for reunification, and there must be systemic and realistic guarantees of the activities of civilian organizations engaged in research and discussion of the reunification issue.

    b.   Both north and south Korea must grant maximum freedom for people who oppose either system or ideology to criticize freely according to their conscience and faith, and both must abide by the International Declaration of Human Rights and the United Nations' Human Rights Covenant.

3.   For a great national unity of the Korean people transcending the differences in ideas, ideologies and systems

If Korea is to realize national autonomy, the people of both north and south will have to transcend their differences in concepts, ideologies and systems, and both populations must be able to clearly confirm for themselves that they are one people sharing a common fate. For such a mutual confirmation, north and south must be able to put firm trust in one another. It follows that those things which enable mutual trust must become the most basic starting point for all efforts directed toward reunification. To foster such trust, all factors giving rise to mistrust and hostility must be eliminated, while mutual exchanges should be expanded to broaden our base of mutual understanding and rapidly restore our sense of common ethnic identity. Because all such measures aimed at fostering trust are the most essential part of the process of overcoming division, even in the case that discussions between the official representatives of the two governments do not show progress, or agreements are

---

* Korean Thanksgiving Day

not forthcoming, there must nevertheless be non-governmental channels through which the citizens themselves may seek progress.

a. North and south Korea must put an end to all mutual hostility and aggressive inclinations, and must eliminate the exclusivism which leads to the slandering and vilification of one another. In addition, each must modify its extreme, emotional censure of the other's differing ideology and system and offer in its place mutually constructive criticism.

b. For the promotion of mutual understanding, north and south need unprejudiced, objective information about each other's situation; therefore exchanges, visits and communications must be opened.

c. In order to restore the sense of common ethnic identity, north-south exchanges and cooperative research must be promoted in such academic areas as language, history, geography, biology and natural resources; while exchanges must also be carried out in the areas of culture, the arts, religion and sports.

d. Since economic exchanges between north and south will not only benefit the people but will also provide opportunities for mutual understanding, they should be opened to the greatest possible extent.

4. For reduction of tensions and promotion of peace between north and south Korea

a. In order to prevent war and reduce tensions on the Korean peninsula, a peace treaty must immediately be concluded to terminate the existing state of war. To this end, it is urgent that negotiations be opened by the governments of north and south Korea, the United States, China which participated in the Korean Conflict, to replace the Armistice Agreement wit Ii a peace treaty which also includes a non-aggression pact.

b. At such time that a peace treaty is concluded, a verifiable state of mutual trust is restored between north and south Korea, and the peace and security of the entire Korean nation is guaranteed by the international community, then the United States troops should be withdrawn and the United Nations Command in Korea should be dissolved.

c. The excessive military competition between north and south Korea is the greatest obstacle to peaceful reunification and is moreover counterproductive to economic progress. Therefore, following negotiations between north and south, mutual military strength must be reduced and military expenditures must be cut, with a switchover to industrial production for peace.

d. Nuclear weapons must never be used under any circumstances. North and south Korea together must block from the start any possibility of the use of nuclear arms on the Korean peninsula. This means that all nuclear weapons deployed on the peninsula or aimed in its direction must be removed.

5. For the realization of national independence

   a. There must be no foreign interference or dependency upon neighboring superpowers in negotiations, conferences, or international agreements between north and south; the Korean people's self-governing and subjecthood must be protected.

   b. Both north and south Korea must either revise or abrogate all diplomatic agreements and treaties which undermine rather than support the life and interests of the Korean people. North and south Korea must also reach mutual agreement in regard to all international alliances and associations, examining them to make certain that the common good of all Koreans is their primary objective.

The Task of the Churches of Korea for Peace and Reunification

We believe that Jesus Christ is the "Lord of Peace" (Colossians 1:20), and that God's mission of salvation and liberation for humankind is being realized also within societies that have ideas and systems different from our own. Even though the confession of faith and the appearance of the churches of Christians living in other social systems may be unlike ours, we believe that since they are bonded to the one God and the one Christ, thereby they are members with us in the same Body (Corinthians 12:12–26).

Within the last few years, in an amazing development, the world ecumenical community has greatly strengthened this conviction of ours, by making contacts with our sisters and brothers in faith in north Korea, and bringing us news of them.

Again we give thanks for God's liberating action in the history of the Korean peninsula, and pray for God's grace and blessing upon our sisters and brothers in the north who are steadfastly keeping the faith even under difficult circumstances.

Based upon this confession, the National Council of Churches in Korea, in order to fulfill its mission for peace and reconciliation, to share in the suffering division has caused, and to respond to the historical demand to overcome the division, now in a spirit of repentance and prayer announces plans to initiate a movement for a Jubilee Year for Peace and Reunification, as follows.

1. The National Council of Churches in Korea proclaims the year 1995 to be the "Year of Jubilee for Peace and Reunification."

   > "The Spirit of the Lord is upon me,
   > because he has anointed me

> to preach good news to the poor.
> He has sent me
> to proclaim release to the captives
> and recovering of sight to the blind,
> to set at liberty those who are oppressed,
> to proclaim the acceptable year of the Lord." (Luke 4:18–19)

The "jubilee year" is the fiftieth year following the completion of cycle of seven sabbatical years totaling 49 years (Leviticus 25:8–10). The year of jubilee is a "year of liberation." The proclamation of the year of jubilee is an act of God's people which reveals their complete trust in God's sovereignty over history and their faithfulness in keeping God's covenant. The jubilee year is the overcoming of all the social and economic conflicts caused by the repressive and absolutist political powers, internal and external: the enslaved are liberated, the indebted have their debts forgiven, sold land is returned to its original tillers, and seized houses are returned to their original inhabitants (Leviticus 25:11–55); the united covenant community of peace is restored through the establishment of *shalom* based on God's justice. The Korean churches proclaim 1995, the fiftieth year after Liberation, as a Jubilee Year, to express our belief in the historical presence of God, who has ruled over those fifty years of history—indeed over all of human history; to proclaim the restoration of the covenant community of peace; and to declare our resolution to achieve this restoration in the history of the Korean peninsula today. As we march forward with high aspirations toward the Year of Jubilee, we should experience a revitalized faith in the sovereignty of God, who works within our people's history, and renewed commitment to the calling of God's mission.

2. As a part of the "Great March toward the Jubilee Year" the Korean churches will carry out a vigorous church renewal movement aimed toward peace and reunification.

   a. In order to fulfill their mission responsibility for peace and reunification, the Korean churches must overcome their self-centeredness and their preoccupation with ecclesiastical power, while greatly strengthening mission cooperation for church unity.

   b. The churches of Korea, proclaiming the Year of Jubilee, must reform their internal structures which have restricted broad participation. Accordingly there must be a resolute opening and expediting of full participation in lay mission activity which will include women and youth.

   c. In order to bring about economic and social justice in our society, the churches of Korea must continue to perform a prophetic role.

3. As a part of the proclamation of the Jubilee Year, the churches of Korea, as a community of faith resolved to achieve peace and reconciliation, will carry out a broad program of education for peace and reunification.

    a. The churches of Korea will widely disseminate Biblical and theological peace studies and peace education materials, and will promote research and exchange of information among the various theological and Christian educational institutions.

    b. To increase concern among the churches for the national reunification issue, the Korean churches will promote unification education which will foster recognition of the historical, social and theological validity of national reunification through an understanding of the structure and history of the division, as well as through a deeper theological understanding of the problem.

    c. Through theological reflection and commitment to the Christian faith, the Korean churches will seek a broader scientific understanding of the communist ideology and will promote research and education on ideology as needed for substantial dialogue.

4. Through the proclamation of a Jubilee Year festival and liturgy for peace and reunification, the Korean churches will seek to bring about a renewal of faith and genuine reconciliation and unity.

    a. The churches of Korea will establish a "Sunday of Prayer for Peace and Reunification" to mark the Year of Jubilee, and will develop a form of worship for this purpose, which will include prayers for reunification, confession of the sin of division, recognition of calling and commitment for unification, prayers of intercession for the victims of division and the divided people, a confession of faith for national reconciliation, proclamation of the Word (proclaiming the Jubilee Year), hymns and poetry, and a sacrament for peace and reconciliation.

    b. Until the time when communication between the churches of north and south becomes possible, we will seek the cooperation of the world churches to enable the joint proclamation in both north and south of the Jubilee Year for Peace and Reunification, and will promote the common observance of the "Sunday of Prayer for Peace and Reunification" and the joint preparation and use of "prayers for peace and reunification."

    c. With the cooperation of the world churches, the churches of Korea will search for ways to confirm the status of separated family members, explore the possibility of exchanging letters, and develop a movement to search out relatives, church members and friends separated between north and south.

5. The churches of Korea will work continuously to develop a solidarity movement for peace and reunification.

a. The proclamation of the Jubilee Year for Peace and Reunification, as an act of confession of faith, will be developed into a continuously expanding "solidarity movement for peace and reunification." This must be a comprehensive movement embracing all the churches at local, denominational and ecumenical levels. The national Council of Churches in Korea especially will make efforts to include not only its member churches, but also non-member denominations and the Roman Catholic Church in this movement for confessional action and practice for peace and reunification.

b. As the mission calling to peace and reunification is the universal task of all Christians on the Korean peninsula, the churches of south Korea will pray for the faith and life of the Christian community in the north and will work for north-south exchanges between our churches.

c. Because peace and reunification on the Korean peninsula is a key to peace not only in Northeast Asia but throughout the world, the churches of Korea will consult closely and develop solidarity movements with Christian communities in the four powerful countries related to the region—the United States, the Soviet Union, China and Japan, as well as with churches throughout the world:*

d. The Korean churches will expand and deepen dialogue with other religious groups and movements, and through joint research and cooperative activities, will work to promote ever stronger solidarity for the realization of peace and the reunification of this nation.

February 29,1988
The National Council of Churches in Korea

---

* Such activity is already in progress, and the National Council of Churches in Korea endorses the proposals and positions which have been expressed in such published consultation reports as: "Findings and Recommendations" of the 1984 Consultation in tozanso, Japan; Message of the Fourth Korean-North American Church Constitution, 1986; the policy statement and declaration of the National Council of Churches of Christ in the U.S.A., "Peace and the Reunification of Korea 1986; and the joint statement of the Sixth Korean-German Church Consultation, 1987.

APPENDIX D

DECLARATIONS OF KOREAN WOMEN THEOLOGIANS ON THE PEACE AND REUNIFICATION OF THE KOREAN PEOPLE

We have just concluded our second seminar on the reunification issue, on March 29–30, 1988. In this seminar we have come to the realization that the overcoming of our national division and the achievement of the reunification of the Korean people is a question of our national survival. We see reunification as the most important mission task of the Korean church, and furthermore we believe it is the way to resolve the sufferings of women in Korean society. Therefore we express our position on peace and the reunification of the Korean people, as follows.

The Division Is a Result of the Patriarchal Culture of Domination

We find the ultimate cause of our national division in the patriarchal culture of domination. In this culture the strong have become the rulers, and this system has continued from the time when tribal societies were formed, right up to the era of modern nation states. The political regimes under this patriarchal culture of domination integrate everything into structures serving the rulers power and interests. In its form, the patriarchal culture of dominance operates as colonialism and imperialism, and is expressed in such forms as the hegemonism of the US and the USSR after World War II. The global form of this patriarchal culture of domination has built up the "science-research-industry complex," which subjugates women, the weak and nature itself.

The results of the national division have been the mobilization of our husbands and children into military service, and the increase of government military expenditures, aggravating the poverty of the people. The economy has been distorted by the multinational corporations, bringing about many irregularities including the invasion of foreign polluting industries that threaten our lives with pollution-related diseases. Furthermore, our women workers are made to suffer miserably under low wages and bad working conditions, and many of our young women have become involved in kisaeng tourism: in the name of earning foreign exchange, they become the sex objects of foreign men, and the victims of sexual violence. Women farmers suffer under the double burden of labor in the fields and in the home. Dark clouds of dehumanization and life-destroying processes are covering our reality.

When women farmers, women workers and women in poverty, who are the victims of economic growth, struggle for their own survival against the unjust economic structures, they are accused of being leftist pro-communists. Industrial mission, the student movement, the youth movement, the women's movement and the democratization movement also are blocked by the anti-communist law and the national security law. The anti-communist ideology has dried up the conscience and human love of the people and is breeding hostility and hatred in the minds of the younger generation, forming distorted personalities that are antipeace. Thus we have reached the comprehensive understanding that all these sufferings and diseases have their ultimate cause in the national division, and that the national division has its cause in the patriarchal culture of domination.

Confession of Our Sin and Guilt

We confess that we women ourselves have been bystanders and abettors in the patriarchal domination which has consolidated the national division. We have abandoned the responsibilities which God has bestowed upon us as the subjects of history. We confess that we have not been faithful women servants in fulfilling our duties, having failed to be awakened to the realities in these times of suffering and crisis of our people. Moreover, we have not stood for justice and truth, while our church has consistently sinned by maintaining a patriarchal authoritarian system that attributes holiness and religious authority to men only. Disregarding the fact that our church did not fulfill its prophetic role in our historical situation because of its narrow minded anti-communist ideology, we have not been able to fulfill our proper task for reconciliation and peace.

What is more, we have not participated in God's special favor and love for the women minjung who suffer under double oppression. We confess that we have been lazy, remaining in a state of apolitical consciousness, and vaguely expecting that all such problems will be solved by themselves.

We confess that we have indulged in an easygoing attitude and "family egotism," in disregard of the passionate aspirations and eager debates for around us.

Our Confession of Faith

We have met God anew in the midst of these historical experiences. We believe that God has created all things (Gen. 1:1), that God is the creator of life

(Deut. 10:14), that God saves the world from its domination by sin and death and restores it to new heaven and new earth full of peace and life (Rev. 21:3–4), and that God protects us like a mother (Is. 49:15).

We believe that Jesus Christ was Killed on the Cross by the logic of violence and death which dominates this world, but that he has declared the non-efficacy of this logic, has risen again from death after three days, and has given us hope for a world governed by peace and life.

We are thankful that the Spirit, who renews freedom, peace and love in humanity, prays, for us even when we do not know how to pray (Rom. 8:18), groans with us in our suffering under the national division, and kindles our expectations for the future our expectations for the future reunification of our people.

Women Minjung as the Subjects of Reunification

Women are the minjung of the minjung in our country, victimized by the structure of division with its political, economic and cultural contradictions in the Korean society, are suffering under the double structure of oppression, exploitation and alienation as a result of the patriarchal ideology.

Therefore we declare that women minjung are the very subjects of national reunification. Our declaration is based on the belief that God always makes the most powerless people the subject of the history of salvation (Luke 1:46–55). With this conviction we are resolved to join in solidarity with the women minjung of the third world and to transform ourselves to change the social system that sustains exploitative relations.

Our Position on Reunification

As we look to reunification, we agree with the three principles of the "July 4 Joint Communique" of 1972, as concluded by the authorities of South and North Korea. In the first place, this statement affirms that the problem of the division of the Korean peninsula must be understood as a problem of the domination of the Korean people by foreign power, and that the solution of the problem is to be sought through the independent self-determination of the Korean people. In the second place, it affirms the principles of peace and reunification, overcoming all means of violence and death. And lastly, it recognizes the survival and unity of the people as the supreme value that must transcend the bondage of absolutized ideological conflict and differences in social systems. In this sense we believe that these principles are still valid today.

Besides these principles, we believe that the overcoming of the national division and the realization of national reunification should move in the direction of dismantling the patriarchal ideology, which brings the suppression of life and the domination of people by violence and death. We believe that the creation of a culture for life and democracy, replacing the culture of violence and domination, should become the foundation for the reunification movement.

Therefore, those who hold political power must be liberated from the ideology of domination; those who have industrial and economic power must be liberated from the development ideology; and soldiers must be liberated from the ideology of power. Finally, Church leaders must be liberated from their patriarchal authoritarianism and church power ideology, because it is only when the church has become renewed as a democratic and open church, that it can pursue democratization of the society.

Our Perspective on the Declaration of Jubilee Year

We support the statement of the NCCK, "Declaration of the, Churches of Korea on National Reunification and Peace," issued on February 29, 1988, and we welcome the declaration of the Year of Jubilee in 1995. We want to emphasize that the subject of the declaration of the Jubilee Year is not church, but God (Lev. 25:17–18). "Jubilee" means God's restoration of the world to its original state as it was created in the beginning. It means the giving up of all privileges by the rulers, and the transformation of authoritarian culture into democratic culture within the church.

In the Jubilee Year of 1995, which is set within the "Ecumenical Decade of Churches in Solidarity with Women," 1988–1998, we believe and hope that women and men will stand before God as partners in equality and harmony, as we were created to be.

Our Strategy for Action

1. We will study and determine the structures of conflict and the causes of suffering due to the national division. We will collect the stories of women who have suffered under the division, and find their theological meaning.
2. We recommend that each denomination and Christian women's organization establish a "study committee on reunification and peace."
3   We will carry out a conscientization program using the mass media and church education texts, for the democratization and humanization of church institutions.
4. In order to free ourselves from our ignorance about North Korea, we will collect data, make it public, and thereby try to transform the anticommunist ideology into a right historical consciousness.
5. We propose a meeting together of Christian women from the south and the north of Korea.

6. Peace on the Korean peninsula is crucial for world peace. All nuclear weapons threatening the Korean peninsula must be removed from both those inside South Korea and those aimed at South Korea from the USSR, and we will work in solidarity with the global peace movement for this goal.

March 30, 1988

NOTES

1. Korean Politics of Isolationism and
Roman Catholic Encounter

1. The Jesuits in China coined the term for the Christian God as *Tien chu,* or the Lord of Heaven.

2. The *Memoirs of Hwang Sa-yong* is one of the most important documents in the study of the history of the Roman Catholic church in Korea. It was written by Hwang during a time of persecution in 1801 to report the persecution to the missionaries in China and to seek help. Hwang, a Korean Catholic, escaped from persecution by hiding in mountain valleys. Afterward, he went to Chechon in Chung Chong Province and wrote down details of the persecution, biographies of noted martyrs and their achievements. This memoir contains over thirteen thousand words and gives a good account of early Roman Catholicism in Korea.

3. William Elliot Griffis, *Corea: The Hermit Nation* (New York: Charles Scribner's Sons, 1904), 377–78.

4. Joseph Schmidlin, *Catholic Mission History* (Techny, Illinois: Mission Press, S.V.D., 1933), 625.

2. Introduction of Protestantism and
the Opening of Korea

1. The account was first written in Dutch and published in Amsterdam in 1668. The story aroused interest among European intellectuals. Hamel's accounts were then translated into French and published in Paris in 1670. The German translation was published in Nuremburg in 1671. The first English version, entitled *An Account of the Shipwreck of a Dutch Vessel on the Coast of the Island of Quelpart, together with the Description of the Kingdom of Corea,* was published by John Churchill in London in 1704 in four volumes. For a recent study see Gari Ledyard, *The Dutch Come to Korea* (Seoul: Royal Asiatic Society, 1971).

2. Charles Gutzlaff, *Journal of Three Voyages along the Coast of China in 1831, 1832, and 1833, with Notice of Siam, Corea, and the Loo-Choo Islands* (London: Frederick Westley and A. H. Davis, 1834), 263.

3. Ibid., p. 273.

4. Harry A. Rhodes, *History of the Korean Mission Presbyterian Church U.S.A., 1884–1934* (Seoul: Chosen Mission Presbyterian Church U.S.A., 1934), 171–72.

5. William Elliot Griffis, *Corea: The Hermit Nation,* 7th ed. (New York: Charles Scribner's Sons, 1904), 422.

6. *Congressional Record: Containing the Proceedings and Debates of the Forty-Fifth Congress,* Second Session (Washington: Government Printing Office, 1878), II, 2324.

7. Griffis, 434–35.

8. U.S. Department of State, *Treaties and conventions concluded between the United States of America and other powers: since July 4, 1776* (Washington: Government Printing Office, 1889), 216.

9. Horace Allen, *Things Korean, A Collection of Sketches and Anecdotes* (New York: Fleming H. Revel Co., 1908), 70.

3. The First Protestant Missionary and Political Involvement

1. "The Hour for Korea," *Foreign Missionary,* 44, 4 (September, 1885), 156.

2. Allen, "Only Square Inch of Royalty," *Foreign Missionary,* 44, 4 (September, 1885), 176.

3. Allen Diary, December 11, 1884. Allen MSS. All the Allen manuscripts used in this book are located in the New York City Library.

4. "The Hour for Korea," 155–56.

5. Allen Diary, April 6, 1885.

6. L. H. Underwood, *Underwood of Korea* (New York: Fleming H. Revell Co., 1908), 14.

7. Allen Diary, September 5, 1886.

8. Allen Diary, December 26, 1887.

9. Horace N. Allen, *Things Korean, A collection of Sketches and Anecdotes* (New York: Fleming H. Revell Co., 1908), 162.

10. Ibid., p. 159.

11. Allen letter to Frazer, September 25, 1889.

12. Allen letter to Min Yong Ik, June 20, 1889.

13. Allen letter to Frazer, September 25, 1889.

14. Allen, Things Korean, 215–16.

15. Ibid., 215.

16. Ibid., 217.

17. Allen letter to Welch, September 21, 1887.

18. Allen Diary, September 23, 1887.

19. Ibid., September 30, 1887.

20. Allen, *Things Korean,* 163.

21. Ibid., 164.

22 Ibid., 255–56.

23. Herman Hagerdon (ed.), *The Works of Theodore Roosevelt* (New York: Charles Scribner's Sons, 1926), 18: 406.

24. Ibid., 21.

25. Allen, *Things Korean,* 250.

26. Ibid., 250.

27. Allen Diary, September 29, 1903.

28. Ibid., September 30, 1903.

29. Ibid.

30. Ibid.

31. Roosevelt letter to John Hay, January 28, 1905. Elting E. Morison (ed.), *The Letters of Theodore Roosevelt* (Cambridge, Mass.: Harvard University Press, 1951), 1112.

32. Allen, *Things Korean,* 251.

33. Allen letter to John Hay, April 14, 1904, in F. A. McKenzie, *Korea's Fight for Freedom* (New York: Fleming H. Revell Company, 1920), 98.

34. Allen letter to Pak Chung Yang, November 30, 1905.

35. Ibid.

4. The Progress of Christianity and
the Awakening of Korean Nationalism

1. *Annual Report of the Missionary Society of the Methodist Episcopal Church for the Year 1884* (New York, 1885), 204.

2. "The Methodist Missions in Korea," *The Korea Methodist* 1, 1 (November 1904), 5.

3. C. F. Pascoe, *Two Hundred Years of the SPG, An Historical Account of the Gospel in Foreign Parts, 1701–1900: Based on a Digest of the Society's Records* (London: Society for the Propagation of the Gospel, 1901), 713–14.

4. Harry A. Rhodes, et al. (eds.), *The Fiftieth Anniversary Celebration of the Korean Mission* (Seoul: YMCA Press, 1934), 22.

5. Ibid., 69.

6. Cornelius Osgood, *The Koreans and Their Culture* (New York: Ronald Press Company, 1951), 278.

7. Korean delicacy made of green peas.

5. The Japanese Colonization of Korea and
Christian Participation in Resistance Movements

1. Hilary Conroy, *The Japanese Seizure of Korea: 1868–1910* (Philadelphia: University of Pennsylvania Press, 1960), 306.

2. George T. Ladd, *In Korea with Marquis Ito* (New York: Charles Scribners' Sons, 1908), 391.

3. *The San Francisco Call,* March 24, 1908, 2.

4. Korean Society of Church History, ed., *The Historical Records of Jesus Presbyterian Church of Korea* (Seoul: Yonsei University Press, 1968), 393.

5. *The San Francisco Call,* March 21, 1908, 1.

6. Ibid.

7. Ibid., March 23, 1908, 1.

8. *San Francisco Chronicle,* March 24, 1908, 1.

9. *The San Francisco Call,* March 24, 1908, 1.

10. Chung Hwan, Song. *Ahn Choong Gon* (Shenyang, China: Ryo Nyung Minjok Chulpansa, 1985), 168–69.

11. *Han Kyorye Shinmun* (one people daily news), March 29, 1990, 8.

6. Christianity and the Japanese
Politics of Oppression

1. A letter of Philip L. Gillett, secretary of the Seoul YMCA to John R. Mott, chairman of the Continuation Committee of the Edinburgh Conference, May 22, 1912, in the Presbyterian Library, New York.

2. The Commission on Relations with the Orient of the Federal Council of the Churches of Christ in America, *The Korean Situation: Authentic Accounts of Recent Events by Eye Witnesses* (New York: The Commission on Relations with the Orient of the Federal Council of the Churches of Christ in America, 1919), 8. Hereafter referred to as *Korean Situation.*

3. Letter from Arthur J. Brown to Masanao Hanihara, February 16, 1912, in the Presbyterian Library, New York.

4. Ibid.

5. Memorandum from missionaries Samuel A. Moffet, Norman C. Whittemore, O. R. Avison, George S. McCune, and C. E. Sharp to His Excellency Count Terauchi, governor-general of Chosen and received by Mr. Komatsu, director of the Bureau of Exterior Affairs, office of the governor-general of Chosen, January 8, 1912, in the Presbyterian Library, New York.

6. Letter from Alfred M. Sharrocks, M.D., to the Hon. M. Komatsu, director of the Bureau of Foreign Affairs of the governor-general of Chosen, December 16, 1911, in the Presbyterian Library, New York.

7. *Annual Report on Reforms and Progress in Chosen,* 1912–1913 (Keijo: Government General of Chosen, 1914), 56. Hereafter referred to as *Annual Report on Chosen.*

8. Special correspondence of the *Japan Chronicle, The Korean Conspiracy Trial: Full Report of the Proceedings* (Kobe, Japan: The office of the *Japan Chronicle,* 1912), 4–5. This is the most comprehensive report of the proceedings of the conspiracy trial. Hereafter referred to as *Japan Chronicle.*

9. Ibid., 130.

10. William Newton Blair, *Gold in Korea* (Topeka, Kansas: H. M. Ives & Sons, Inc., 1957), 175.

11. Letter from missionary Samuel A. Moffett, reporting the conspiracy case to the Presbyterian Board of Foreign Missions, August 26, 1912, in the Presbyterian Library, New York.

12. Arthur Judson Brown, *Korean Conspiracy Case* (Northfield, Mass.: Northfield Press, 1912), 15.

13. "Extracts from Statement given to the Press" by the delegation of church officials, dated July 29, 1912, in the Presbyterian Library, New York.

14. Brown, *Korean Conspiracy Case,* 22–23.

15. Blair, *Gold in Korea,* 76.

16. *Annual Report on Chosen,* 1912–1913, 200, and 1913–1914, 127.

17. *Annual Report on Chosen,* 1916–1917, 174–75.

7. Christianity and the Japanese Politics of Cultural Rule

1. The Rev. D. Frank Herron Smith, *The Other Side of the Korean Question* (Seoul: Seoul Press, 1920), 6.

2. *Kodae Minjok Munhwa Yonguso, Minjok, Kukkasa* (history of the Korean people and the nation) (Seoul: Koryo Daehak Minjok Munhwa Yonguso, 1964), 657.

3. Board of Foreign Missions, Presbyterian Church in U.S.A., *The Eighty-Third Annual Report,* 1920, 193.

4. For the Underwood report, see "First Account of Massacres and Burning of Villages," *Korean Situation,* 68–72.

5. Keiichiro Hara (ed.), *Hara Takashi Nikki* (diary of Takashi Hara) 9 vols. (Tokyo: Kangen-sha, 1950), 8: 216.

6. Quoted in *Korean Situations,* 3–4.

7. Quoted in Ibid., 3.

8. *Hara Nikki,* 8: 260.

9. *Annual Report on Chosen,* 1918–21, 204.

10. Ibid., 205.

11. Robert C. Armstong (ed.), *The Christian Movement in Japan, Korea and Formosa: A Year Book of Christian Work* (Tokyo: Federation of Christian Missions in Japan, 1921), 333.

12. *Korean Situation,* 2, 9–10.

13 Ibid., 10–12.

14. Government-General of Chosen, *Outline of Administrative Reforms in Chosen* (Seoul: Seoul Press, 1920), 19. Hereafter referred to as *Outline of Reforms,* 18.

15 *Address of Dr. Rentaro Minzuno* (n.p., 1921), Korean file, The Missionary Research Library, Union Theological Seminary, New York.

16. These figures are based on *Chosen Sotoku-fu Tokei Nenpo,* 1924 (annual statistical report of Chosen Government-General, 1924) (Keijo: Chosen Sotofu-fu, 1924), 7: 86–87.

17. Harry A. Rhodes, *History of the Korean Mission Presbyterian Church, 1884–1934* (Seoul: Chosen Mission Presbyterian Church U.S.A., 1934), 503.

18. L. T. Newland, "Is the Church Meeting Korea's Economic Problems?" *The Korean Mission Field* 25, 4 (April 1929), 69.

19. Samuel H. Moffet, "Missionaries Contributed to Korea," In *D.R.P.: The Official Bulletin of the Democratic Republican Party* 10, 11 (November, 1975), 72.

20. Quoted in Ibid., 16.

8. Christianity and the Japanese Politics of War

1. The following figures show the growth of shrines from 1923 to 1933. These figures are based on *Chosen Sotoku-fu Tokei Yoran,* 1925, 195, and *Tokei Nenpo,* 1934, 294.

Year	Number of Jinja	Number of Jinshi
1923	40	77
1924	41	103
1925	42	108
1926	43	107
1927	43	129
1928	47	152
1929	49	177
1930	49	182
1931	51	186
1932	51	199
1933	51	215

2. *Annual Report on Chosen,* 1933–34, 86.

3. D. C. Holtom, *Modern Japan and Shinto Nationalism* (New York: Paragon Book Reprint Corp., 1963), 98.

4. Personal interview with Rev. Edward Adams, New York, 1964.

5. Sacra Congregatio de Propaganda Fide, "Instructio," *Acta Apostolicae Sedis,* annua 28, series 2, 3, (Romae: Typis Polyglottis Vaticanis, 1936), 408–19.

6. The Board of Foreign Missions of the Presbyterian Church in the U.S.A., *Chosen Mission, Annual Report,* 1937, 27.

7. This statement was adopted in the mission meeting in February, 1936, at Chinju. See "The Situation in Korea," *The Mission Chronicle* 33, no. 3 (March 1939), 15.

8. *Minutes and Reports of the Chosen Mission of the Presbyterian Church in the U.S.A.,* 1936, 37.

9. Takushiro Hatsutori, *Taitoa Senso Jenshi* (the complete history of the war of great East Asia) (Tokyo: Hara Shoho, 1965), 8. This, the most comprehensive history on the subject, was written by a former high-ranking Japanese army officer. According to the author, the first shots were fired by the Chinese soldiers on the night of July 7 against a small platoon of drilling Japanese soldiers. The author also claims that Japan did not intend to escalate the war, at least at the time of the Marco Polo Bridge incident.

10. Sotoku-fu Chosen, *Shisei Sanjunen-shi* (history of thirty years' administration) (Keijo: Sotoku-fu Chosen, 1940), 4. Hereafter referred to as *Sanjunen-shi.*

11. *Sanjunen-shi,* 856. This account is based on an official Japanese government source. However, it is questionable whether a large number of Christian leaders actually attended the meeting to form such a federation. Korean and English Christian sources are silent on this matter.

12. Report of the Special Committee on Relationships between the Japan Methodist Church and the Korean Methodist Church, Korea file in the Methodist Library, New York. (Mimeographed.) The report is only one page long.

13. Darley Downs (ed.), *The Japan Christian Year Book* (Tokyo: The Christian Literature Society, 1941), 89. The Japan Christian Year Book of 1941 is the last year book published before the end of World War II.

14. Church and Mission in Korea: Report of a Visit to Korea by Bishop James C. Baker and Dr. R. E. Diffendorger to the Board of Missions and Church Extension of the Methodist Church, (Mimeographed, 1941), 16.

15. Ibid., 18.

16. Ibid., 14–15.

17. J. Manning Potts (ed.), *Grace Sufficient: The Story of Helen Kim by Herself* (Nashville, Tenn.: The Upper Room, 1964), 105.

9. The Division of the Nation, the Korean War, and the Churches

1. Harry S. Truman, *Memoirs of Harry S. Truman, vol. 1, Year of Decisions* (Garden City, N.Y.: Doubleday and Co., 1955), 444–45.

2. Quoted in Soon Sung Cho, *Korea in World Politics, 1940–1950* (Berkeley: University of California Press), 62–63.

3. Dong A. Ilbo Sa (ed.), *Han Mi Sugyo Baeknyunsa, Kwankye Jaryo Mit, Nyunpyo* (one hundred years history of Korea-U.S. relations, documents and chronology) (Seoul: Dong A. Ilbo Sa, 1982), 155. Hereafter Dong A. Ilbo.

4. Ibid, 116.

5. *New York Times,* November 10, 1946, 10.

6. Kim Hae-chul, *Tongil Munje Ui Jongchaeksajok gochal* (historical study of the Korean reunification policies) (Pyongyang: Pyongyang Chulpansa, 1989), 29.

7. Ibid., 81.

8. Harry A. Rhodes and Archibald Campbell, *History of the Korean Mission: Presbyterian Church in the U.S.A.,* vol. 2, 1939–1959 (New York: Commission on Ecumenical Mission and Relations, The Presbyterian Church in the U.S.A., 1965), 379–80.

9. Ibid., 380–81.

10. Bruce Cummings, *The Two Koreas* (New York: Foreign Policy Assocation, 1984), 36.

11. "Truman Statement on Korea," in Harold C. Syrett (ed.), *American Historical Documents* (New York: Barnes and Noble, Inc., 1960), 406.

10. The Politics of Anticommunism and the Unification Church

1. Yong Oon Kim, *Divine Principle and Its Application* (Washington, D.C.: The Holy Spirit Association for the Unification of World Christianity, 1969), 193.

2. *Divine Principle* (Washington, D.C.: The Holy Spirit Association for the Unification of World Christianity, 1973), 20.

3. Sun Myung Moon, *Christianity in Crisis: New Hope* (Washington, D.C.: The Holy Spirit Association for the Unification of World Christianity, 1974), 27. Hereafter, *Christianity in Crisis.*

4. *Divine Principle,* 143.

5. Ch'oi Syn-duk, "Korea's Tongil Movement," *Transactions of the Korean Branch of Royal Asiatic Society* 43 (1967): 175.

6. "Declaration of the Unification church," *Hanguk Shinmun* (Korean daily news), May 3, 1975, 6.

7. Song Hun Lee, *Communism: A Critique and Counter Proposal* (Washington: The Freedom Foundation, Inc., 1973), 233.

8. Ibid., 233.

9. Young Whi Kim (ed.), *The Way of the World* (Seoul: The Holy Spirit Association for the Unification of World Christianity, 1972), 103. Hereafter, *The Way of the World.*

10. Ibid., 57.

11. *Christianity in Crisis,* 55.

12. Ibid., 59.

13. Ibid., 61.

14. Ibid., 64.

15. Sun Myung Moon, *Answers to Watergate* (Washington, D.C.: The Holy Spirit Association for the Unification of Christianity, not dated), 3.

16. Ibid., 8.

17. *The Christian News,* February 10, 1975, 13.

18. Ibid., March 1, 1976, 16.

19. *St. Louis Globe Democrat,* December 13–14, 1975, 11.

20. *St. Louis Post-Dispatch,* November 8, 1976, 13a.

21. Ibid., November 15, 1976, 10a.

22. *Victory for Freedom* (Washington, D.C.: The Committee to Defend the U.S. Constitution, 1985), 5.

23. *Unification News* 2, no. 2 (Jan. 1992), 7.

11. The Military Junta and the Politics of Conservatism
in the Nation and the Church

1. *Emergency Measures Proclaimed by the President of the Republic of Korea under Article 53 of the Constitution* (Seoul: Korean Constitutional Research Institute, 1974), 7.

2. *Emergency Measures No. 9* (Seoul: Korean Overseas Information Service, 1975), 25.

3. Ibid., 26.

4. Ibid., 28.

5. Ibid., 14.

6. Declaration Drafting Committee, *The Declaration of the Korean Churches on the Occasion of Korea's 30th Anniversary of Liberation* (Seoul: Korea Christian Leaders' Association, 1975), 1.

7. Ibid., 2.

8. Religious News Service, "South Korean Churchman Defends Rights Limitations as Necessary," April 9, 1976, 9.

9. "Religious Leaders Resolve to Protect Constitution," in *D.R.P.: The Official Bulletin of the Democratic Party* 10, no. 1 (January 1975), 26.

10. Ibid., 26.

12. Christian Opposition to
President Park Chung Hee

1. Samuel H. Moffet, "Missionaries Contributed to Korea," in *D.R.P.: The Official Bulletin of the Democratic Republican Party 10, no. 11, (November, 1975),* 19.

2. *Report on an Amnesty International Mission to the Republic of Korea* March 27–April 9, 1975, 18.

3. For the entire text of the theological declaration, see Appendix.

4. Statement of Reverend James P. Sinnott before the Subcommittee on International Organizations, n.d., 1.

5. Ibid., 2.

6. For the complete text of the declaration, see Appendix.

7. Kim Chi Ha, "A Declaration of Conscience," *New World Outlook* (January, 1976), 28.

8. Ibid.

9. *St. Louis Post Dispatch,* December 15, 1974, 7b. The eight men charged in this case were executed by hanging within twenty-four hours after sentencing on April 9, 1975.

10. Ibid., May 28, 1975, 3b.

11. Ibid.

13. The Christian Movements for Democracy and the Assassination of the President

1. Park Tae Sun, "Upon Resigning as President," April 3, 1975, 1.

2. Printed Letter of Dr. Park Tae Sun, June 9, 1976.

3. Ibid.

4. "Facts Concerning the Metropolitan Community Mission Committee" (Seoul: Metropolitan Community Organization, April 4, 1975), 5.

5. "Statement of William P. Thompson, Stated Clerk of the General Assembly of the United Presbyterian Church, U.S.A. before the Subcommittee on International Organizations & Movements of the Committee on International Relations of the House of Representatives," June 10, 1975, 3.

6. "News Release" East Asia Office NCCUSA, May 9, 1975, New York, 1.

7. "What Is the Seoul Metropolitan Community Organization?" (Seoul: SMCO, 1976), 2.

14. Democratization and the Anti-American Movement during the Rule of General Chun Doo Hwan

1. The North American Coalition for Human Rights in Korea, *Korea '88: The Bigger Picture* (Washington, D.C.: NACHRK, 1988), 29.

2. Dalle Kim and K. C. Lee, "1980 Kwangju People's Uprising Revisited," *Korean Diaspora* 65 (May 1990), 30.

3. Ibid., 31.

4. Ibid.

5. Korean Overseas Information Service, *Forging a New Era* (Seoul: Samhwa Printing Co., 1981), 15. Hereafter, *Forging a New Era.*

6. Ibid.

7. United States Congress, *Congressional Record* (Washington, D.C., 1980), E4675.

8. *Forging a New Era,* 52.

9. Gregory Henderson, "Why Koreans Turn Against Us," *The Washington Post,* July 1, 1986.

10. North American Coalition for Human Rights in Korea, *Korea Update* 15 (January 1984), 1.

11. *Korea '88: The Bigger Picture,* 35–36.

12. Ibid., 39.

15. Christianity and the Politics of Reunification

1. *Korea '88: The Bigger Picture,* 45.

2. International Christian Network for Democracy in Korea, *Minju Dongji* 41 (March 1988), 4.

3. Ninan Koshy (ed.), *Peace and Reunification of Korea* (Geneva: World Council of Churches, 1990), 87.

4. Christian Conference of Asia and International Christian Network for Democracy in Korea (eds.), *Reunification, Peace, and Justice in Korea* (Hong Kong: Christian Conference of Korea, 1988), 94.

5. See appendix D for the entire text.

6. Gregory Henderson, "Why Koreans Turn against Us," *The Washington Post,* July 1, 1986.

7. *The Christian Century* (January 20, 1982), 48.

8. Korean Ecumenical Education Programs and Catholic Institute for International Relations, *The Reunification of Korea* (London: Third World Publications, Ltd., 1989), 41.

9. Dorothy L. Ogle, "Testimony before the Subcommittee on Asian and Pacific Affairs: Committee on Foreign Affairs, Reunification of Korea," May 24, 1988, (mimeographed), 4.

10. See the appendix for the entire text.

11. International Christian Network for Democracy in Korea, *Minju Dongji* 42 (April 1988), 7.

12. Ibid., 6–7.

13. *The Washington Post,* June 11, 1988.

14. *South-North Dialogue in Korea* (Seoul: International Cultural Society of Korea, 1988), 11–12.

15. See the appendix for the entire text.

16. The Christian President and the Politics of Reform

1. Korean Foundations, *Korea Focus* 1, no. 4 (July–August, 1993), 132.

2. Korean Overseas Information Service, *The Dawning of a New Era* (Seoul: Korea Overseas Information Service, 1993), 41.

3. Korea Press Service, *Achievements of the Kim Administration during its First Two Years* (Seoul: Korea Press Service, 1995), 9.

4. Korea Foundation, *Korea Focus* 1. no. 31 (May–June, 1993), 125.

5. Ibid.

6. Korean Center for World Missions, *Korean Torch for World Missions* 2, no. 1. (January–March, 1994), 12.

7. Korea Foundation, *Korea Focus* 1, no. 6 (November 1993), 10–11.

8. "Statement of the Government of the Democratic People's Republic of Korea," quoted in Korea Church Coalition, *Urgent Action Appeal* (New York: Korea Church Coalition, 1993), 5.

9. Program Ministry Committee for World Community, National Council of Churches of Christ—U.S.A., *Resolution on North and South Korea* (New York: NCC-USA, March, 1993), 1.

10. Reunification Committee, National Council of Churches in Korea, *Statement of NCC in Korea* (Seoul: NCC in Korea, March 16, 1993), 1.

11. Korean Foundation, *Korean Focus* 2, no. 3. (May–June, 1993), 127.

12. *Statement of NCC in Korea*, 1.

13. National Unification Board, *The Three-Stage, Three-Basis Reunification Policy* (Seoul: National Unification Board, 1993), 1.

14. Korea Foundation, *Korea Focus* 2, no. 2. (March–April, 1994), 171.

15. Ibid., 2, no. 4 (July–August, 1994), 179.

16. Jimmy Carter, "Report of Trip to North Korea" in *Korea Report* 20 (Fall, 1994), 8.

17. Ibid.

18. Korean Information and Resource Center, Inc., *Korea Report* 20 (Fall, 1994), 11.

19. "USA and DPRK 'Agreed Framework'—Geneva, October 21, 1994," in the Korean Society, *The U.S.-Korea Review* 2, no. 10 (September/October, 1994), 9.

20. Korea Press Service, *Achievements of the Kim Administration During its First Two Years* (Seoul: Korea Press Service, 1995), 4.

Conclusion: Christianity in North Korea and Its Future in Relation to Christianity and the Politics of South Korea

1. Roy E. Shearer, *Wildfire: Church Growth in Korea* (Grand Rapids: W. B. Eerdmans Publishing Co., 1966), 224–25.

2. Kim Yang Sun, *Hanguk Kidokkyo Haebang Simnyonsa* (ten-year history of Korean Christianity after the liberation) (Seoul: Korea Yesu Presbyterian Church, Dept. of Religious Education, 1956), 68.

3. The personal accounts of the Shinuiju student demonstration were often told by General Chang Do Young in Korean study conferences at Western Michigan University in Kalamazoo where General Chang taught.

4. For the North Korean account of the land reforms, see Chun Young Ryul, et. al (eds.), *Chosun Tong Sa* (general history of Korea) (Pyongyang: Sahoe Kwahak Chulpansa, 1987), 316–20.

5. Kim, 68.

6. Ibid., 69.

7. Raymond A. Lane, *Ambassador in Chains: The Life of Bishop Patrick James Byrne* (New York: P. J. Kennedy & Sons, 1955), 223.

8. Ibid., 237.

9. Ibid., 249.

10. Kim Il Sung, *Segi wa Dubulo* (together with the century) (Pyongyang: Chosßn Rodongdang Chulpansa, 1992), 1: 102–4. This is a rough translation of Kim's autobiography.

11. Kim Jong Il, *On the Juche Idea* (Pyongyang: Foreign Language Publishing House, 1982), 8.

12. Ibid., 9.

13. "Reconciliation in Korea," *Christian Century,* August 16, 1972), 825

BIBLIOGRAPHY

Allen, Horace N. *A Chronological Index: Some of the Chief Events in Foreign Intercourse of Korea from the Beginning of the Christian Era to the Twentieth Century.* Seoul, Korea: Press of Methodist Publishing House, 1901.

————. *Korea: Fact and Fancy.* Seoul, Korea: Methodist Publishing House, 1904.

————. *Things Korean: A Collection of Sketches and Anecdotes Missionary and Diplomatic.* New York: Fleming H. Revell Company, 1908.

Baldwin, Frank, ed. *Without Parallel: The American-Korean Relationship Since 1945.* New York: Random House, Inc., 1974.

Barclay, Wade C. *History of Methodist Missions.* 6 vols. New York: The Board of Missions of the Methodist Church, 1957.

Barnds, William J. *The Two Koreas in East Asian Affairs.* New York: New York University Press, 1976.

Biernatzki, S. J., William E., Luke Jin-Chang Im, and Anselm K. Min. *Korean Catholic Catholicism in the 1970s.* Maryknoll, New York: Orbis Books, 1975.

Bishop, Isabella. *Korea and Her Neighbors: A Narrative of Travel with an Account of the Vicissitudes and Position of the Country.* New York: Fleming H. Revell, 1898.

Blair, William Newton. *Gold in Korea.* Topeka, Kansas: H. M. Ives & Sons, Inc., 1957.

Board of Foreign Missions, Presbyterian Church in the U.S.A. *The Eighty-Third Annual Report.* Philadelphia: Presbyterian Foreign Mission Board, 1920.

Bock, Kim Yong, ed. *Minjung Theology: People as the Subjects of History.* Singapore: The Commission on Theological Concerns—The Christian Conference of Asia, 1981.

Boettcher, Robert, and Gordon L. Freedman. *Gifts of Deceit: Sun Myung Moon, Tongsun Park and the Korean Scandal.* New York: Holt, Rinehart, and Winston, 1980.

Brown, Arthur Judson. *The Korean Conspiracy Case.* Northfield, Massachusetts: Northfield Press, 1912.

Brown, George Thompson. *Mission to Korea.* Nashville: Board of World Missions, Presbyterian Church U.S.A., 1962.

Byas, Hugh. *Government by Assassination.* New York: Alfred A. Knopf, 1942.

The Carnegie Endowment for International Peace. *Dialogue with North Korea.* Washington, D.C.: Carnegie Endowment for International Peace, 1989.

Cho, Soon Sung. *Korea in World Politics, 1940–1950: An Evaluation of American Responsibility.* Berkeley: University of California Press, 1967.

Choi, Ho Chin. *The Economic History of Korea: From the Earliest Times to 1945.* Seoul, Korea: The Freedom Library, 1971.

Christian Conference of Asia-Urban Rural Mission. *From the Womb of Han: Stories of Korean Women Workers.* Hong Kong: Christian Conference of Asia—Urban Rural Mission, 1982.

————. *Rev. In Myung Jin's Prison Letters.* Hong Kong: Christian Conference of Asia, 1980.

Chung, Henry. *The Case of Korea.* New York: Fleming H. Revell Co., 1921.

Clark, Allen D. *A History of the Church in Korea.* Seoul: Christian Literature Society of Korea, 1971.

Clark, Charles Allen. *First Fruits in Korea.* New York: Fleming H. Revell, Co., 1921.

Clark, Donald N. *Christianity in Modern Korea.* Lanham, Maryland: University Press of America, 1986.

Cohen, Warren I. *New Frontiers in American-East Asian Relations.* New York: Columbia University Press, 1983.

Commission of the Churches on International Affairs of the World Council of Churches. *Human Rights in the Republic of Korea.* Geneva: Commission of the Churches on International Affairs of the World Council of Churches, 1979.

Committee for a New Direction for U.S. Korea Policy. *Conference for a New Direction in U.S. Korea Policy.* New York: Committee for a New Direction for U.S. Korea Policy, 1977.

Conroy, Hilary. *The Japanese Seizure of Korea: 1868–1910.* Philadelphia: University of Pennsylvania Press, 1960.

Cumings, Bruce. *The Two Koreas.* Headline series. New York: Foreign Policy Association, 1984.

Dong, Wonmo, ed. *Korean-American Relations at Crossroads.* Montclair, New Jersey: The Association of Korean Christian Scholars in North America, Inc., 1982.

England, John C., ed. *Living Theology in Asia.* London: SCM Press Ltd., 1981.

Fabella, M. M., Virginia and Sun Ai Lee Park, eds., *We Dare to Dream: Doing Theology as Asian Women.* Hong Kong: Asian Women's Resource Center for Culture and Theology, 1989.

Fisher, James E. *Democracy and Mission Education in Korea.* Seoul, Korea: Yonsei University Press, 1970.

Fukuda, Tsuneari. *Future of Japan and the Korean Peninsula.* Translated by K. Jahng. Elizabeth, New Jersey: Hollym International Corp., 1978.

Grayson, James Huntley. *Early Buddhism and Christianity in Korea.* Leiden, the Netherlands: E. J. Brill, 1985.

Han, Woo-keun. *The History of Korea.* Translated by Lee Kyung-shik. Seoul, Korea: Eul-Yoo Publishing Company, Ltd., 1970.

Hanson, Eric O. *Catholic Politics in China and Korea.* Maryknoll, New York: Orbis Books, 1980.

Harrington, Fred Harvey. *God, Mamon and the Japanese: Dr. Horace N. Allen and Korean-American Relations, 1884–1905.* Madison: The University of Wisconsin Press, 1944.

Holy Spirit Association for the Unification of World Christianity. *Divine Principle.* New York: HSA-UWC, 1973.

Hulbert, Homer B. *Hulbert's History of Korea.* 2 vols., Seoul, Korea: The Methodist Publishing House, 1905; Clarence N. Weems, ed., reprint ed., New York: Hilary House, 1962.

———. *The Passing of Korea.* New York: Doubleday and Page, 1906.

Hunt, Jr., Everett N. *Protestant Pioneers in Korea.* Maryknoll, New York: Orbis Books, 1980.

Janelli, Roger L., and Dawnhee Yim. *Ancestor Worship and Korean Society.* Stanford, California: Stanford University Press, 1982.

Kang, Wi Jo. *Religion and Politics in Korea under the Japanese Rule,* vol. 5, *Studies in Asian Thought and Religion.* Lewiston, New York: Edwin Mellen Press, 1987.

Kim, C. I. Eugene, and Dorethea E. Mortimore, eds. *Korea's Response to Japan: The Colonial Period 1910–1945.* Kalamazoo: Western Michigan University, 1977.

Kim, C. I. Eugene, and Han-Kyo. *Korea and the Politics of Imperialism, 1876–1910.* Berkeley and Los Angeles: University of California Press, 1967.

Kim, Han K., ed. *Reunification of Korea: 50 Basic Documents,* Monograph no. 2. Washington, D.C.: Institute of Asian Studies, 1972.

Kim, Helen. *Grace Sufficient: The Story of Helen Kim.* Nashville, Tennessee: The Upper Room, 1964.

Kim, Soo Dong, and Byong-suh, eds. *Human Rights: In Minority Perspectives*. Montclair, New Jersey: Association of Korean Christian Scholars in North America, Inc., 1979.

Kim, Young Oon. *Unification Theology*. New York: HSA-UWC, 1980.

Korean Overseas Information Service. *Forging a New Era: The Fifth Republic of Korea*. Seoul: Korean Overseas Information Service, 1981.

Kwak, Tae-Hwan, John Chay, Soon Sung Cho, and Shannon McCune, eds. *U.S.-Korean Relations, 1882–1982*. Ithaca: Cornell University Press, 1963.

Lane, Raymond A. *Ambassador in Chains: The Life of Bishop Patrick James Byrne*. New York: P. J. Kennedy & Sons, 1955.

Lauterbach, Richard E. *History of the American Military Government in Korea*. Seoul, Korea: Kukche shinmun-sa, 1948.

Lee, Chong-Sik. *The Politics of Korean Nationalism*. Berkeley and Los Angeles: University of California Press, 1963.

Lee, Jung Young, ed., *Ancestor Worship and Christianity in Korea*, vol. 8, *Studies in Asian Thought and Religion*. Lewiston, New York: Edwin Mellen Press, 1988.

———. *Korean Shamanistic Rituals*. New York: Mouton Publishers, 1981.

———. *The Theology of Change: A Christian Concept of God in an Eastern Perspective*. Maryknoll: Orbis Books, 1979.

Lee, Yur-Bok, and Wayne Patterson, eds. *One Hundred Years of Korean-American Relations, 1882–1982*. University: The University of Alabama Press, 1986.

Meskill, John, trans. *Ch'oe Pu's Diary: A Record of Drifting across the Sea*. Tucson: The University of Arizona Press, 1965.

Moffett, Samuel Hugh. *The Christians of Korea*. New York: Friendship Press, Inc., 1962.

Nahm, Andrew C., ed. *Korea under Japanese Colonial Rule*. Kalamazoo: Western Michigan University, 1973.

Oliver, Robert. *Why War Came in Korea*. New York: Fordham University Press, 1950.

Osgood, Cornelius. *The Koreans and Their Culture*. New York: The Ronald Press Company, 1951.

Paik, L. George. *The History of Protestant Missions in Korea 1832–1910*. Seoul, Korea: Yonsei University Press, 1971.

Palmer, Spencer J. *Korea and Christianity*. Seoul, Korea: Hollym Corporation, 1967.

Rhodes, Harry A. *History of the Korea Mission Presbyterian Church U.S.A.* Seoul: Chosen Mission Presbyterian Churrh, 1933.

Rhodes, Harry A., and Achibald Campbell, eds. *History of the Korea Mission: Presbyterian Church in the U.S.A.,* vol. 2, 1935–1959. New York: Commission on Ecumenical Mission and Relations—The United Presbyterian Church in the U.S.A., 1965.

Ryang, J. S. *Facts about the Korean Methodist Church.* Seoul: Korea Methodist Headquarters, 1938.

Sauer, Charles August. *Methodists in Korea 1930–1960.* Seoul, Korea: The Christian Literature Society, 1973.

Shearer, Roy E. *Wildfire: Church Growth in Korea.* Grand Rapids, Michigan: Wm. B. Eerdmans Publishing, 1966.

Sohn, Pow-key, Kim Chol-choon, and Hong Yi-sup. *The History of Korea.* Seoul: Korean National Commission for UNESCO, 1970.

Suh, Dae-Sook. *The Korean Communist Movement 1918–1948.* Princeton: Princeton University Press, 1967.

Sullivan, John, and Roberta Foss, eds. *Two Koreas—One Future?* Lanham, Maryland: University Press of America, Inc., 1987.

Sunoo, Harold Hakwon. *America's Dilemma in Asia: The Case of South Korea.* Chicago: Nelson-Hall, 1979.

———. *Repressive State and Resisting Church: The Politics of CIA in South Korea.* Fayette, Missouri: Korean American Cultural Association CMC, 1976.

Sunoo, Harold Hakwon, and Dong Soo Kim, eds. *Korean Women: In a Struggle for Humanization.* Memphis: Association of Korean Christian Scholars in North America, Inc., 1978.

T. K. *Letters from South Korea.* Translated by David L. Swain. Tokyo: Iwanami Shoten, 1976.

Truman, Harry S. *Memoirs.* New York: Doubleday, 1956.

Weems, Benjamin B. *Reform, Rebellion, and the Heavenly Way.* Tucson: University of Arizona Press, 1964.

INDEX